I Know What I Know

I Know What I Know

The Music of Charles Mingus

TODD S. JENKINS

Foreword by Sy Johnson

Westport, Connecticut
London

Library of Congress Cataloging-in-Publication Data

Jenkins, Todd S., 1968–
    I know what I know: the music of Charles Mingus /
  Todd S. Jenkins; foreword by Sy Johnson.
      p. cm.
    Includes bibliographical references (p.) and index.
    ISBN 0–275–98102–9 (alk. paper)
    1. Mingus, Charles, 1922–1979—Criticism and interpretation. 2. Jazz—Analysis,
  appreciation. I. Title.
  ML418.M45J46   2006
  781.65092—dc22   2006001241

British Library Cataloguing in Publication Data is available.

Library of Congress Catalog Card Number: 2006001241
ISBN: 0–275–98102–9

First published in 2006

Praeger Publishers, 88 Post Road West, Westport, CT 06881
An imprint of Greenwood Publishing Group, Inc.
www.praeger.com

Printed in the United States of America

(∞)™

The paper used in this book complies with the
Permanent Paper Standard issued by the National
Information Standards Organization (Z39.48–1984).

10 9 8 7 6 5 4 3 2 1

Copyright Acknowledgments

The author and publisher gratefully acknowledge permission to reproduce lyrics from the
following songs by Charles Mingus: "Weird Nightmare"; "Eclipse"; "Oh, Lord Don't Let Them
Drop That Atomic Bomb On Me"; "Original Faubus Fables"; "Freedom"; "Don't Let It Happen
Here"; and "The Chill of Death."

All songs are written by Charles Mingus and published by Jazz Workshop, Inc.

*This book is dedicated to
my beloved wife, Christie*

Contents

Foreword   ix
A Note from Sue Graham Mingus   xv
Acknowledgments   xvii

Introduction   1

Central Avenue Swing   5

New York and the Bebop Revolution   17

Breaking into Freedom   41

The Poetic Blues of Mingus   53

Triumph: Columbia Records, 1959   63

Into the Past, Into the Future   71

Resurgence: The Impulse Albums   97

The 1964 Tour   107

Falling Away   123

A Slow Climb   131

Denouement   153

Coda   165

Bibliography   177
Index   179

Foreword

Charles Mingus was a Primitive. Before you reach for your poison pens, let me point out that Duke Ellington was also a Primitive, as was Thelonious Monk, as is Ornette Coleman.

Let me define "Primitive" as I mean it. A Primitive is an artist who either willfully ignores the rules of his art, or can't or won't learn them. When an artist is so driven to realize his vision that he steamrolls ahead despite his limitations, the result can be genius.

Genius and talent, however extraordinary, are not the same thing. A supremely talented man like André Previn knows thirty-five time-tested solutions to any musical problem he may pose himself. He can thumb through them like a deck of cards and make a beautiful choice before you can blink. He can build a musical structure for any occasion from his successive choices—a movie score, an opera, a ballet, a jazz trio recording—all absolutely first-rate, all absolutely equal to the task at hand. And yet he seems never, and perhaps he doesn't want, to break new ground, to push the envelope to the limit.

A Primitive such as Charles Mingus had no backlog of tested solutions. He had certain doors he could enter to break through the start of a new piece. He could put his hands down on the keyboard in the key of D-flat, particularly a D-flat major seventh chord, and his hands would begin to shape melodies and harmonies, some borrowed from himself, some from outside himself (Billy Strayhorn's "Lush Life," for example), and some new. Check out his "Duke Ellington's Sound of Love" or "Sue's Changes." You can hear ghosts of other melodies, but the totality is pure Mingus.

He loved to set up a bass ostinato, then pile riffs on top—"Haitian Fight Song" and "Boogie Stop Shuffle," for example. The strength of the rhythmic force field he set up still powers these pieces today, whether it be a high school band or the Mingus Big Band. His unmatched energy and spirit is an essential component of his composing. You can feel something of the man by playing his music. I've heard members of the Mingus Big Band come off the bandstand and say, "Mingus is in the room tonight."

Mingus was an impatient man, with no interest as a composer in the classic motivic development techniques, inversion, retrograde, and the like. He had tons of new melodies and new motifs at hand, and to satisfy his need to make longer and more important compositions, he would drop any motif he had grown tired of or had exhausted, and move to another idea, another tempo, another mood. Frequently, there was no attempt to bridge one to the next. They were just jammed together. And further, Mingus expected each soloist to negotiate these landscapes (or, as I felt playing for him, obstacle courses). He gave soloists less help from the bass than one would expect from the composer, making it difficult when he felt the soloist was getting lazy or facile.

The result was a new kind of extended jazz composition, increasingly influential, and a generation of jazz musicians who never played better than (or as well as) they had with Mingus.

If Mingus' reputation had remained where it was at the time of his death, he would have been acknowledged as a great bassist and a powerful bandleader, but his compositions judged too difficult to play, with the exception of the "hits": "Goodbye Porkpie Hat," "Better Get Hit in Your Soul," "Haitian Fight Song," "Jelly Roll," and half a dozen others.

When Sue Mingus formed the first Mingus Dynasty with myself and Jimmy Knepper organizing and writing the book, her stated intent was to demonstrate to the world that Charles was the great composer she knew him to be. And she has succeeded beyond even her wildest expectations. He is now acknowledged as the second most prolific composer in jazz after Duke Ellington. His posthumous epic, "Epitaph," is recognized as a triumphant summary of his life and performed the world over. The Library of Congress is the repository of his scores. School bands all over the globe are embracing his Hal Leonard "Big Band" series. His recordings are always surfacing under commercials, films, TV shows, and being sampled in hip-hop and rap records. High school marching bands are marching furiously up and down football fields playing "Children's Hour of Dream" from "Epitaph," a piece that Gunther Schuller, its conductor, declared "almost unplayable" at the 2006 IAJE convention.

Mingus still appeals to the rebels, to the energy and passions of young musicians. They respond to the raw edge that Mingus brought to his music and the challenge he laid down for future generations to find themselves in this music.

My first encounter with Mingus was in the late 1940s. My friend, Roger Brousso, got tickets for a charity concert at Woolsey Hall, on the Yale campus in New Haven, Connecticut. Mel Powell had been the successor to Teddy Wilson in Benny Goodman's band. Mel was, by this time, a protégé of Paul Hindemith and a professor of music at Yale. Mel used the occasion of this concert to reunite his old boss, Benny Goodman, and his Goodman bandmate, Lionel Hampton. I remember the concert as marvelous, with Goodman, Powell, and Hampton obviously enjoying themselves intensely. They played in various combinations, with Hampton playing drums as well as vibes, until they introduced the rest of the musicians. Benny had brought his drummer, Charlie Smith, and Hamp had brought his bassist, Charlie Mingus. What I remember about the two Charlies was their deference and support throughout.

My next Mingus sighting was at the Embers in New York in the early 1950s. I was on furlough from the Air Force during the Korean War, and dropped in to see Red Norvo's trio, with Red on vibes, Tal Farlow on guitar, and Mingus on bass. The group played jaw-dropping fast tempos with watch-like precision. It didn't take much listening to discern that Mingus was the engine propelling the trio, easily dominating the musical flow and tempos of the group.

I had known of his writing and playing from the famous recording with Hampton, "Mingus Fingers," but actually hearing him so strong in the company of his peers, and in New York City, opened my ears.

I was discharged from the USAF in 1955 and went to Los Angeles to study law. But I soon found myself entangled in the jazz scene, and had abandoned law by the time I graduated from UCLA in 1958. In the meantime, Mingus was making waves, and records, to New York. The two most important records from 1959, *Mingus Ah Um* and *Mingus Dynasty*, swept through the L.A. jazz scene, followed closely by the great Atlantic LPs—*The Clown, Blues and Roots*. Mingus had arrived. I learned some of the tunes like everybody else: "Goodbye Porkpie Hat," "Better Get Hit in Your Soul." Even bands such as Woody Herman's were covering his pieces. The year 1959 was a banner year for jazz records; *Kind of Blue* and the Miles Davis-Gil Evans collaboration on *Porgy and Bess* were just a few of the seminal recordings, and Mingus' stood out among them.

In December of 1959 I left Los Angeles for New York, preceded by friends such as Paul Bley and Ornette Coleman. In particular, one evening in front of Jazz City, Ornette told me he was starting an open gig at the Five Spot, and that I should come to New York as soon as I could to join them on piano. When I did get here, it was very apparent that Ornette had no intention of adding a piano to his by-then famous (or infamous) quartet. After a week of hanging around at the Five Spot, I heard that Paul Bley was working with Mingus at the Showplace, just a short walk across town. I walked over, climbed the stairs, and heard Booker Ervin on tenor, Ted Curson on trumpet, Eric Dolphy in his first week with the band, Dannie Richmond on drums, Mingus, and the great Baby Lawrence tap-dancing, but no Paul Bley, no piano.

When the group took a break, I approached Mingus to ask about Paul Bley. He said, "He's not here. You a musician?"

"Yeah, piano."

"Can you play?"

"Yeah."

"Stick around and I'll call you up next set, if you want."

So I stuck around, and on the last tune, "Billie's Bounce," Baby Lawrence's signature tap tune, he called me up. As I squeezed between Mingus and the piano, he said, "You better be able to play, motherf***er!"

When the set was over, he told me to play the whole last set, and then invited me to play the next two weeks until Baby Lawrence left, upon such time I would get the piano player's salary (then currently going to Baby Lawrence). I agreed, and gradually accumulated assurance and some classic Mingus stories.

On my first paid night, I showed up at the Showplace and found the group already playing—no piano, but Yusef Lateef on tenor. I sat at a prominent table under a spotlight and glared at Mingus the whole set. When he came off, he started to walk right by my table, but then paused and backed up. He leaned over and said in my ear, "If you was me, and you had the chance to hire Yusef Lateef or you, who would *you* hire?" He then walked away, sure that he had resolved the situation.

Mingus walked back into my life (or, more precisely, climbed a flight of stairs) in the fall of 1971. I had buzzed him in, listened to him laboring up the stairs, and opened the door, not knowing who was there.

"This Emile Charlap's office?"

"Yeah. What do you say? How can we help you? Come on in. Take that comfortable chair. Can I get you something?"

"No, thanks. I have a meeting with Emile Charlap at 3:00. I want him to arrange some stuff."

"Emile's not an arranger, he's a copyist. This is his office. Lots of arrangers around. I'm sure he'll take care of you when he gets here. He's on a record date that went into overtime."

I sat him down, sure that he remembered me from the Showplace. I chatted away to keep him entertained until Emile arrived. After twenty minutes or so he said, "Why am I waiting for Emile Charlap if he's not an arranger? You an arranger?"

I said yes, and he said, "Where can we talk?" I took him back to the little room with the piano, and when he left I had *Let My Children Hear Music* to arrange.

I worked with Mingus for the next five years until the effects of Lou Gehrig's disease began to make their impact. *Let My Children Hear Music, Charles Mingus and Friends at Philharmonic Hall, Mingus Moves, Changes One, Changes Two.* He recorded two of my originals, "Wee" and "For Harry Carney," commissioned a blues suite for the Montreux Jazz Festival, and nominated me for a Guggenheim Award to follow his own. We were friends, and spent time together with our wives. Charles died in 1979, and I am still involved with Mingus Music.

You'll learn much about Mingus and his life and legacy from the book you hold in your hands. Todd Jenkins has done a wonderfully insightful and thorough job of documenting a life's work and a unique man. This book should find an essential place among the many Mingus volumes already available, and those sure to come.

Sy Johnson
February 2006

A Note from Sue Graham Mingus

Record piracy and counterfeiting have adversely affected the recording industry since its earliest days. Unlike a legitimate record company, the pirate bears none of the initial cost of searching for talent, creating, producing, marketing and publicizing a recording. Nor does he pay union fees, artists, back-up vocalists and musicians, publishing and songwriting royalties. Pirate recordings are produced by procuring legitimate recordings and re-issuing them; bootlegs by taping live concerts, tapping into the venue's sound system, or illegally procuring studio outtakes; and counterfeiting by duplicating both the music and packaging so they are indistinguishable. Not only are musicians and record companies cheated out of their share of the royalties, but their reputations are damaged when consumers unknowingly purchase poor quality copies of their work. In the case of Mingus, clues to unauthorized copies include misspelled song titles, "Danny" instead of Dannie Richmond (Mingus's longtime drummer); misspellings of other musicians' names like Jaki Byard or "Cliff" instead of Clifford Jordan, and especially "Charlie" rather than Charles Mingus.

Adding to the problem of illegal releases is the accompanying praise of reviewers that lend them an air of legitimacy. The music community is hardly served by badly recorded tapes, purloined photographs, incorrect liner notes and inflated prices. The irresponsibility, and often criminality, of entrepreneurs who fail to observe copyright laws and who wish nonetheless to appear to be dedicated collectors retrieving music for us from the past, do not need plaudits from writers. While it is understandable that reviewers call attention to formerly out-of-print or rare recordings for the buying public when they are released legitimately, they would do well to examine the shoddy behavior of entrepreneurs masquerading as collectors. I bring this to the reader's attention, because some of the Mingus material discussed in this book falls within that category.

In 1981, the Smithsonian Institution had in its possession Mingus material from the 1940s and was interested in releasing a "Baron Mingus in the Forties" album. Being a responsible institution, they were reluctant to do so until they had obtained permission from the various record labels, such as Fentone and Excelsior, which had originally released the material, as well as the Mingus estate. Uptown Records, whose owner, Robert Sunenblick, decided for himself that possession equaled ownership, released this material without permission from either the estate or record labels. When illegal recordings of Mingus's legendary 1964 European concerts were released years ago, I started a record label called Revenge Records and issued the material myself, correcting musical errors, adding historical notes and paying sidemen who had never been reimbursed. (See my liner notes to this release, which can be found on our website, http://www. mingusmingusmingus.com). Presently, Universal Music France, the European distributor of our new imprint, SueMingusMusic, will issue similar performances of indisputable value from the past while respecting copyright ownership, licensing and established payments. The recent release of the Thelonious Monk/John Coltrane material acquired from the Voice of America archives is an example of an historical find being offered to the world in honest, laudable fashion. It is important that music reviewers understand the distinction.

Sue Mingus
March 24, 2006

Acknowledgments

One of the most valuable assets a writer could ask for is an understanding family, and in that way I have been blessed immeasurably. I began my previous book project, the two-volume *Free Jazz and Free Improvisation: An Encyclopedia* (Greenwood Press, 2004), a year before I met my wife, Christie. It was completed nearly seven years after we wed. Christie was constantly supportive throughout that long, frustrating period, giving me the encouragement I needed to press onward despite multiple changes of direction on the part of the publisher (and myself as well), major loss of data (thanks to computer glitches), and the niggling demands of everyday life. The volume you are now holding took about one-fifth as much time as the free jazz books, and if it weren't for my wife's patient grace in minding the kids and taking on extra responsibilities at home, it might still be unfinished to this day. For that, and many other reasons, I lovingly dedicate this book to Christie.

I owe a tremendous debt of thanks to several people, including the members of the online Mingus and Jazz-L mailing lists. These Internet fellowships of jazz aficionados provided me with invaluable factual and material support as this project developed. Their memories and opinions about Mingus' recordings, concerts, and compositions provided me with the necessary inspirational fuel to keep the book alive. The inimitable Alan Saul dipped into his vast fountain of knowledge to share information and insight about Mingus and Eric Dolphy. Bill Hery was gracious enough to provide me with copies of the more elusive recordings covered in this book. Mingus biographer Brian Priestley and archivist Andrew Homzy filled in many blanks about who performed what on which session.

Esa Onttonen's exhaustive online discography was a tremendous help in piecing together all of the official and bootleg releases of this material.

Thanks also to Jack Walrath, Ozzie Cadena, Charles McPherson, and others who consented to being interviewed for the umpteenth time about their experiences with, and perceptions of, Mingus' music. Sy Johnson and Sue Graham Mingus were gracious enough to provide their contributions fairly late in the game, and they have my undying respect and gratitude. Dan Harmon, my editor at Greenwood/Praeger, has been more than patient as I slogged through this process. And, last but certainly not least, profuse thanks to my longtime friend Simon Barley, one of the finest DJs the jazz world has to offer, for his assistance and encouragement. I love you madly.

Introduction

As a child growing up in the declining Los Angeles suburb of Watts, little Charlie Mingus used to collect scraps of broken glass and pottery, and cart them down the street to the otherworldly homestead of Simon Rodia. The short-statured Romanian immigrant would reward Charlie and the other neighborhood kids with spare change to buy candy and ice cream, then add their odd little baubles to the bright, freakish towers that were consuming much of his time. As young Charlie grew into manhood, the structures known as the Watts Towers crept higher toward the sky, resplendent in tiles, paint, mirrors, and wire, to become one of the defining monuments of the Los Angeles area.

As a composer and recording artist, Mingus' sizeable body of work can be viewed as a musical parallel to Rodia's Watts Towers. Both can be daunting and foreign upon first encounter, though they are composed of recognizable, perhaps comfortably familiar elements. Both are larger than life, greater than sum, the fruits of dedication and hard labor, both tainted by derision and strengthened by encouragement. And, despite the wear and tear of time and tide, both have endured as distinctly American symbols of creativity.

At first, little Charles probably gathered detritus for Rodia because of the coins he knew would be forthcoming. But in time, he surely understood that what was being done with all those little chips and scraps would be timeless. By the same token, as his musical career progressed, Mingus usually had something well beyond finances as his principal motivation, even if the need for cold, hard cash did override other priorities at times. One does not take the kind of risks Mingus did with his art, if commercialism is the end-all. Those risks led Charles Mingus to become one of the greatest bass players in jazz, and one of its most outstanding composers, arrangers, and bandleaders as well.

Brian Priestley and Gene Santoro have written markedly different and engaging biographies of Charles Mingus, the man, but comparatively little has been committed to print about his lifeblood, the music he created over more than three decades. Mingus' autobiography, *Beneath the Underdog* (New York: Vintage, 1991), is an interesting look into his fantasy world but bears scant resemblance to his actual life and sheds almost no light on his music. In Italy, Stefano Zenni has committed years to a musicological study of Mingus' works, but most of his research is yet to be printed in English. The book you are holding, then, is intended to fill the gap as a listener's guide to the recorded works of Mingus. It begins with the CD reissues of his earliest 78 rpm sides, waxed in Los Angeles and San Francisco, and ends after his exhausting final sessions, where he was little more than a shell in a wheelchair, before his death from Lou Gehrig's disease in 1979.

*   *   *

The sheer scope of the Mingus canon makes trekking through it all an intimidating prospect, especially when faced with myriad inconsistencies in titling, arrangements, and history. My aim is to cast light on the many facets of Mingus' work, make connections between related compositions and their inspirations, and clarify misconceptions about a *corpus* so unparalleled in the arts that many have simply labeled it "Mingus Music," for lack of a better term. Because the majority of the readers will lack a functional background in musicology, and perhaps even basic music theory, this book avoids technical terminology and notation in favor of a layman listener's analysis of Mingus' music. The aim is to get the word out about this remarkable assortment of works, guide listeners through Mingus' substantial discography, and perhaps answer some intriguing questions: How many ways did Mingus retitle "Weird Nightmare" over the years? Why does the session with Lionel Hampton in 1977 include a single track with a lead trombone and rhythm section, while there is no trombonist on the rest of the album? What were all those tunes quoted by the soloists during the 1964 tour? Why did Mingus completely disappear from the jazz scene at the end of the 1960s? All these subjects and many more will be addressed in time. We will also look at the evolution of compositions such as "Dizzy Moods," "Orange Was the Color of Her Dress, Then Blue Silk," and "Portrait" over different spans of time.

After a long period of experimentation and soul-searching, the core characteristics of Mingus' works were in place by the beginning of the 1960s. A strong emphasis on the blues and gospel pervades many of his most popular tunes: "Wednesday Night Prayer Meeting," "Haitian Fight Song," "Better Get Hit In Your Soul," "Slop," "Moanin'," and so on. Mingus owed a tremendous debt to the example of Duke Ellington, and he paid his due not only by covering a number of pieces from the Ellington songbook, but also by echoing the master's style in his own compositions, from the early "Shuffle Bass Boogie" and "Make Believe" to "Boogie Stop Shuffle," "Duke's Choice," and "Duke Ellington's Sound of Love." He likewise paid homage to jazz pioneer Ferdinand "Jelly Roll" Morton ("Jelly Roll"), pianist Thelonious Monk ("Jump Monk," "MDM," "Monk, Bunk and Vice Versa"), bassist Oscar Pettiford ("O.P."), and alto saxophonist Charlie "Bird" Parker ("Parkeriana," "Reincarnation of a Lovebird," "Bird Calls," "Something Like A Bird"), all of whom had lasting impacts upon his musical concepts and personality.

Mingus had a deep fondness for certain structural elements, particularly the ever present triplets (three notes uniformly crammed into what would normally be the space of two). He tried out less common meters, such as 6/8 (six eighth-note beats per measure, as heard in the gospel-jazz trilogy "Wednesday Night Prayer Meeting," "Better Get Hit In Your Soul," and "Slop") and 5/4 (five quarter-note beats per measure, as heard in the first measure of "Free Cell Block F, 'Tis Nazi USA," which also contains five sets of triplets in a row!). He liked to layer two, three, and even four melodic lines on top of one another, giving greater weight to classic compositions such as "Moanin'" and "Open Letter to Duke." Early in his career he tried to combine elements of jazz and classical music, largely in his Jazz Composers Workshop of the 1950s, but he had abandoned most of those notions by the mid-1960s; "Canon," from 1973, is one of the significant exceptions. Admittedly, the few concepts listed here make up but a minute portion of Mingus' ideas about the nature of music. Few composers have embraced a wider scope of stylistic elements in the course of their careers, making his one of the most diversified, interesting, and difficult bodies of work in jazz.

Daniel Harmon, my editor at Praeger, suggested this book's title as a glimpse of Mingus' personal and musical character. In the background of "Moanin'" (on *Blues and Roots*, Atlantic Records, 1959), Mingus shouts "I know . . . what I know" with the raw vehemence of a preacher. If Charles Mingus was sure of anything, it was that he knew what he knew. Or at least he *thought* he did. He knew women: being married four times, with several affairs in between, had been quite educational. He knew business: having record labels and a publishing company come crashing down at his feet taught him solid lessons. At the same time, even subtle moves like changing the titles of his compositions indicated some business savvy. As archivist Andrew Homzy suggests, not only would it make his catalog of tunes look larger, it kept newly recorded versions from competing in the marketplace with older versions on other labels. And Mingus knew his music. From his childhood studies of cello (which was deemed inappropriate for an African-American in the 1930s, since there was little hope of securing a job in classical music) to his radio-born love of Duke Ellington, from his teenaged experiments in jazz composition (some of which he finally recorded more than two decades later) to his later forays into jazz-rock and world-music fusions, from chartbuster to oblivion and back, Mingus spent his hard, fleeting life having the ups and downs of the music business hammered into his head. He knew many things, but chiefly Mingus knew how to create distinctive music of durable character and quality. This is the story of the timeless art known as Mingus Music.

Trumpeter Jack Walrath played in Mingus' bands for the last several years of the bassist's life. He provided a great analysis of why Mingus' music has endured so well. "It's very organic, for one thing. It was very down to earth in a lot of ways. The blues, for example, will be there forever. And also, I think there really are some people that would like to hear a melody that's more than just a two-bar soundbite. Charles would write these melodies like Duke Ellington would write, that had a range of more than a minor third. He wrote music that was meant to be listened to; it wasn't meant to be background music. It's a novel thing today to listen to music instead of using it for some other activity."

"There are a lot of other factors," Walrath said. "Nowadays you have all these powerful corporations that look for a formula. They can't come up with things on their own, so they just take other things and market them. They will find someone who manages to break through, and then they will find twenty other guys who sound the same. I think there's a feeling of helplessness, in that people are afraid if they like something the whole group doesn't like, then they don't fit in. If you hold a contrary opinion, then people think you are trying to hurt them. The computer was supposed to save us time, but it takes more hours out of our day. People are getting their information in the condensed form of *Reader's Digest*. But I think things like Mingus' music will hold up because there is development to it. It goes from point A to point C and you can follow the development of it. Even though this music is written, it has the feeling of improvisation. I think that Beethoven did like most of us do. He heard a lick in his head, so he put it in his notebook, sat down at the piano and began to develop it. If you listen to a Beethoven symphony, it sounds like a piano improvisation that has been orchestrated. It is the same with Mingus' music. It's rough, it's energetic, it's soulful and it sounds spontaneous." And, more than a quarter-century after Mingus' death, his work remains as vital and popular among jazz listeners as it was during his peak years.

One final note: as he liked to do with his instrumental scores, Charles Mingus frequently rewrote the lyrics to his songs as well. Throughout this book, lyrics are quoted from particular versions of songs being discussed within the chapters. To avoid confusion, keep in mind that subsequently recorded versions of these same songs might contain altered lyrics. Please refer to *Mingus's More Than a Fake Book* (Jazz Workshop/Hal Leonard, 1991) for alternate lyrics, should you find any discrepancies between versions.

Central Avenue Swing

Charles Mingus Jr. was born on the U.S. Army base in the desolate town of Nogales, Arizona, on April 22, 1922. His half-white, half-black father was a stubborn and often violent career military man who moved the family to Watts, a suburb of Los Angeles, a few months later. Charles' half-black, half-Chinese mother, Harriet, suffered poor health and died when the little boy was only seven months old. Charles Jr. and his siblings were raised by their father and stepmother, Mamie, who tried at times to still her husband's harsh hand but never made any close connections with his children.

As the sole male heir, Charles was called "Baby" with as much affection as his parents could muster, and in his early life he was disciplined less harshly than his sisters. His light skin, the product of two biracial parents, was a source of discomfort to Charles for years, giving him a sense of confused dissociation from any of his bloodlines. In fact, when Mingus began writing his rambling, mostly fictitious autobiography in the 1950s, its unsubtle working title was *Memoirs of a Half-Schitt-Colored Nigger*.

Mingus Sr. had no musical education, but he perceived that the formal study of classical music was a symbol of intelligence and class. Until then, the only music that the Mingus children had heard was the gospel songs of the Baptist and Holiness churches. At the age of eight, Charles Jr. began learning to play a trombone his father had bought out of the Sears catalog. But his pudgy arms wouldn't cooperate, and a few months later he took up the cello. He also studied with his sister Vivian's piano instructor and demonstrated great promise. Soon he became a member of the Los Angeles Junior Philharmonic, but at the same time he was taunted by kids at school who told him that black children didn't play classical music. And that was true, for the most part: orchestral opportunities for a black musician in the 1930s were almost nonexistent.

One day, when Charles was twelve, he was fiddling with his father's crystal radio set when he heard a new kind of music he had never experienced before. It was different, exciting, and loud. It was the Duke Ellington Orchestra playing their theme song at the time, "East St. Louis Toodle-Oo." Charles sat there captivated, the hot jazz music making a lifelong impression on his soul. He knew right then what he wanted to do. It has been suggested that without a Duke Ellington there wouldn't have been a Charles Mingus. It is a silly speculation at heart—who knows what other influences might have stepped in to similarly shape the direction of Mingus' art—but the stamp of Ellington on much of the bassist's lifelong body of work is unmistakable.

It took a couple of more years for Mingus to dump the cello. Saxophonist Buddy Collette, his friend and bandmate at Jordan High School, convinced Charles that there was no future for an African-American cellist in the 1930s, and encouraged him to take up the bass instead. Britt Woodman, another friend, played trombone in the school band. Woodman's father, William, had actually played with Ellington, which helped to cement Mingus' relations with the family. William Woodman had helped his sons organize their own orchestra, and Collette was also playing in a band by that time. Mingus' racist music teacher pushed him further from his classical studies by suggesting that blacks made inferior musicians. Finally, Britt Woodman smoothly talked Mingus' father into trading in the cello for a bass.

Charles immediately got into the big new instrument, practicing it as often as he found the time. Collette remembers that Mingus used to sit in the back of the trolleys that serviced Los Angeles and work out music for hours. Collette and Woodman landed more professional gigs. Their pals, drummer Chico Hamilton and clarinetist Eric Dolphy, also began to make names for themselves around Los Angeles. Mingus' father had wanted Charles to take the postal service exam and join his dad in his post-military career, but he recognized that he could not prevent his son from becoming a musician.

Mingus Sr. arranged for his son to take lessons with Lloyd Reese, one of the most respected black music teachers in the city. Reese knew many of the Ellington sidemen, who would come by his home and demonstrate jazz and instrumental techniques to the young students. He didn't forget to emphasize classical music, which Mingus still loved. Charles found himself in hog heaven, learning quickly alongside friends like Collette and saxophonist Dexter Gordon, who would also become a giant of the bebop movement.

For all his growing knowledge of musical mechanics and forms, however, Charles felt that Reese wasn't doing much to improve the specific skills he needed as a bassist. To fill that need, Mingus collared his slightly older friend, Red Callender, an expert bass and tuba player. Callender had just come to Los Angeles from New York, where he had been freelancing for a while. He taught Mingus to find his way around the fingerboard, how to position his hands to prevent cramps and injury, how to build speed and accuracy. Callender then fixed up Mingus with his own teacher, a former New York Philharmonic bassist named Herman Rheinschagen. But that experience wasn't as rewarding as working with Callender directly, because Rheinschagen insisted that Mingus had to do things "the right way." Still, those lessons built up Mingus' bass technique enough that, in 1937, he joined Collette and Hamilton to tour the West Coast in Floyd Ray's band. He was fifteen years old and out on his own.

The Ray group wasn't any great shakes musically, but they kept busy traveling the length of California between Los Angeles and Oakland. On one of the band's trips up north, Mingus met a artist named Farwell Taylor. The two hit it off immediately in spite of their dissimilar backgrounds; Taylor was a white painter whose studies of the Vedantic Hinduism of India gave him an appreciation of all cultures and races. Mingus moved in with the painter and his wife, Faye, for a time, and he absorbed as much new literature, culture, and music as he could. The Hindu studies were especially convincing to Charles. Prior to his death in 1979, he requested that his ashes be scattered into the Ganges River according to Hindu tradition.

Years down the road, Mingus immortalized his unlikely friend in a composition he entitled "Far Wells, Mill Valley"; after the artist's death, Mingus also wrote "Farewell Farwell." While staying with Taylor, Mingus began composing some tunes inspired by his spiritual awakening. It was some time before he finished either of the pieces, one of which was "Half-Mast Inhibition" (a pun on his teenaged sexual neuroses), the other a murky narrative poem called "The Chill of Death." Even as a young man, Mingus was quite preoccupied with life and death, so much so that he tried to will himself to die during this period. His views of life were rarely celebratory and most often stained with the spittle of racism, lost loves, and economic difficulties.

When he was eighteen, Charles returned home to Watts. It was an exciting time in the jazz world, particularly when a young bass phenomenon named Jimmy Blanton made his debut with the Ellington band. Blanton was one of the first bassists to approach the big instrument like a horn, playing long, fluid, melodic lines instead of the staid, plunking four-beat that had been the jazz bassist's lot up to that time. Ellington tunes such as "Jack the Bear" and "Jumpin' Punkins" were enlivened by Blanton's fearless bravado. So when the Ellington band spent an extended period of time in Los Angeles in 1941, Mingus went to check out Blanton's style at every available opportunity. It was as if the universe opened up and poured its bounty into Mingus' musical soul, revealing to him that the bass could be anything he wanted it to be.

Mingus had begun playing in the clubs along Central Avenue, an L.A. street that some had dubbed "The Brown Broadway" because it was the best place to go hear black musicians. In the 1940s Central Avenue was a prosperous African-American community, the living and stomping grounds of blacks who had come out west to work in the defense plants. There were jazz clubs aplenty there, hosting jam sessions on Sunday afternoons and after-hours on most other nights. Some of Duke Ellington's sidemen had effectively jumped off the bandwagon in Los Angeles to establish their careers in what seemed to be a bottomless well of opportunity for black jazzmen in California. And it was, at least for a while. The scene would change in the mid-1950s, when the white musicians who played with the bands of Woody Herman and Stan Kenton settled in and gave a paler hue to the face of jazz in Los Angeles.

Nineteen-year-old Charles had the fortune to play a few times with Art Tatum, a blind pianist who was revered by musicians and fans alike for, among other things, his skill at interpolating classical motifs into his virtuosic approach to jazz. That was another revelation to the young bassist who had been torn between two musical worlds. Alvino Rey, whose orchestra had an unusual lead feature in Rey's steel guitar, regularly used Mingus as a pickup bassist while in town. Charles also gigged with drummer Lee Young, whose brother, tenor saxophonist Lester Young, was making waves of his own. Lester had picked up the nickname "Prez," which was short for "president of the tenor sax," a nod to the jazz hierarchy then topped by the Duke (Ellington) and the Count (Basie). Within a few short years he would be the most influential tenor saxophonist in jazz, emulated by legions of white players such as Stan Getz, Brew Moore, and Zoot Sims. A few years beyond that Lester Young would be dead, fallen victim to the jazz lifestyle alongside Charlie Parker, Billie Holiday, and an unconscionable number of other stars.

Faced with the draft, Mingus faked diabetes to get out of military service, an act which might have sent his father into conniptions but ensured his ability to stay active on Central Avenue. He wanted to grow as a composer and arranger, so Lloyd Reese sent Mingus to Dimitri Tiomkin, a film-score composer who not only taught Mingus the art of orchestration, but also the convenience of parting out work on his own scores to willing arrangers. The daring scope of Tiomkin's scores had some effect on Mingus' writing as well, despite his protests about the dull, workmanlike labors that the composer saddled him with.

In August 1942 Mingus was hired by clarinetist Barney Bigard, whose ensemble included the hot New Orleans trombonist Edward "Kid" Ory. Bigard brought Mingus one step closer to his Ellington ideals, having played in Duke's band since 1927. Bigard had quit the Ellington group earlier in 1942, having grown tired of the constant touring. For the time being he was settling down in Los Angeles with his own band, and Mingus was his choice for the bass chair.

The Bigard gig was a class act but didn't last very long. Mingus soon joined the local orchestra of Les Hite, backing Louis Armstrong during his stay in California. In 1943 he appeared on his first recordings, which were some broadcast transcription sessions with Armstrong. That same year Lee Young landed a job heading the house band at Club Alabam, and Mingus was his bassist of choice once again. He had now become the most talked-about bass player on Central Avenue. But despite all of this lucrative, educational activity, Mingus' heart burned to explore his own musical ideas. He had a huge pool of them circulating in his brain and crying for an outlet.

The Strings and Keys was a trio that Charles had assembled to play around Long Beach. The name of the guitarist has practically been lost to the ages, but the pianist was Spaulding Givens, a cousin of Art Tatum. Givens worked occasionally with Mingus for the next few years, recording a duo session that would inaugurate the bassist's own label, Debut, in 1952. The Strings and Keys became popular and widened Mingus' profile in the Los Angeles area. He began to bill himself as "Baron Mingus" (or sometimes "Baron Von Mingus"), boldly placing himself amidst the jazz royalty of Duke Ellington, Count Basie, and his friend Lester "Prez" Young. During this same period, in January of 1944, Mingus married his first wife, Jeanne Gross, in Los Angeles.

When the bebop band of Dizzy Gillespie came to town for eight weeks at the end of 1945, Mingus was not impressed by the new wave of jazz sounds from New York. To him, bebop was little more than ugly noise, compared to his beloved Ellington. He had become familiar with some of Charlie Parker's records, but in Mingus' mind the young alto saxophonist couldn't yet match the urbane skillfulness of Johnny Hodges, Ellington's alto star, or even his friend Buddy Collette.

Things would change once Mingus got to New York himself in 1947 and was able to perceive bebop in the proper context. He would get the gist of bebop as a retaliation against the white musicians who kept copping black creations and claiming them as their own. It had happened in 1917, when the falsely titled, all-white "Original Dixieland Jazz Band" got a recording contract with Columbia Records and became the first jazz group ever put to wax, beating authentic jazzmen such as Freddie Keppard to the punch. And it was still happening three decades later, as white audiences bought records by white musicians playing black music. The New York beboppers took the chord changes to standards such as "Indiana," "How High the Moon," and "Sweet Georgia Brown" and affixed new, insanely quick-tempoed, densely notated melodies such as Parker's "Ornithology," "Donna Lee," and "Anthropology." (These compositions on old changes are called "contra-facts," a term to be encountered throughout this book.) In effect, they aimed to make a music so wild and complicated that the white musicians couldn't begin to keep up with them.

But for now, bebop was all still a bit lost on Mingus. He put together a new band he dubbed the "Stars of Swing," with Collette (usually the ostensible leader), Spaulding Givens, Britt Woodman, tenor saxophonist Eli "Lucky" Thompson, and later, vibraphone player Teddy Edwards. The ensemble was never recorded, but the Stars of Swing served as a flexible workshop for the new ideas that Charles and the others were developing.

In 1945 Mingus was signed to Excelsior Records, run by the songwriting brothers Leon and Otis Rene. He recorded some long-lost sides with Givens, Buddy Collette, Britt Woodman, and bebop drummer Roy Porter, but it is not known whether Excelsior ever intended to release those 78s. In the fall of 1945 Charles put together a sextet with Porter, William "Brother" Woodman and Maxwell Davis on tenor saxophones, N.R. "Nat" Bates on trumpet, and pianist Robert Mosley. They recorded the very first Mingus compositions to be put onto shellac: "The Texas Hop," "Baby, Take a Chance With Me," and "Swingin' an Echo." These three tracks, along with "Lonesome Woman Blues," start off *Charles "Baron" Mingus: West Coast, 1945–49* (Uptown, 2000), a CD compilation of two dozen Mingus recordings from his days in California. This terrific set gives us the chance to see Mingus' early evolution as a composer and bassist, with multiple versions of the same tunes given different names and arrangements. As a bass player he progresses from a four-to-the-bar supporting role in the earliest records to a lead voice in "Mingus Fingers" and "Say It Isn't So." Likewise, his compositions evolve from straightforward blues and swing structures to expansive works that embrace classical and Latin forms.

At first spin, there is little to distinguish this primal Mingus music from anything else that was happening in jazz in the mid-1940s. Porter adds a bebop flair to what would otherwise be well-done but undistinguished R&B/jazz tunes. An unknown singer named Oradell Mitchell croons through the swinging "Texas Hop" with spirit, but the voice is so androgynous it is impossible to tell whether we're hearing Mr. or Ms. Mitchell. The solos are decent, with heavy vibrato in the tenor saxes and a nice clarity in Bates' trumpet tone. Also forgotten is Everett Pettis, who sings the slower "Baby, Take a Chance With Me" above the florid piano of Mosley. "Lonesome Woman Blues" is actually credited to one Jack Griffin, who is also listed as cocomposer of "The Texas Hop." Nothing is known of Griffin beyond these sides, and it might have actually been a pseudonym, or possibly the record producer taking some credit and extra pay for the music. On this languid blues it is now possible to tell that Oradell Mitchell is a woman, and a fine blues singer at that. "Swingin' an Echo" possesses a totally different character from the prior tracks, leaning more towards the bebop side of the fence. Mingus' bass is now more prominent in the mix, and Woodman tears it up on his solo turn. The "echo" involves a sharp arrangement wherein Mosley's piano echoes the last few notes of each horn passage. It's a neat chart that stands out from the rest of the session.

Mingus must have had a special place in his heart for "Baby, Take a Chance," or at least he thought it had the potential to become a smash single. He recorded it again in January 1946, with an expanded ensemble that included vocalist Claude Trenier, fresh out of the Jimmie Lunceford band and a rising star at Club Alabam. Henry Coker's bright trombone begins this version (track 6 on the CD), and Trenier's delivery is more soulful and relaxed than Everett Pettis' interpretation. Even nicer is the billowy tenor sax solo by the young Lucky Thompson. Mingus' bass stands forward with beautiful triplet figures before Trenier takes the piece out. On "Ain't Jivin' Blues" the singer effects a humorous, hiccupping quirk, something akin to what Little Richard would do a decade later during the rise of rock-and-roll. The band shifts gears once more on "Shuffle Bass Boogie," the closest predictor yet of where Mingus would go in the future. It's an obvious nod to Duke Ellington's jazzy train songs ("East St. Louis Toodle-Oo," "Take the 'A' Train"), and it has one of the first substantial Mingus bass solos on record. Even this early in his career he is obviously possessed of great technique and confidence. The tune has a distinctive harmonic and rhythmic structure which reflects the contemporary currents of swing while leaning a bit forward.

Trenier returns on the artsy, morose "Weird Nightmare," which still stands as one of the strangest, yet most compelling tunes in the Mingus canon. He changed its title time and time again—"Pipe Dream," "Vassarlean," "Smooch" when Miles Davis recorded it—but it remained gripping with each interpretation. It was one of the very few tunes from his early years to reappear in his later recordings and live sets. Mingus was always more interested in advancing as a composer than in revisiting the past, so "Weird Nightmare" must have held some particular magic for him.

Mingus often had difficulty writing for vocalists, fighting to reconcile his poet's heart with the special demands of jazz singing. "Weird Nightmare" typifies the awkward structure and flow of some of Mingus' songs, clunky and perhaps forced, yet it possesses a true, enduring charm. It begins with a minor dissonance from the horns, a downward piano arpeggio, then:

> Weird Nightmare, you haunt my every dream
> Weird Nightmare, tell me, what's your scheme
> Can it be that you're a part
> Of a lonely, broken heart?
> Weird Nightmare, why must you torment me?
> Weird Nightmare, there's such pain and misery
> In a heart that's loved and lost
> Take away the grief it's caused
> Can't sleep at night
> Turn and twist in fright

With the fear that I'll live it all again in my dreams
You're there to haunt me
When you said she doesn't want me
I've been hurt, oh, do you know what that means?
Weird Nightmare, take away this dream you've borne
Weird Nightmare, mend the heart that's torn
And has paid the cost of love a thousandfold
Bring me a love with a heart of gold...

A couple of months later Mingus switched over to 4 Star Records, another small, visionary local label. This time the group was "Baron Mingus and His Octet," including the Woodman brothers, Buddy Collette, trumpeters Karl George and John Anderson, Lee Young on drums, guitarist Louis Speigner, and a pianist billed as "Lady Will Carr." The impact of Duke Ellington and his arranger, Billy Strayhorn, becomes more palpable in Mingus' music during this period. These arrangements alternate between derivative and inspired. "Make Believe" is in the first camp, very Dukish in its conception (in the CD's liner notes, Andrew Homzy suggests that it is a partial rip-off of Ellington's "Everything But You"). The third, and final, version of Mingus' expectant hit single is here entitled "Honey, Take a Chance On Me," even though Trenier sings "Baby" instead of "Honey." On the earlier recordings it seemed that the cascading piano was being used as a device to cover up some holes in the chart, but by this point it is sublimated in service to the whole concept. The horn lines are now smoother, more sinuous, and everything blends together quite well. Britt Woodman and Collette have a great time on the saxophonist's own tune "Bedspread," the most Ellingtonian track of the session.

Mingus' interest in composing and arranging on a grander scale emerges on "This Subdues My Passion," which Homzy, in the liner notes, terms "virtually a serenade for a chamber music ensemble." Strayhorn's "Chelsea Bridge" is an obvious inspiration, but in this case Mingus has much to say on his own behalf. Collette, however, pays homage to the Ellington band in both his bubbly clarinet playing and an alto sax solo which directly channels Johnny Hodges' swoops and tremors. The next track, "Pipe Dream," is simply "Weird Nightmare" recast as an instrumental feature for Lady Will Carr's piano. The use of a Chinese gong in the intro, and Carr's abstracted flits and runs on the keyboard, predict some of the later pieces in which Mingus expanded the jazz ensemble's sonic palette.

Mingus' marriage fell apart in 1946, and he spent some time in San Francisco hanging with Farwell Taylor and working at the post office. But by the next summer he was back to gigging in Los Angeles. Mingus took time off from his own projects to tour with Lionel Hampton's big band for a while. The vibraphonist/drummer had first made a name for himself with the racially integrated Benny Goodman band in the 1930s, and in the mid-1940s he set off on his own path with huge success.

Mingus took the opportunity to compose a feature for his bass playing, the bebop-informed "Mingus Fingers," which Hampton called up often during the next tour. It can be found on an anthology, *Charles Mingus' Finest Hour* (Verve, 2002), and must be one of the most avant-garde things ever attempted by the vibraphonist. The unusual intro with clarinet and flute was ahead of its time for 1947, presaging Mingus' Jazz Workshop experiments in New York several years later. The bassist definitely asserts himself here, sparring with Hampton and the horns throughout the entire track. Check out the sizzling solo that begins with an upward bowed run at precisely one minute into the tune. *Finest Hour* also includes the hip "Zoo-Baba-Da-Oo-Ee" from the same session. Also composed by the bassist, it's a plodding but fun tune with a collective scat vocal by the band (one must assume that Mingus' voice is included). The bass sticks to a firm four-beat rhythm for the entire track, so it's not Mingus' most interesting work on upright, but as a contrast to "Mingus Fingers" it serves as evidence of his wide-ranging vision as a composer.

While working with Hampton, Mingus spent several weeks in New York City. He met some of the beboppers there and started a new friendship with trumpeter Fats Navarro. The younger man not only gave Charles a deeper appreciation of what the bop movement was trying to accomplish, his atrocious heroin habit (which killed him in 1950) reminded Mingus that drugs would damage both his body and career. Charles' uncle, pianist Fess Williams, and his cousin, saxophonist Rudy Williams, helped him work out the new chart for "Mingus Fingers" that the bassist taped in November 1948 for Dolphins of Hollywood, the house label of the Dolphins record shop. Mingus' bass tone is titanic, his technique quick and accurate as he doubles the melody lines with Collette's clarinet. As represented on the Uptown CD compilation, this track and "These Foolish Things," again with Mingus handing the melody, mark an increase in Mingus' assertiveness as he steps to the fore in a fashion rare for bassists at the time.

In 1949 Charles returned to San Francisco where he put together a big band that he billed as "Charles 'Baron' Mingus Presents His Symphonic Airs." The group cut two sides for the Fentone label in February of 1949. "Story of Love" had a Spanish emphasis, lying in the middle ground between Gerald Wilson's Latin big-band experiments in Los Angeles and the Cuban-influenced bop of Dizzy Gillespie's orchestra in New York City. Tambourine, Latin drums, and a saxophone pulse set the stage for layers of hard-swinging themes, reminiscent of Wilson pieces such as "The Golden Sword." Mingus does not quite have a grip yet on orchestrating for such a large group: the horn sections tend to fall over themselves, and soloists are washed away in a relentless tide of sound. It's an interesting precursor to his later works for big band, however, especially the use of multiple themes layered in a single composition.

Vocalist Herb Gayle is featured on "He's Gone," ushered in by the lush, opulent tones of flute, clarinet, and cello. This piece characterizes Mingus' long desire to unite the separate worlds of jazz and classical music, which would eventually immerse him in the 1950s movement known as the Third Stream. Gayle stuck around later in the day, when Mingus cut back to a quartet with baritone saxist Herb Caro, drummer Warren Thompson, and pianist Buzz Wheeler. Their "Pennies from Heaven" is slow with a certain charm, worlds removed from the usual cheery interpretations, and Caro's embellishments behind Gayle's vocals are a nice touch. "Lyon's Roar" is a short run through a twelve-bar blues, with the undersung Caro taking the lead without any apparent written melody. The bright young saxophonist showed tremendous potential, and he followed Mingus back to Los Angeles when the Fentone sessions were wrapped up.

Right after he got home, Charles organized a quick sextet date for Dolphins of Hollywood, and he placed Caro in the tenor saxophone seat with good results. The band cut Irving Berlin's "Say It Isn't So," another showcase for Mingus' lead-bass technique wherein he uses a series of sliding notes that would become a recurrent motif in his solos for years to come. Singer Helen Carr (no relation to Lady Will Carr, Mingus' erstwhile pianist) was then married to Donn Trenner, the pianist on this session, and had sung with Skinnay Ennis' big band. Her only appearance with Mingus was her soft-spoken, languid delivery of "Say It Isn't So." In the 1950s she cut two albums for Bethlehem before dying of breast cancer in 1960. The flip side of the sextet's 78 was "Boppin' in Boston," where Mingus not only burns through a mighty bass solo but offers up a respectable scat vocal. Caro effects a cool Lester Young tone on his short solo turn before the tune ends with an unexpected crash and boom.

Next, Mingus went back to the score of "Story of Love" and made some helpful changes in the ponderous chart. He eliminated the tambourine and much of the intro, let go of the more grating dissonant parts in the horns, and apparently had enough rehearsal time to get the different sections comfortable with their parts. His L.A. big band included Caro, trumpeters Buddy Childers and Hobart Dotson, trombonists Britt Woodman and Jimmy Knepper, Eric Dolphy and Art Pepper on alto saxes and other reeds, pianist Russ Freeman, and probably Red Callender taking over the bass parts (it doesn't sound like Mingus, who most likely wanted to concentrate on conducting the date). The big band's second piece was "Inspiration," which Mingus later retitled "God's Portrait," then simply "Portrait." This composition takes a step even further into the classical-jazz confluence, with a slowly building, ever tenser introduction worthy of Scriabin. The melody is stately and slow, with the trumpet particularly effective in conveying the laconic mood. Further into the tune come clarinet and flute swoops, fleeting passages of swing rhythm, and light percolations like the ticking of a clock. It is an amazingly sophisticated piece of work for a young man such as Mingus, and this early record offers an interesting comparison point with the later "Portrait" recordings. Solos by Childers and Caro are among the many high marks. Tragically, Caro soon went to New York City and got embroiled in the drug scene there, dying of a heroin overdose at the age of twenty-two.

As a bonus, the Uptown CD includes an eight-minute excerpt of one of Mingus' rehearsals, as he tries to work out the arrangement of "He's Gone" on the piano. It has a surplus of down time, of course, but might be of interest to those who are curious about the process of putting arrangements together. Except for this rehearsal excerpt, all of the West Coast material is also available, in exactly the same track order, on the 2002 Jazz Factory CD, *Complete 1945–1949 West Coast Recordings*. However, the Uptown disc's extensive, well-organized liner notes, by reissue producers Chuck Nessa and Robert Sunenblick, make it an essential document of early Mingus.

A prior LP issue called *The Young Rebel* (Swingtime) combined some of the same material with recordings led by Earl "Fatha" Hines and bassist/cellist Oscar Pettiford, who was another of Mingus' key influences on bass and would sometimes hire Charles for support. That extra material with Mingus as a sideman is also of some interest, but has not been available for some time. In 2004 the Proper label released *The Young Rebel* as a four-CD set including all of the above West Coast material; some additional tracks from that era; the Hines and Pettiford sessions; and dates led by pianist Billy Taylor, Charlie Parker, Red Norvo, Bud Powell, and Mingus himself in the early days of the Debut label. It is a wonderful, reasonably priced overview of the bassist's career up to the early 1950s.

The year 1949 was a series of ups and downs for Mingus. He met a white woman named Celia Gemanis, who would become his second wife, although for now she was engaged to trumpet player Jon Nielsen. He was rehired by Lionel Hampton, but fired during a tour for fighting with the band's drummer and refusing to go along with Hamp's notions of showmanship. He soon met another girl named Shirley Holiday, started a new group with Richard Wyands on piano and Shirley singing, got her pregnant, then got evicted and had to go slouching back to his stepmother's house with his expectant girlfriend. Shirley left him the following summer, after their daughter Yanine was born.

Mingus wrote a slow, somber song called "Eclipse" for Billie Holiday but never got her to sing it before she went to jail on drug charges. "Eclipse" was more than just a bluesy lament. It was a parable of miscegenation and racial inequality, disguised in the form of a song that might, to inattentive ears, simply be about the crossing of planets. He held onto the song and cut different versions in 1953 and 1960, but one expects that the definitive interpretation would have been Billie's had it come to pass.

In 1950, on the recommendation of pianist Jimmy Rowles, Mingus was hired by vibraphonist Red Norvo to work in his trio with a gifted guitarist named Tal Farlow. The music they played was extremely fast, complex, and invigorating, and Mingus had trouble adjusting to the demands of the Norvo book. But there were few bassists better equipped to handle such charts, and soon Mingus had carved out his niche in the trio. The CD *Move!* (Jazz Heritage/Denon, 1997) is a good collection of sides that Mingus cut with the trio in 1950 and 1951, after he decided to follow Norvo to New York. They rode the line between cool jazz and bebop, revamping tunes like George Wallington's "Godchild" and Denzil Best's "Move" that had recently been recorded by Miles Davis' "Birth of the Cool" ensemble. A passel of chestnuts like "Zing! Went the Strings of my Heart" and "I Get A Kick Out Of You" were reinvented with a smooth bebop flair. Mingus was on equal ground with the vibraphonist and guitarist in all things; he was expected to contribute much more than a rhythmic foundation. It was not the ideal setting for Charles, who wanted to do more innovative things than the purely entertaining displays of virtuosity that were Norvo's stock-in-trade. But it did open his mind to new things. And more importantly, it took him to New York City, which had become the heart of jazz innovation in the United States.

Central Avenue would remain the hub of Southern California jazz for a few more years, until the cool-leaning, progressive-minded sidemen of Kenton and Herman shifted the scene to white-owned clubs such as the Lighthouse and Haig. Mingus' timing in leaving California was spot-on, and the change of locale was just the catalyst Charles needed to move further with his career. His reputation did not exactly precede him from the West Coast, although some of the people he met were aware of what he had been doing in Los Angeles. For the most part, like every other transplanted musician, Mingus had to work his way up the ladder in his new home city.

New York and the Bebop Revolution

Mingus came to New York seeking bold new opportunities, and he found them awaiting him in spades. The city was alive with the excited pulses of bebop, and Charles was soon networking with other musicians to find the prime job openings. He was also pursuing Celia, whose short marriage to Jon Nielsen was already on the rocks. Finally she acquiesced, and when the trio returned to California, Celia came along. She and Charles were married in San Francisco in April 1951. When the trio toured the Southern states, Celia often had to register at hotels as "Mrs. Tal Farlow" so the issue of miscegenation wouldn't rear its head. By that fall they were back in New York, ready to commence their life together. The city's Musicians Union wouldn't let Norvo work in its clubs if he retained the bassist, ostensibly because Mingus didn't have a local union card. But the race issue was an unspoken yet implicit factor, so Norvo reluctantly let Mingus go.

Miles Davis stepped in and offered Mingus a job in his band, which was working at Birdland. Pianist Billy Taylor was also happy to use the bassist, and gave him valuable instruction in the Afro-Cuban flourishes that had begun to color jazz around the city since Dizzy Gillespie had integrated Latin music into his bebop. It meshed a little with some of the Mexican music Charles had been exposed to in California, so he took to it well.

Also of interest was the "cool school" music of Lennie Tristano, a blind white pianist who was pursuing the kind of classical formality in jazz structures that Charles had been interested in. The pianist was already assembling a cult following among young players who were enraptured by every word and idea that came from Tristano's mouth, although many jazz fans couldn't connect to what they perceived as a cold detachedness in the music. In the future Mingus would successfully overcome that lack of emotion as he worked out his own classical-jazz fusions. Gigging with Tristano and alto saxophonist Lee Konitz for the time being nudged him further in directions outside of bebop.

Mingus reached a settlement with the musicians' union, having sued them for his unfair termination from the Norvo trio. He used the money to establish a record label he called Debut, inspired by Dizzy Gillespie's recent venture into Dee Gee Records. Tired of seeing black jazz musicians taken advantage of by white-run labels, Gillespie, Mingus, and other performers had decided to take charge of their own careers so they could reap the financial and artistic benefits they deserved. Celia helped Charles administer the new label, handling the accounting, distribution, liner notes, cover art and other matters while her husband tended to the artists and their art. Max Roach and his girlfriend were also partners in the fledgling label, and they frequently battled with Mingus over business and artistic issues. It was hardly a big-budget enterprise: a 1953 recording session with singer Jackie Paris cost them $400 to produce. They effectively doubled their money on sales, clearing just enough to record and issue the next Debut disc. That kind of hand-to-mouth financing characterized artist-owned labels for many years, and to a degree the numbers have only changed due to inflation. "DIY" (do-it-yourself) independent labels are still a risky proposition, and in the early 1950s they represented something close to financial suicide. But Mingus was convinced that he was the one best suited to determine where his music would go and who would get the money.

In 1990 Fantasy Records, which had held the rights to Debut's catalog for many years, issued an impressive twelve-CD boxed set entitled *Charles Mingus: The Complete Debut Recordings*. It collects every recorded performance on which Mingus had appeared during the label's lifetime, the fruits of over twenty sessions held between April 1951 and the end of 1957. Among the titular leaders of these dates were pianists Bud Powell, Paul Bley, Hazel Scott, and John Dennis; bassist Oscar Pettiford; trumpeters Thad Jones and Miles Davis; and trombonists Kai Winding, J.J. Johnson, and Jimmy Knepper. To keep a sense of continuity in this listener's guide, these albums will be discussed chronologically as they were recorded, and as they are ordered in this landmark boxed set.

*   *   *

The first Debut release was *Strings and Keys* (on disc 1 of *The Complete Debut Recordings*), a duet date that Mingus had made with his friend, pianist Spaulding Givens, in 1951 before he left Los Angeles. Sometimes the sound is spare and subtle, as on their opening version of "What Is This Thing Called Love"; other times Givens' piano is busy as a tumbling waterfall, as demonstrated on his masterful solo piano interpretation of "Yesterdays." Mingus takes the melodic role on "Body and Soul," which had become an anthem for tenor saxophonists after Coleman Hawkins cut the definitive version in 1939. His tone on bass is magnificent, tender, but confident. Givens had worked with Mingus long enough to know when and how to sublimate his own playing in service to his mate, and the session works exceptionally well as a result. Mingus' technique is percussive to the point that the lack of a drummer becomes moot within a few bars. Givens has a rather cool-school approach to some of the tunes, light and blocky. His own composition, "Blue Tide," has a slow majesty that is complemented by Mingus' restrained bowing. The full session was rounded out by "Darn That Dream" (two takes, one released for the first time in the boxed set), "Blue Moon," and two unreleased takes of "Jeepers Creepers" that find Givens leaning toward Bud Powell and the more lucid moments of Thelonious Monk. *Strings and Keys* was not a big seller, but it served notice that Mingus was serious about his new enterprise.

The next recording date under Mingus' supervision involved several disciples of Lennie Tristano, who acted as engineer for the session. It featured alto saxophonist Lee Konitz, pianist Phyllis Pinkerton, drummer Al Levitt, and NBC Symphony cellist George Koutzen, with Mingus on bass. There is a shadowy, haunted air about this entire set of music, reflective of the dark, often cold classical edge of Tristano's own works, though all of these selections were written by Mingus. The first track is "Portrait," which was "Inspiration" augmented with nature-glorifying lyrics that were inspired by his spiritual conversations with Farwell Taylor. It is sung by a promising young vocalist named Jackie Paris, whose gentle jazziness perfectly conveys the spirit of the lyrics. The airiness of Lee Konitz' alto and the formal cello lines further buoy the pastoral feeling. A second, little-known singer, Bob Benton, gives "I've Lost My Love" a quavering, stiffer interpretation that is more reminiscent of older-style big-band vocalists. Some of the instrumental parts are well-conceived, but the lyrics are somewhat pretentious and, as a whole, the tune just doesn't come together well.

"Extra-Sensory Perception" is a more dissonant, avant-garde piece without any vocals. At first the ensemble seems to have trouble getting started, and Konitz seems very unsure of himself. There is a good, and humorous, reason for this. He was contracted to producer Norman Granz' label at the time, and Konitz' contract stated that he could not *improvise* for any other record label. With that in mind, Mingus wrote out, note-for-note, the solo that he wanted Konitz to take. The rhythm as it was written out was different from what Konitz was hearing in his head, so he had to fight to correlate his instincts with the notations. Except for a cobbled-together version of "Extra-Sensory Perception" which was pieced together from two takes, none of these tracks had been issued except on 78s before the Fantasy set. It's just as well; although these pieces are interesting as historical items, they are not the best documentation of Mingus nor of the Tristano aesthetic. "Portrait," however, is valuable for demonstrating the early promise of Jackie Paris. Mingus dusted off the tune on several occasions during his career, changing its structure each time.

Mingus worked with Jackie Paris again in September of 1952, cutting three more sides for Debut 78s. They were the only carry-overs from the prior session; this one was manned by Juilliard School piano instructor John Mehegan, cellist Jackson Wiley, flute and alto sax player Paige Brook, and drummer Max Roach, who was Mingus' business partner in the Debut venture. "Make Believe" is another of the bassist's typical songs of love, fear, and rejection, with sinuous lines that would be difficult to sing if one weren't of Paris' caliber. Here he sings like a suave, prototypical hipster in the Mel Tormé manner. The first few seconds of the song are marred by tape wow, but it's a nice feature for the singer. "Paris in Blue" is a put-on, acted out in the studio to appear as if Paris were singing for a live nightclub audience. He states, "Thank you, thank you, ladies and gentlemen. This next number will be my interpretation of the blues." Roach, a bowing Mingus, and the others immediately begin playing arhythmically and aton-ally, at which point Paris slyly admonishes them that he will teach them what the blues is really about. That said, "Paris in Blue" is more of a cabaret cliché than anything resembling authentic blues, again due to Mingus' difficulty in reconciling his jazz roots and classical ambitions. The cello-flute combo is a nice addition, certainly. The third track from this session, "Montage," was long believed to have been recorded that April at the Tris-tano date, perhaps, because Paige Brook's alto playing was a little reminis-cent of Konitz'. This is an upbeat, light-hearted instrumental piece that would be at home in the soundtrack to some European-vacation film of the era, and Mingus gets to flaunt his solo chops freely. As blessed as their partnership was, Mingus and Paris didn't work together again for almost a quarter-century. Finally, in 1974, Mingus would call upon the stylish singer once again for one of the bassist's last hurrahs.

Mingus got the call to fill Duke Ellington's bass chair in January of 1953, and one more dream had come true. Unfortunately, Mingus' temper and ego worked him out of the job within a month. He couldn't resist the temptation to show off his skills to the new boss whom he had already worshipped for twenty years, so he played inappropriate bop lines and brought in his original compositions, which impressed many of his bandmates but didn't endear him to Ellington. On February 3, before a gig at the Apollo Theater in Harlem, Mingus and valve trombonist Juan Tizol got into a racially motivated scuffle. In the aftermath, Ellington had words with the bassist and convinced him to resign. What a blow to Charles' swelling ego, being effectively fired by the man he had idolized since childhood.

In April 1953, Mingus called Spaulding Givens out to join him for another album in New York City. The two friends were joined by Max

Roach for a session that went unissued in any form until they were dusted off for the Fantasy boxed set. The trio cut two takes each of Billy Strayhorn's sumptuous "Day Dream," Gershwin's "Rhapsody in Blue," and a tune called "Jet" that was in Nat "King" Cole's repertoire. The music on this date was attractive and engaging, particularly the tight swing feel they struck up on the Gershwin standard. It works so well in a jazz context that one almost forgets its orchestral roots. Roach's hard-hit drums give the first section of "Jet" an almost tribal undercurrent, which would likely have a completely different feel if the kit had been recorded with a bit more clarity. It shifts moods dramatically in an episodic fashion, foreshadowing the quick alterations that would characterize later Mingus works like "Slop."

On April 29, 1953, Mingus and Roach brought in pianist Hank Jones, the eldest of three brothers (the others were drummer Elvin and trumpeter Thad) who were taking the city's jazz scene by storm. They laid down a delicately beautiful rendition of "You Go To My Head" that showcased Jones' unhurried, sophisticated piano style. Given the fact that the track ends with an abrupt edit, general consensus is that it was originally the first part of a medley that has now been lost. The rhythm trio cut four other tracks in support of a singer named Honey (sometimes Honi) Gordon, who cowrote all of the songs. Possessed of an interesting contralto voice, she is reminiscent of Sarah Vaughan more than anyone, and her very low range enables her to tackle material that might be unsuitable for other female singers. "Can You Blame Me" is an engaging, buoyant song of teen love, while "Cupid" is slower and a bit affected. The other two tracks present The Gordons, which is Honey's vocal ensemble with her father, George, and her brothers, Richard and George Jr. Their harmonies on "You and Me" are tinged with a gospel flavor and recall groups such as the Ink Spots, with Ms. Gordon taking the lead. Jones' piano is the real highlight, while Mingus tends to get lost within the concept. "Bebopper" is sort of a period piece that doesn't work so well. A song about a bebop musician should likely be more up-tempo and energetic, but this one is so slow and wavering that it sounds as if there were something wrong with the master tape. Upon subsequent listens, evidence builds that perhaps there *was* some technical problem, but it should have been fixed with the technology that digitized it for CD release.

*   *   *

That spring, Charles was invited to take part in a momentous concert in Toronto, Canada. Bud Powell, Max Roach, Dizzy Gillespie, and Charlie Parker would be playing a full set of bebop at Massey Hall, one of the city's premier concert venues, at the behest of the New Jazz Society of Toronto. Oscar Pettiford had originally been selected as the bass player, but for some reason he was not available for the May 15 concert so Mingus was asked to fill in. He thought this would be an ideal opportunity to get some hard-core bop onto the Debut label, so he offered to record and release the concert. It became one of the many times that Mingus' good intentions turned into a near-disaster.

Despite some technical gaffes and a half-full house, the concert itself went off successfully. Roach had the first hurrah with a humongous solo improvisation he called "Drum Conversation" that gave clear reason for his prominence in the bebop movement. Powell and Mingus joined him onstage for a trio session that was issued on Debut as *The Amazing Bud Powell: Jazz at Massey Hall, Volume Two*, a fact that has often been lost on people who assumed that the only music played that night was captured on *Quintet of the Year: Jazz at Massey Hall*. The pianist was starting to suffer some of the mental and emotional difficulties that continued to plague him until his death in 1966—in fact, he had just been released from Bellevue mental hospital before the gig—but the Massey Hall performance is all wonder and facility. Mingus' solo on "Embraceable You" is vibrant and sensitive, meshing brilliantly with the jaunty piano. Roach is miked a bit too loudly on "Cherokee," almost shutting out the bass at times, but all three men play hell-bent for leather. "Sure Thing" is an original by Powell with such a stately structure that it sounds like a classical étude gone to seed, until the bebop pulse picks up. Powell's left-hand dexterity alone makes the piece work well. Vincent Youmans' "Hallelujah," which was inexplicably titled "Jubilee" on almost every issue of this material, and George Shearing's "Lullaby of Birdland" bear witness to just how tightly the three boppers could mesh onstage.

Next, Gillespie and Parker joined the rhythmists for a long, hot set of fresh bebop. Due to a contractual obligation, Parker was billed as "Charlie Chan" on the Debut release of the Massey Hall concert, although there was no mistaking his dazzling tone and fleet flow of ideas. The quintet begins with Denzil Best's "Wee," a.k.a. "Allen's Alley," which sets a rapid pace for everyone to follow. The tune is in a typical bop form: the horns blow the main melodic phrase twice, Bird and Diz both improvise for a few bars, then play the key phrase once again before Parker goes sailing off into an intense solo flight, followed by the trumpeter's improvisation. Each member solos in turn—Roach practically tears off the roof and screams through the chasm—before they reconvene to take out the theme. Mingus gets in a hot, heavy solo turn before the exit on Tadd Dameron's unusually keyed "Hot House." The Massey Hall version of Gillespie's "A Night in Tunisia," one of the authentic bebop anthems, is an absolute landmark in the evolution of jazz and belongs in every collection; the same goes for "Salt Peanuts," the full lyrics of which are found in its title and sung by Gillespie and Parker in a particular break. Juan Tizol's "Perdido," drawn from the Ellington book, is transformed into a bebop treasure, while the theme of "All the Things You Are" is maintained for about one-and-a-half phrases before Gillespie starts to take it to the roof. Mission accomplished, the band closed out with a forty-four second blast through Thelonious Monk's "52nd Street Theme."

After the show was over, disappointment set in. The New Jazz Society of Toronto had not sold enough tickets to pay the band, so they offered them the tapes of the concert in lieu of cash. Mingus latched onto them and said he would issue an album on Debut. Then, after he had the tapes in hand, Mingus did something that became the subject of controversy for decades to come. Whether he was being self-absorbed and disingenuous, or whether he was really trying to make a genuine artistic decision about sound quality, is still a bone of contention in the jazz world. Mingus went into the studio and overdubbed new bass lines onto the Massey Hall quintet tracks to make his parts stand out better, as he felt the bass wasn't miked well enough the first time. In hindsight, he might have had a point. The Fantasy boxed set includes the original, pretampering tracks as well as those with Mingus' added bass lines. It's true that his instrument is not especially audible much of the time, but whether that justified "tampering" with the tapes is dubious.

What Mingus had done was bring pianist Billy Taylor and a drummer (neither Art Taylor nor Max Roach by their own recollections, so Lord only knows who it was) in to listen to the original tapes and duplicate their pace and character as much as possible. The musicians could hear each other playing, but afterward Mingus pulled out the bass tracks and overlaid them onto the Massey Hall concert tapes. We'll leave it up to the individual listener to compare the boxed set tracks and determine whether the effort was worth the end product. Whatever the case, it made Debut Records a force to be reckoned with.

An interesting artifact of Mingus' subterfuge is "Bass-ically Speaking," an extra tune from the Billy Taylor session. Actually, four different takes exist, all of them in the Fantasy boxed set. This is a tune that Mingus recorded with Bud Powell and Max Roach after the Massey Hall concert, but all four takes are included in the CD issue of Powell's *Massey Hall, Volume 2* recording. The applause at the end of the fourth track, following Mingus' magnificent bowed outro, was obviously added on after the fact, but the bass redub is fairly smooth. The "Untitled Blues" in the Fantasy boxed set showcases Mingus in top form, with only minimal accompaniment from the piano to stall his flow of ideas. It hardly seems possible that this master of blues bass was the same man who supported a cadre of Tristano acolytes on avant-leaning jazz a year prior.

Mingus continued to work on and off with the beboppers for the next couple of years while developing his own concepts. An especially interesting artifact is "If I Love Again" (on the anthology *Charles Mingus' Finest Hour*, Verve, 2002), from a Charlie Parker date on May 25, 1953. The tune was arranged by Gil Evans, a few years after his "Cool School" work with Miles Davis, and features the Dave Lambert Singers. Mingus doesn't even solo on the tune, but he and Max Roach keep a constant simmer going under the unusual musical mix.

*   *   *

In September 1953, Debut recorded a trombone quartet-plus-rhythm, one of the more unusual sessions in their catalog. Trombonist J.J. Johnson was one of the first and best slidemen to tackle the complexities of bebop, holding his own easily among Dizzy and Bird. Kai Winding, a Danish immigrant, was becoming a marvelous stylist of his own and would remain a frequent partner of Johnson's well into the 1970s. Bennie Green and Willie Dennis were two lesser-known but talented trombonists who rounded out the unique quartet on *4 Trombones*. Pianist John Lewis had just cofounded the Modern Jazz Quartet, which would become his primary outlet. He and drummer Art Taylor joined the bassist in the rhythm section here.

Johnson's "Wee Dot (Blues for Some Bones)" kicks off this live set (recorded at Brooklyn's Putnam Central Club) in a red-hot fashion, with Lewis getting into a burning swing mood as he would rarely do in his cool/Third Stream explorations. Mingus and Art Taylor boot the pianist along for a full minute before Bennie Green's greasy horn bursts out. Winding follows in like manner, then Johnson rips in with his signature high notes and smooth effortlessness. Dennis is less precise in his delivery, hitting the occasional "clam" and with a rougher edge in his tone, but his rhythmic and harmonic concepts are perhaps more advanced than his bandmates'. "Stardust" presents Green solo, bubbly and almost nostalgic in the way he slides, smears, and vibrates his way beautifully through the Hoagy Carmichael chestnut. Mingus' high-velocity walking introduces "Move," which he had cut a couple of years previously with Red Norvo. This is a hellacious tune for any trombonist to tackle, much less four, but the quartet hacks through it fairly well and the solos are uniformly good. Mingus' powerful bass meshes with Taylor's propulsive drum torrents to drive the horns on to new heights. Lewis plays staccato clashing tones on the intro to "I'll Remember April," on which Winding seems a bit breathless but weaves a nicely conceived solo with nods to "Tea for Two." The ensemble interplay later in the track is the real selling point. Charlie Parker's "Now's the Time" (similar and possibly identical to the tune "The Hucklebuck") gives Mingus a great solo spot where he works with a lazy hand at tempo, dragging the beat a little to accentuate the blues feeling.

The other half of the *4 Trombones* gig, on Disc 5 of the Fantasy set, begins with what is probably the high point of the date. Spaulding Givens' "Trombosphere," which was apparently composed especially for this group, reverberates with the kind of rich, heady harmonies that characterized the best of the cool-era recordings. The liner notes give no clue, but this may have been arranged by John Lewis, given his hand in charting the classic Miles Davis "Birth of the Cool" nonet. It ends on a rather strange note, with hard minor tones and tumbling drums. Dizzy Gillespie's "Ow!" brings us back into the bebop mold, with the 'bones harmonizing on the first part of the melody and playing in gloriously effective unison elsewhere. When Art Taylor trades blows with each horn he kicks up the energy level substantially. Following "Chazzanova," which we will address in a moment, the band kicks off "Yesterdays" with a false start. Lewis begins the tune with a stream of interesting ideas, but the horns apparently drop the ball and Johnson has to kick it off again in a different spirit. The moment is all his as that bright, ringing tone fills the club. The concert ends with Winding's "Kai's Day," a sprightly theme that is most typical of his later quintet work with Johnson. Winding is in better form here than on "I'll Remember April," taking command with the first of a string of tight solos.

"Chazzanova," the sole Mingus composition of the date, offers an abrupt change of pace. Nearly orchestral in scope, it is very indicative of where the bassist's head was compositionally, from the dissonant piano introduction and bowed bass to the layering of horn voicings. It advances Ellington's ideas into new territory, and is captivating at that, but very unlike anything else presented in the concert. There are many of the unexpected touches that would be found in Mingus' music from then on: a sudden traffic-bustle in Lewis' piano that lasts but a couple of measures before Dennis' solo, subtle shifts in the chord pattern from minor-key bitterness to major-key optimism. "Chazzanova" is sort of an overlooked landmark in Mingus' development as a composer, a step well beyond his trial-and-error works such as "Story of Love" and "Inspiration," and his more blatant tries at emulating Ellington's formulas. The spirit of Duke can still be felt here, but it is more definably Mingus at its soul.

*   *   *

Before Debut had really gotten off the ground, Mingus had the opportunity to record a couple of sides for Prestige Records. As Ira Gitler relates in the booklet for *The Complete Debut Recordings*, Prestige president Bob Weinstock asked Gitler to look into whether Mingus' new group was worthwhile. "[Mingus] was rehearsing a large ensemble and Weinstock asked me to report on whether or not it had merit . . . I listened for several hours on a Sunday afternoon in some midtown studio, then Mingus drove me home. During the ride he was pressuring me to persuade Weinstock that everything was in order for the date to become a reality. I was in the uncomfortable position of middle-man. Finally I told him that, although I thought the compositions were indeed worthy, the band's execution was not yet to the point of necessary readiness." Mingus acquiesced as he thought about it, and the Prestige date never came off. But on October 28, 1953, the bassist convened a similar group to record Spaulding Givens' arrangements of the music that Mingus had been working on during Gitler's sojourn. And, in fact, the compositions were even older: Mingus had written them at the age of twenty-one, in 1943, except for Givens' own "Blue Tide" which they had recorded in duo in 1951.

Debut issued the EP record as *Charles Mingus Octet*, deemed in the liner notes as "a synthesis of old and new." It was an idea he would revisit later on his 1960 album *Pre-Bird*, which also contained tunes written before Mingus had come in contact with Charlie "Bird" Parker. This octet date is more blatant in its attempted fusions of Ellingtonia and classical forms. The ensemble is Mingus, John Lewis, trumpeter Ernie Royal (a former sideman in the Woody Herman band), Willie Dennis on trombone, Eddie Caine on alto sax and flute, tenorman Teo Macero, baritone saxophonist Danny Bank, cellist Jackson Wiley, and bebop drummer Kenny Clarke, who had just begun exploring similar fusions with Lewis in the Modern Jazz Quartet. "Pink Topsy" is jazzy but a bit busy, enhanced by the brilliance of Royal's clean trumpet sound and Wiley's deft, assertive bowing. On the boxed set's alternate take Royal loses his train of thought, but John Lewis' piano solo is charmingly concise and jovial. The song title, by the way, is a veiled racial reference (according to Mingus) to someone who is neither quite white nor black and is trying to see where she fits in.

The firm, almost boogie-woogie pulse of "Miss Blues" rescues it from the cool-school staleness which could have befallen it. Royal's trumpeting is bright and airy again, but the restrained feel of the arrangement gives an impression that more could have happened here. "Miss Blues" is notable as one of the earliest instances of self-reference, a thread that would occur time and again throughout his later compositions. The supporting passages behind the bass solo are drawn from "Mingus Fingers," the tune that Charles had written up for the Lionel Hampton band in 1946.

Singer Janet Thurlow joins the band on an evocative vocal rendition of Givens' "Blue Tide," which bears the same sort of languid, depressed mood as many of Mingus' own vocal ballads. Still, she is more effective than if the tune had been arranged with a horn as lead. Thurlow also sings "Eclipse," the ballad which Mingus had composed for Billie Holiday to no avail. The mood is frighteningly avant-garde, low-toned chords and rattling drums battering sharply bowed figures from Mingus and Wiley. The lyric, at first glance, seems an intriguing slice of poetic philosophy about the cosmic event. But it takes on a completely different character when viewed properly, as a statement about the mixing of the black and white races:

> Eclipse, when the moon meets the sun
> Eclipse, these bodies become as one
> People go around, eyes look up and frown
> For it's a sight they seldom see
> Some look through smoked glasses, hiding their eyes
> Others think it's tragic, staring as dark meets light

But the sun doesn't care and the moon has no fear
For destiny's making her choice...

Following a passage of tense dissonance over a swing pulse, bowed cello
and bass wail mournfully in the darkness. The tension builds further as flute
and trombone peep out like something from a *Twilight Zone* soundtrack,
then Thurlow sweetly sings the last two lines before drawing out
"Eeeeeeeee-cliiiipse" for the chilling finish.

*   *   *

Mingus had met Wiley, Macero, and some other band members after
joining the Jazz Composers Workshop, a collective of artists who were
exploring new avenues in composition and arrangement. A principal interest of the group was the attempted fusion of the forms and ideas inherent in
jazz and classical music, a concept that was soon dubbed the Third Stream
as a confluence of two flows of art. As we have seen in many instances
already, this was exactly the kind of company amongst which Mingus
wanted to place himself. Among his other associates in the workshop
were alto saxophonist and clarinetist John LaPorta and pianist Wally
Cirillo. The bassist worked closely with these new friends for a few
years, ironing out wrinkles in the disparate concepts they hoped to defini-
tively unite. (More on them later, once we get past the next few Debut
releases.)

Another new associate was a young pianist named Paul Bley, who
had come from Montréal, Canada, to join the New York jazz scene. He
spent several months in the Big Apple before going to Los Angeles, where he
undertook some groundbreaking free jazz excursions with Ornette
Coleman. In November 1953, Debut recorded *Introducing Paul Bley*, a
trio date with Mingus and drummer Art Blakey. Aside from cocreating
the blues improvisation "Spontaneous Combustion," Mingus didn't
have a compositional hand in this session, but his supportive presence
and solos are vital to the success of the record. Blakey is heard here
well before the founding of his seminal Jazz Messengers hard-bop outfit,
which introduced players such as Lee Morgan, Wayne Shorter, Chuck
Mangione, and Wynton Marsalis to the jazz public over the course of
more than thirty years. In those later years Blakey was acknowledged
as a titan of the drums, but here he plays more of a reliable workman
role for the most part. Bley's playing is utterly beautiful in conception,
informed by the melodicism of Oscar Peterson, perhaps, more than anyone
else. While in Montréal, the members of Bley's working trio had formerly
been employed by Peterson, and the big man had been one of Canada's
brighter jazz stars before coming to the United States, so the influence is
only appropriate.

This is a breathtaking session highlighted by "Opus 1," which is a Bley original, not the Sy Oliver piece of Tommy Dorsey renown. On better sound systems, the listener should be able to hear Bley singing along with his playing on the piece, a mannerism now associated more with the younger Keith Jarrett. "Teapot," later known as "Walkin'," hurtles from the speakers on the torrents of Blakey's ferocious drum intro. During the trade-offs we can hear the bassist's verbal exhortations to the drummer, just as he would do with Dannie Richmond in the years to come. "Like Someone in Love" is tender and heartfelt, while "I Can't Get Started" bears an unusually avant-garde prologue before the ballad melody arrives. "Spontaneous Combustion" is a themeless B blues improvisation on which Bley and Mingus both solo with an organic silkiness. As mentioned in the liner booklet, "The Theme" was a common feature of bebop ensembles throughout the 1950s, but no one seems to know who actually composed it. The trio here does as nice a job with it as any on record. A Latin flair emerges on Horace Silver's "Split Kick" before a segue into bebop, a few stuttered-rhythm bars, then back into the bop. "This Time the Dream's On Me" is taken at a fast pace. The even speedier "Zootcase" was written by tenorman Al Cohn in honor of his bandmate Zoot Sims, although it's often attributed to Sims himself. This really shows off the trio's collective chops more than anything on the disc; Mingus' ability to simply hang on while the pianist rips through the tune is testament enough to his amazing bass dexterity. They have a great deal of fun on "Santa Claus is Coming to Town," rushing certain phrases and leaving plenty of room between for drum riffs.

*   *   *

In mid-December of 1953, Mingus supported Teo Macero on a session led by the saxophonist. It was a highly unusual affair with two bassists, an accordionist, and drums by Ed Shaughnessy, who would later gain renown with Doc Severinsen's *Tonight Show* band. Although the tapes were licensed to Debut for initial release, Macero held contractual ownership and they were not made available for *The Complete Debut Recordings*. As there is so much more Mingus material to be addressed, this book will not address the Macero recordings.

A couple of weeks later, a session for Debut was made by Oscar Pettiford, who was one of Charles' bass idols. Like Mingus, "O.P." had translated the speed-and-lead innovations of Jimmy Blanton to the bebop vocabulary. But on *Oscar Pettiford Sextet* the leader stuck strictly to cello, his other love, and left the bass chair to Mingus. An unusual front line of French horn (Julius Watkins) and tenor sax (Phil Urso, a lesser-known Lester Young disciple) chugs through oddly titled themes such as "The Pendulum at Falcon's Lair," a nod to Rudolph Valentino's California homestead, and "Jack the Fieldstalker." On the latter tune Urso tears away from the cool Prez tone and blows hot and heavy, recalling his fellow tenorman Stan Getz' more extroverted moments. Watkins is simply tremendous, handling the difficult French horn as if it were a mere toy, and Pettiford's pizzicato cello is dexterous and vibrant (even if the twangy tone does take some getting used to). Walter Bishop Jr. on piano and Percy Brice on drums round out the rhythm section as Mingus rules the roost much of the time. On his solo spots Mingus almost seems to hold back his technique, as if he were deferring to the leader's authority. Bishop swings and flits lightly on Quincy Jones' "Stockholm Sweetnin'," a joyfully bouncy piece with more greatness from Urso and Watkins. The pianist also starts off the unthemed blues "Low and Behold" before Pettiford's cello takes the reins. His interactions with Mingus are especially nice. Charles was becoming a master at playing precisely in the higher range of the bass, which meant that the cello and bass here could have trod all over one another if played by two less attentive and respectful musicians. That they blend together so well is a testament to their keen musicianship.

Mingus and Debut introduced to a wider audience trumpeter Thad Jones, a young man from Detroit whose elder brother, pianist Hank, had recorded with Mingus the previous year. In 1954 Jones was only known to the jazz world for his solo on Count Basie's "April in Paris," and when Mingus gushed endlessly about him to the press (just as he had in comparing Buddy Collette favorably to Charlie Parker) people were skeptical. So into the studio went the band, and out came *Thad Jones* on Debut. Taped in August 1954, this album features a quintet with Jones, Mingus, Hank Jones on piano, Basie bandmate Frank Wess on tenor sax and flute, and Kenny Clarke on drums.

Jones and Wess practically dance on the trumpeter's quick-legged "Bitty Ditty," a spirited theme with interesting intervals and solid bebop pacing. "Chazzanova" is redone much less effectively by this ensemble. It's not bad in itself, but the conceptual scope of the piece is so ambitious that the trombone septet was just naturally a better vehicle for it. In comparison it loses much of its character when reduced for the trumpet and tenor, fine musicians though they are. Brother Hank's appealing piano style comes to light on "I'll Remember April" and the plaintive original "Sombre Intrusion," which bears the slightest harmonic resemblance to George Benson's "This Masquerade" in places. "Elusive" is upbeat yet poignant with a Miles Davis cool edge. The record ends on a downbeat tone, with a deep blue reading of "You Don't Know What Love Is" that affirms all of the lip service that Mingus had been paying the trumpeter.

*   *   *

At this point, we'll set the Debut box aside for a while and investigate what else was going on with Mingus in the mid-1950s. As stated earlier, Mingus was involved with the Jazz Composers Workshop, which had been convened by *Metronome* magazine jazz writer Bill Coss and a handful of concordant musicians who wanted to explore some new directions for jazz. Mingus liked the core notions of the group but felt that too little was happening of real consequence. His visionary heart led him to break the group apart and establish his own Jazz Workshop with more cohesive ideas and less infighting. But, as fate would have it, the bassist's ego drove him to emphasize his own compositions over the other members', and he allegedly took credit for others' accomplishments as well. For these reasons, the initial Jazz Workshop only lasted for a couple of years before its ugly disintegration. Although Mingus kept the Jazz Workshop name alive for many moons, the concepts upon which it was originally founded were left to fade after 1955.

Mingus' Workshop recorded their first tracks on Halloween of 1954, at Rudy Van Gelder's studio in Hackensack, with Ozzie Cadena as the producer. The personnel were Mingus, LaPorta, Macero, tenor and baritone saxist George Barrow, pianist Mal Waldron, and drummer Rudy Nichols, most of whom were young men equally intent on changing the status quo of jazz. The all-reeds front line gave this lineup a very distinctive flavor.

The tyros of Mingus' Workshop faced widely disparate futures. Mal Waldron, in particular, was on the cusp of greatness when he joined Mingus. He had already been working with saxophonist Ike Quebec, and by the end of 1956 he would move on to lead his own groups and accompany Billie Holiday in her final days. Further on, the pianist would play some groundbreaking duets with soprano saxophonist Steve Lacy, who in 1955 hadn't yet made the move from Dixieland to free jazz. John LaPorta's greatest successes lay in the halls of academia, as he would become a beloved music educator. Teo Macero is now best known as a producer, specifically of later Mingus albums and Miles Davis' controversial electric-funk period. Barrow and Nichols remained more marginal figures, with the saxophonist gaining some attention for his work under tenorman Oliver Nelson.

Jazz Composers Workshop (Savoy) includes both the October 1954 session and one from January 30, 1955, led by pianist Wally Cirillo, a Lennie Tristano disciple from whom little has been heard beyond this release. The music, by and large, is representative of the early Third Stream, with complicated chord changes and classical leanings. Most of the tracks are unlike the compositions that would make Mingus' fortune a few years down the road, but some do smack of the future.

"Purple Heart," driven by LaPorta's clarinet and Barrow's forceful baritone sax, is similar in spirit to the cool-school material recorded in 1949 and 1950 by Miles Davis with John Lewis, Gil Evans, and Gerry Mulligan (*Birth of the Cool*, Capitol). The sense of swing is notably subdued, and the dynamics are marked by innumerable surges of breath in the horns. Through much of the tune the three horns are playing separate lines that may or may not be improvised. At 2:17, right in the middle of the interwoven tenor/baritone lines, LaPorta injects an atonal element by blowing long tones that conflict glaringly with the other activity. Such tonal clashes would become a Mingus hallmark from now on.

The introduction to "Gregarian Chant" features Mingus' mournful bowed bass, a pained lament that is answered in stages by the other performers. About a minute into the piece, Mingus begins playing the pizzicato theme. One by one, the horns tear themselves away from their improvised wailings and fall into place for harmonic support. "Eulogy for Rudy Williams," dedicated to a passed musical relative of Mingus, is closest to his later Ellington-inspired compositions; the melody played by LaPorta on alto could have fit into many of Mingus' subsequent records for Columbia or Atlantic. It is not as bitter in tone as "Gregarian Chant," but still mournful. Mingus' gift for collaged compositions is evident here: the multivoiced horn lines of the intro spread out into a suspended-time feel at 0:35; the pulse rises again around 1:00; the leader solos at 1:24 with the wailing of LaPorta distant behind him; the horns swell into a new theme at 1:52; Waldron takes the reins around 2:13 as another thematic stretch is brought up. Macero's tenor solo is lyrical and owes much to Lester Young, and the main melody blown by LaPorta is a classic of *film noir* intensity.

For the first several years that he was in New York, Mingus toyed with layered medleys, having the ensemble play two or three separate themes woven together instead of in sequence. Vincent Youmans' "Tea for Two" is the earliest of these in the Mingus catalog, fused here with "Prisoner of Love," "Body and Soul," and a figure in the clarinet part that recalls Juan Tizol's "Perdido," from the Duke Ellington band-book. Forty-five seconds into the track, the pace slows to an eerie ballad style before Mingus picks things up again with an upbeat bass solo. His interaction with the horns here is humorous and prescient of his musical communications with Eric Dolphy in 1960. "Tea for Two" winds down with a marvelous Dixieland-style collective exchange.

The last two tracks on the 2000 Savoy CD reissue are also from the Halloween 1954 session, so we will address them now. "Getting Together" is a jazz fugue of sorts, with each player entering in turn to build layers gradually. Rudy Nichols' drums provide the first rank of sounds, laying down an intriguing beat that would make a cool loop for a modern dance programmer. Eight bars later, the baritone sax (probably Macero) enters, followed by the clarinet, then tenor, then the leader's muscular bass. Nearly a minute into the tune, LaPorta solos with firm backing from Mingus and Nichols. At 1:36, Waldron steps in with a fragmented, dystonal improvisation that amounts to barely a handful of notes but grips our ears daringly. After a short horn burst, Mingus' solo begins at 2:20 and is pierced at intervals by pointed clarinet pokes. Barrow's tenor takes a turn before being supplanted by the baritone. The three horns meld in a happy melange of jazzy lines, then the bari sax is left alone for a spell. Nichols' tumbling drums lead the track out.

"Body and Soul" is one of the most revered standards in jazz, usually a testing ground for tenor saxophonists following in Coleman Hawkins' wake (his 1939 solo take is definitive). LaPorta delivers it here on alto sax in this album's most beautiful, moving performance. Unlike most of the other tracks, this melody is permitted to dominate with only the most suitable brocading by the tenor and bari saxes. Mingus solos exactly two minutes in, a staccato message of love that twists and turns unpredictably. Then the horns return, and LaPorta smears on some excellent blues sensibility before the end.

Tracks four to eight were composed by Cirillo and ostensibly taped under his leadership. The band is a simple quartet of piano, tenor sax (Macero), bass (Mingus), and drums (bebop giant Kenny Clarke). Although Mingus' development as a composer was nowhere near complete, it's obvious that these four tunes, good though they are, did not come from his pen. "Smog L.A." is effectively built upon variations of a couple of phrases, and Cirillo's piano soloing brings mostly linear streams of eighth notes. "Level Seven" is highly unusual and might be based upon dodecaphonic (twelve-tone) theory, in which the twelve notes of the traditional Western musical scale are sequenced so that no note is repeated until all twelve have been played. Macero's attractive tenor solo and its accompaniment are in a more traditional jazz mode, however. At 2:29 the piano brings us into a dreamlike reverie, and Mingus' ensuing solo is suitably spare. "Transeason" flows smoothly in an essentially cool mode, built upon the chord changes of "All the Things You Are." It's a lovely piece. The last track is a comfortable but unmemorable melody called "Rose Geranium," nice enough but not of enduring consequence.

*   *   *

In December 1954, between the sessions presented on *Jazz Composers Workshop*, Mingus brought the group back to the studio to tape some adventurous pieces that were a little more in line with his background: the Holiness Church, Ellington, blues, Central Avenue. He had decided that his music had only been representing part of his expansive interests, and he felt that more of his experiences should be expressed in his compositions. Some of these were penned in collaboration with John LaPorta, although the reeds player usually only receives joint credit for "Four Hands," if even that. The Period label initially issued these sides on *Jazzical Moods, Volumes 1 and 2*, and they have been reissued on LP and CD under such titles as *Intrusions* and *The Jazz Experiments of Charles Mingus* (most recently by Rhino/Atlantic under the latter title).

Jazzical Moods was a tentative step in the direction that would later seal his place in jazz history. The session was held with a sextet featuring Mingus alternating on bass and piano, LaPorta, Macero, cellist Jackson Wiley, drummer Clem DeRosa, and young Thad Jones on trumpet. The studio engineering has as much to do with the effect of this recording as the tunes or musicianship. The distinctive reverb, especially clear in Jones' case, adds a fullness that makes the ensemble seem larger than reality.

Cole Porter's "What Is This Thing Called Love" is taken pretty straight at first. Macero, LaPorta, and Jones rotate through the roles of lead voice and harmonies, arriving at the point where all three are simultaneously improvising on the chord changes. Jones is off on a solo turn before we know it, playing with the assuredness, clarity, and vigor that would mark his career from then on. The melodies of Tadd Dameron's "Hot House" and Dizzy Gillespie's "Woody 'N You" are also woven into the arrangement. After LaPorta takes a cool-toned solo, the influence of Lennie Tristano is palpable in Mingus' piano improv. Jackson Wiley presents a fine walking-bass technique on cello, taking over the master's supportive role. Jones returns at 4:40, exchanging ideas fluently with Macero. DeRosa's drumming is spot-on, and it's a shame that he never received better exposure. The band's version of "Stormy Weather" is similarly distinctive, and much too short at less than three and a half minutes.

As mentioned earlier, one of the cornerstones of the bebop movement was the contrafact, a new melody built upon the chords of an older work. For example, Charlie Parker's "Anthropology" and Ellington's "Cottontail" are among dozens of contrafacts written on the chords of George Gershwin's "I Got Rhythm." On *Jazzical Moods*, "Spur of the Moment," composed by pianist Horace Parlan, is a contrafact on Gershwin's "'S Wonderful." Its multilevel structure falls in line with Mingus' vision in that era, but at times it becomes so heavy with sound that the whole thing bogs down. Jones takes a long, well-conceived solo, with Macero picking right up on the last note. Especially effective are the little, far-away horn phrases that pop up throughout Mingus' bass solo. LaPorta emerges from that fog for his own fast-paced, rhythmically interesting improvisation, and the second he is done, the band immediately lands on the melody without pause.

LaPorta switches to clarinet, and Macero to baritone sax, for the lead voices in "Thrice Upon A Theme." This Mingus composition is more along the lines of his Third Stream work and would have fit well on *Jazz Composers Workshop*. DeRosa steers with a quiet but tightly swinging hi-hat ride as the two reedmen do their cool musical dance. At about 3:48 things switch gears, with Mingus emerging to solo as the horns blow long tones and languid lines behind him. The mood changes once again at about 5:38, as the clarinetist blows a series of ascending note pairs, several hard tones, then a tumble down the scale, where Mingus hammers down on the piano to call things back to order. Though much of the piece is composed, the style is so loose and improv-like that it's hard to pin down the theme they've allegedly played thrice.

"Four Hands" is a contrafact on "Idaho," with Mingus' piano track overdubbed along with his bass. This is more accessibly jazzy and melodic than the two prior tracks, which gives the players great inspiration for their excellent solos. LaPorta, in particular, really has a ball here. Mingus has a too-heavy left hand on the piano, but he fares well as he explores some repetitive patterns with his right. He's certainly more at home with the strong bass solo that follows Macero's turn.

Now and then Mingus produced a memorable blues-that-isn't, with the feeling of the blues but lacking the expected chord structure. "Minor Intrusions" is one of those, and jazz-wise it is probably the most effective piece on this session. After the horns state the plaintive, high-ranged theme, the strings of Mingus and Wiley harmonize beautifully in variations upon it. The horns slink back in sumptuous layers, providing a rudimentary Ellingtonian feeling. Mingus and crew do an excellent job of blurring the lines between composition and improvisation, due in part to the sinuousness of the written material.

Typical of the material he wrote in this era, Mingus apparently never returned to these compositions in his live concerts or later recordings. Nevertheless, they represent valuable stepping stones in his evolution as a composer.

*   *   *

In 1955 Mingus stepped away from the Third Stream ambitions of the workshop to concentrate more on the jazz end of things. He gathered a new lineup for his band that now included George Barrow, Mal Waldron, trombonist Eddie Bert, and drummer Willie Jones, who had been working on the outer fringe of bop with Thelonious Monk. It was this Mingus Jazz Workshop that performed at New York's Café Bohemia on December 23, 1955, as captured on *Mingus at the Bohemia* (Debut/Original Jazz Classics).

The Bohemia had only reinstated its jazz policy a few months before Mingus got the gig there, and that was only due to the success of other nightclubs such as Nick's, Eddie Condon's, and the Village Vanguard. Manager James Garofalo had planned for Charlie Parker to inaugurate the Bohemia's jazz program, but Bird's death on March 12, 1955, caused the club to scramble. Oscar Pettiford was the new headliner, and in his wake came a number of up-and-comers and veterans: young alto saxophonist Julian "Cannonball" Adderley, a schoolteacher by trade; pianist George Wallington; the original edition of the Jazz Messengers, with pianist Horace Silver and drummer Art Blakey; and Miles Davis' new quintet, which would immediately reshape the face of mid-decade bebop. Mingus walked through the Bohemia's door into good company.

Mingus at the Bohemia begins with "Jump Monk," a portrait of the bebop pianist that does not reveal much direct Monk influence except for rhythmic elements. The title stemmed from Monk's constant level of motion, whether he was playing, conversing, or off in the corner. The solo bass introduction, with its rapid clusters of sixteenth notes, is one of Mingus' finest and offers a clear testimony of where he was taking the instrument. George Barrow gets into a tasty blues improvisation, accompanied later by Bert before the melody comes. The theme is constructed of descending eighth notes figures that cover over two full octaves, from a high C above the staff to G below it. This is followed by eight bars of collective improvisation. This scheme is repeated once more—melody, then group improv—then a softer bridge with long ascending phrases, staccato (short accent) playing, and a couple of ear-catching jumps to higher intervals. Barrow takes a solo that begins smoothly but takes on a rough, bluesy edge at times. At 3:51 the tenorman wraps up and Waldron hits a couple of long notes prior to his own rich piano improvisation. In one section, from 4:10 to 4:20, he plays a pedal point (a single bass note maintained across several changes of chord) with his left hand to build tension.

The 1990 CD reissue on Original Jazz Classics appends a longer alternate take of "Jump Monk." This one is enjoyable, but not quite as cohesive in the horn lines. At about 8:33 and 8:53, during the drum solo, the musicians play a couple of high tremolos that seem rather unnecessary, and were missing from the shorter take that was chosen for the original album release.

The Gordon and Warren standard "Serenade in Blue" receives an intriguing new treatment, with the tempo and chordal character changing several times. Mingus, bowing his bass, and Barrow play the melody low and slow, with trombonist Bert adding subtle counterpoint. Thirty-three seconds in, Barrow takes up the counterpoint instead and the bass and trombone play the theme twice as fast. At 0:50 Waldron augments the melody as the other instruments spread out into long tones. The pianist is left alone for a bit to play beautifully expanded figures, then at 1:22 the double-time melody returns. A stronger, bustling rhythm is brought out behind Bert's swinging solo. Willie Jones gets excited in the midst of Waldron's piano improvisation, kicking up the volume and energy so that Barrow is floating on a bright cloud of sound when his solo turn arises. Four minutes in, Mingus plays a brilliant solo with a few variations on the theme's rhythm and a couple of wittily suspenseful figures. At 4:47 the full band begins to play fun, broken figures that precede the return of the slow melody.

Drummer and Debut Records partner Max Roach was in the house that night at the Bohemia, and he stepped onto the stage to engage Mingus in a spontaneous duet. You'll immediately notice two bass parts on "Percussion Discussion." This is because Mingus went into the studio as these tapes were being prepared, and overdubbed a second part on the higher-pitched piccolo bass. It was a better, less controversial experiment in studio trickery than his notorious tampering with the Massey Hall concert tapes. The exchanges between Mingus and Roach onstage at the Bohemia were interesting enough, but the high overdub permitted the bassist to expound even further on what had happened during the live duet.

The track begins with bowed passages from both basses and minimal response by Roach, just a cymbal tap here and there. At 1:06 Roach plays a tom-tom roll, to which the bassist responds with a couple of hard, low notes and a quick, high skitter. This pattern is repeated, then we're back to the bitter lament. At 1:39 Roach executes a loud snare-drum roll, a light dancing pattern, then a more martial cadence that brings out more energetic bowing by Mingus. The clean, crisp sound of the drums tells us that Roach is a performer who takes his kit seriously, tuning the heads precisely and selecting the most absorbing, inspiring patterns in his exchanges with the bassist. At 4:16 the overdubbed piccolo bass (or perhaps it's Mingus' original bass line, plucked up in the higher register) engages in a most wonderful give-and-take with the previously recorded drums. After the five-minute mark the two players trade off in the finest jazz tradition, egging one another on to new heights of creative energy. Around seven minutes in, the slow, lamenting bowed passages return even as Roach continues to up the ante in volume and power. Eventually he gives up the chase and settles in to quiet punctuation, but not without a final burst of noise.

"Work Song" is Mingus' evocation of slaves laboring on the chain gang, and we can clearly visualize the strikes of their sledgehammers on rocks as George Barrow's sax groans out the theme. Chordally, this is the blues at its most basic, essentially an eight-bar melody instead of the more typical twelve-bar form. This tune is orchestrated as a canon, with Eddie Bert answering the tenor lines. Mingus' composition "Canon," written in the early 1970s (see *Mingus Moves*), is tangentially related to this earlier work, not only in form but in the use of a triad of notes as the first statement of the theme. The foreboding spirit of Waldron's hammer-strike clusters is carried over to his piano solo, which begins with jerky variations in a minor mode. The solos of both Bert and Mingus are soaked in the despondent, yet ultimately hopeful, spirit of the blues. In the 1960s pianist Bobby Timmons composed his own "Work Song," which became a hit for Julian "Cannon-ball" Adderley's band, and once again when singer Oscar Brown Jr. put words to it. Duke Ellington wrote his own piece by that title as well. Due in part to the immense success of the Timmons tune, Mingus' own "Work Song" has often been forgotten, but it is one of the greatest statements of his early New York period.

As shown in the workshop recording of "Tea for Two," one of Charles' interests was blending two or more compositions into one unit, which was not difficult if the chord patterns were all compatible, but proved to be a challenge otherwise. At Café Bohemia he presented two such unions. "Septemberly" is a confluence of "September in the Rain" and "Tenderly." Mingus subtitled this contrafact "the song of the thief" as a witty poke at plagiarism because the two original source tunes are so similar. It's ironic because the act of writing a contrafact is a more acceptable form of plagiarism. Stealing the chords of an existing piece, lock, stock and barrel, brings no penalty from the copyright officials, but borrowing too heavily from a composed melodic line is another matter. All of the politics aside, this is a beautiful performance that features Bert and Barrow in marvelous trades. As Mingus' solo fades, the suspended feel of the theme returns.

"All the Things You C#" is another medley, this time fusing "All the Things You Are," Rachmaninoff's "Prelude in C# Minor," and Debussy's "Clair de Lune." It begins with Waldron's thunderous pounding of the "Prelude," then the horns blowing the odd, three-note clusters of the "All the Things" introduction. Barrow later plays its melody as Bert blows long, often clashing notes alongside him. "Clair de Lune" is mostly hinted at in the piano but ties in thematically nonetheless. After the string of solos—Barrow, Bert, Mingus—everyone trades bars with the dynamic Willie Jones. The structured tune then returns, with the crushing piano "Prelude," the horns blowing "All the Things" and such, and winds down after a restatement of the "Things" introduction.

On the CD reissue, Mingus introduces the nearly eleven-minute alternate take of "All the Things You C#" by explaining the title. The band does a false start, but the sax is off-rhythm and Mingus calls for a do-over. Even then, the horns have a hard time getting the rhythmic structure of their parts aligned with the pianist. At the Bohemia, Waldron proved himself as a suitable rhythmic partner for Mingus, a little more inventive and freer than he had been at the earlier workshop session. The pianist's liner notes, by the way, give good insight into this seminal music and should be read while listening to the CD.

*   *   *

More material was recorded that same night at the Café Bohemia, and was issued on Debut as *Charles Mingus Quintet+Max Roach* (sometimes reissued under the title *Chazz*). Roach took over the drum chair from Willie Jones and prodded the quintet into a frenzy. This set was a sort of test-run for some material that Mingus would tackle on his next two studio albums.

"A Foggy Day" explores the kind of urban-noise motifs used so successfully by George Gershwin in "An American in Paris." The concept is fleshed out much better on *Pithecanthropus Erectus*, Mingus' next studio album, but it's interesting to hear the early genesis of the arrangement. The sound effects are more sparse; Mingus, Barrow, and Bert toss around ideas for a few moments before the tenorman takes up the stylish melody. In sticking with the concept, the trombone occasionally injects a quiet foghorn sound in the background. Barrow does likewise when Bert solos, giving a humorous edge to the tune. As Mingus winds up his own articulate improvisation, the horns once again introduce the foghorn motif, then trade off with it during the last run-through of the melody.

"Drums" is an avant-garde improvisation of sorts, with long tones and fragmented ideas played over the constant tide swell of Roach's drums. At about 2:18, following the first drum solo, the horns and piano play a series of high-range trills to which the drums suitably respond. Roach becomes more frenetic, pounding out a series of short, repetitive ideas until the trills come back. At times Mingus plays bowed bass figures to complement the drummer. At around 3:44 the dire bass is more than a little reminiscent of the "Jaws" soundtrack! It's not Mingus' most effective exploration of free improvisation, but it is a good document of his rapport with Roach.

Next is "Haitian Fight Song," which Mingus would develop further over the next few years, ending up with the definitive version on 1957's *The Clown* (Atlantic). As done at the Bohemia, it lacks the extreme tension caused by the insistent eighth-note triplets of that later version. Still, it is a very compelling minor blues tune, and the canon effect of trombone against tenor sax is ear-catching.

Tadd Dameron's "Lady Bird" was a favorite among beboppers of the time, and Mingus gives it his own characteristic polish with an arrangement that features intensely clashing tonalities in the tenor sax and trombone. Bert plays many of the phrases a half-step lower than Barrow, causing an almost painful dissonance. The band breaks the tune up further by having the rhythm section drop out for a few bars at a time, leaving those unharmonious horns suspended in midair. It is a very strange version of a classic theme, with some strong improvisations. Waldron is particularly noteworthy, not only for his maintenance of the dissonance behind the other soloists, but his distinguished use of the same tensions in his own solo. Mingus, for his part, sticks to melodious thoughts in his improvisation, even as he quotes "I'm An Old Cowhand!"

A thirteen-minute take on "I'll Remember April" is full of tension and beauty. It begins with throbbing note-pairs from the bass, soon assaulted by a rattling drum pattern. That gives way to a slow simmer as soon as George Barrow begins playing the melody with a beautiful tenor tone. At about 1:08, the rhythm section drops out for a solo tenor riff, which is immediately answered by Eddie Bert's trombone. Bert contributes a warm counterpoint during Barrow's next improv. Waldron's piano solo, beginning around 5:07, is interesting for the solitary bass notes he uses to accentuate his improvised theme. At about 7:15 the horns, starting with Barrow, trade off four-measure lines with Roach. The drummer has a great deal of fun, sliding between hot swing riffs, rapid sprays of cowbell or woodblock, and hard quarter-notes on the bass drum. After a snare swell and some tom rolls, Roach returns to a basic pulse rhythm for the final theme statement. Barrow shines on this album, and it's a shame that he never became better known as a performer. Bert fared a bit better in his career, but also remained mostly a section player. Tracks like this one are fond reminders of how well these two men conformed to the Mingus aesthetic.

As he did with "A Foggy Day," Mingus would reevaluate "Love Chant" a few weeks later on *Pithecanthropus Erectus*. This earlier test run has its own clear-cut charms, chiefly the embraceable sweetness of Eddie Bert's trombone sound. Waldron's piano vamp, too, is a key selling point of this marvelous creation, providing a quiet brook of sound on which the horns are set afloat. During most of the track, Barrow and Bert slide between silken harmonies and abrupt clashes. Their mutual use of dynamics is striking as well. The fast upward climb heard at about the two-minute mark is evocative of Gil Evans' cool-school arrangements; the switch to a buoyant, major-key mood at 3:03 is pure Mingus.

The Debut box includes alternate takes of several tracks from the Bohemia date, including two more versions of "Drums," an interesting Waldron piano solo entitled "A Portrait of Bud Powell," and a barn-burning variation on "Jump Monk." These fine live tracks pointed the way to the next significant breakthrough in Mingus' career: taking a role in the development of free jazz as a viable art form.

Breaking into Freedom

If the Café Bohemia sessions gave notice to the world that Charles Mingus was a force to be reckoned with, *Pithecanthropus Erectus* was his manifesto. It compiled many of the features that would characterize his music for years to come: an outspoken racial awareness, subversive handling of standard material, special effects, and an emphasis on tone color that gave Mingus' ensembles their distinctive air.

Alto saxophonist Jackie McLean was the latest addition to the group. A native of New York City, McLean was the son of guitarist John McLean, who had played with the swing orchestra of Tiny Bradshaw in the 1940s. Young Jackie made a serious impression on the city's jazz circles while he was still a teenager, gigging with Sonny Rollins when he was sixteen, and recording with Miles Davis before he hit twenty. McLean had most recently worked with George Wallington at Café Bohemia when he made the acquaintance of Mingus. McLean only worked with the bassist for a few months before joining Art Blakey's Jazz Messengers, but would come back to Mingus briefly in 1959. This documentation of their early time together is a true landmark of jazz' evolution.

Tenorman J.R. Monterose was a more reluctant member of the quintet, stating in later years that he was never comfortable with what Mingus was trying to accomplish at the time. Mal Waldron and Willie Jones were held over from the prior workshop band, giving some needed stability to what could have been a very difficult session.

Recorded for Atlantic Records on January 30, 1956, *Pithecanthropus Erectus* was a bold step forward for Mingus as a composer and visible figure in New York jazz. The title track was intended as a parable of man's evolution and collapse through hubris and hatred. Mingus described it in the liner notes as:

> My conception of the modern counterpart of the first man to stand erect—how proud he was, considering himself the "first" to ascend from all fours, pounding his chest and preaching his superiority over the animals still in a prone position. Overcome with self-esteem, he goes out to rule the world, if not the universe, but both his own failure to realize the inevitable emancipation of those he sought to enslave, and his greed in attempting to stand on a false security, deny him not only the right of ever being a man, but finally destroy him completely.

This thinly veiled stab at the white man's history of oppressing minorities did not sit well with some, but the composition carrying this message stands as one of Mingus' finest achievements. It is reminiscent of "Jump Monk" in its inclusion of collective improvisations, but the theme is more interestingly composed. The dynamics are one of the keys to this piece as it begins at low volume, skulking along the ground, crescendos with huge drama to a long note, and immediately quietens down again. The full scope of jazz can be heard in the improvised sections, from bebop to stride piano to purest blues. The theme is repeated again, and the next group improv is far more unrestrained: squeals and moans from McLean, hard blues by Monterose, a manic waltz in the rhythm section. A piano tremolo brings the energy down to a thud before Monterose's unsure but nicely worked-out tenor solo. At 3:50 Waldron subtly ushers the collective improvisation back in behind Monterose. Mingus moves into a very stiff four-beat, highly unusual for him, then opens up into a steady walk as Waldron solos. Listen especially at 4:58, when the pianist plays a staccato figure that is instantly, brilliantly answered by the bass. The same occurs at 5:38, not long before McLean lets out with a series of anguished alto sax wails before his own solo turn. The altoist is considered a pioneer of free jazz for a series of albums he cut for Blue Note Records, though much of his work has been outside the free vein. His ambitious ideas are a great complement to Mingus' notions, and presage the arrival of quintessential free thinker Eric Dolphy at the bassist's door in 1960. After the solo sections, the pattern of theme and group improv returns, becoming so unfettered that the bassist screams frantically during the last exchanges.

"A Foggy Day" (subtitled "In San Francisco," Mingus' personalized displacement of Gershwin's opus from London) is here more thoroughly developed than it had been when he tested it out at Café Bohemia a few weeks prior. The sound effects are louder and more prevalent now, ranging from foghorns and klaxons to dropped change. "Love Chant" is not as significantly altered from the Bohemia version; the twin saxophones are an ideal pairing on this complicated but eminently enjoyable composition.

The distinct personalities of McLean and Monterose are given much elbow room on this album. In fact, by now it had become Mingus' practice to sculpt his arrangements in accordance with the character of his sidemen. Nowhere is that more evident than on "Portrait of Jackie," created as a showpiece for the talented young alto saxophonist. Little gets in the way of McLean's unbridled virtuosity. He demonstrates taste, maturity and no small measure of chops at an age when many contemporary jazz students are just finding their way out of music school.

At the 1956 Newport Jazz Festival, Mingus took some further risks and performed two new pieces that comprised his full set. "Tonight at Noon" was an ambitious, nearly atonal work that leaned toward the free jazz being formulated by such fringe artists as pianist Cecil Taylor and alto saxophonist Ornette Coleman. Mingus may or may not have been aware of those two upstarts; Taylor had just debuted on the small Transition label, and Coleman was still in Los Angeles, recording for Contemporary Records and hanging at with Mingus' former associate, Paul Bley. But all three men were interested in pushing jazz' boundaries outward in their own fashions, and "Tonight at Noon" was the bassist's next step out. The more accessible but no less expansive "Tourist in Manhattan" was recast the following year as "New York Sketchbook." (*A Modern Jazz Symposium of Music and Poetry*, to be assessed later.) Reactions to the Newport set were mixed but could hardly be considered catastrophic. As he had done with *Pithecanthropus Erectus*, Mingus was still serving notice that the shape of jazz would be changing at his hands.

*   *   *

Although it would not be released on LP for seven more years, Mingus recorded "Tonight at Noon" in the spring of 1957 along with other material that made it onto his next album, *The Clown* (Atlantic). McLean and Waldron were out, replaced by Shafi Hadi (a.k.a. Curtis Porter) on alto and tenor saxes, Jimmy Knepper on trombone, and Wade Legge on piano. Perhaps the most significant arrival was a young drummer named Dannie Richmond, who would become Mingus' most faithful and longest-tenured sideman. Richmond possessed one of the finest techniques of any drummer since Ellington's Sonny Greer, capable of the full gamut of expression from tiny cymbal rides to full-kit explosions. This brilliance was tempered by a large measure of taste and good judgment. The whole spirit of the Mingus band changed with *The Clown*, setting a new precedent for experimentation and energy. And, as a bassist, Mingus offered up some of the most inspired and inspirational performing of his life.

"Haitian Fight Song" is one of Mingus' most unique adaptations of the blues, an impressively powerful tune with tremendous bass playing and a hard-pounding sixteenth-note triplet line that recurs time and again. As you might recall, the band played an early version of "Haitian Fight Song" at Café Bohemia in December 1956, but it was lacking some of the structural elements heard here. Mingus hints at the sixteenth-note form as he solo-improvises the introduction. Then, as the bass sets up the rhythmically loping initial theme, Knepper's trombone begins to slowly emerge with that recurrent motif. He and the other horns alternate between that line and the principal melodic phrase. In the rear Mingus can be heard howling and exhorting the musicians onward before Knepper's solo turn. The trombonist immediately demonstrates the distinctive technique and good sense of melody that made him a favored Mingus sideman for several years. Pianist Legge is a solid player, not in the same league as Waldron or the later Jaki Byard, but well-suited to this phase of Mingus' development. He and the bassist trade some interesting rhythmic ideas during the piano solo. Hadi alludes to the sixteenth-note motif in his alto sax solo, which reveals him to be in a similar place to McLean at this point. Then Mingus provides a well-built bass improvisation, working on repetitive figures and conveying a deep sense of the blues. The ending is especially effective: the sixteenth-note motif slows down to a dramatic standstill.

Mingus didn't revisit "Blue Cee" very often once it was recorded, but it is a good, basic blues. It alternates between B and C, and the theme is quite spare considering who composed it. From this simple framework the band constructs some enjoyable variations on the blues. Legge's understated solo is followed by more relative mildness from Hadi, then a creative improv by Mingus. Partway through the solo Mingus plays some sliding double-stopped figures that he would echo, at a much faster pace, in a later work called "E's Flat, Ah's Flat Too" (alternately titled "Hora Decubitus"). Knepper's solo is rather reminiscent of the blues-drenched smoothness of Quentin "Butter" Jackson, Ellington's longtime trombonist.

"Reincarnation of a Lovebird" is yet another of Mingus' tributes to Charlie Parker. Like the later collage "Parkeriana," it blends several snippets of Bird's favored themes—"Parker's Mood," "Salt Peanuts," "Embraceable You" and what have you—but unlike the later work, "Reincarnation" has an original theme composed by the bassist. The Bird quotes come early in the track, alternately stated by bass and horns. A dire theme follows, choppily blown by Hadi and Knepper, then the lovely principal theme is heard. This is one of Mingus' most charming creations, a sing-songy melody that unites Bird with the Ellingtonian aesthetic. At about 1:52 a slower, Dukish theme is played, then the pace is doubled most subtly to herald a return to the primary melody. Parker's spirit is still palpable in Hadi's alto solo; though he rarely approaches the virtuosic speed of the bebop pioneer, the homage is clearly heartfelt. After an up-tempo romp by Knepper, the pace dies down briefly for the first part of Legge's piano improvisation. The quicker tempo is soon resumed, however, not long before the main theme is revisited.

The title piece is completely unique in Mingus' canon, not only for its style but its conception. The bassist had created this multilayered piece at the piano, envisioning it as the basis for a story about an unsuccessful clown. Mingus shared the idea with comedian Jean Shepherd, one of New York's most popular radio personalities of the time. They got the idea to record the composition with Shepherd improvising the story, and that became the album's centerpiece. Its length and relative strangeness meant "The Clown" was less than radio-friendly, but by this point Mingus was hardly concerned with such things.

Mingus and the band easily convey the off-kilter spirit of the circus, and the horns add perfect counterpoint to Shepherd's tale of the clown who was "a real happy guy... he had all these greens and all these yellows and all these oranges bubbling around inside him, and he had just one thing he wanted in this world: he just wanted to make people laugh. That's all he wanted out of this world. He was a real happy guy." The problem, as laid out by Shepherd and the band, was that no one thought the clown was funny until he fell down and really hurt himself. There are a number of brilliant instrumental passages and solos serving as *entr'actes* to this improvised narration; Legge's solo is a particular highlight. When it pulls away from the circus emulations, "The Clown" stands out as one of the leader's more impressive compositions of this period.

There may or may not be something autobiographical about the clown in Mingus' story. He occasionally compared himself to a clown in his writings and conversations, and returned to the subject in song as well—"Don't Be Afraid, The Clown's Afraid Too"; "sad clown with his circus torn down" ("Duke Ellington's Sound of Love")—and at this time in his life, Mingus might have had some self-degrading perception that people only valued him when he was down. This preceded the era when he entered into depression and mental illness that resulted in his commitment to Bellevue Mental Hospital, but this vision of the clown might have been an early indicator of his emotional difficulties.

"Tonight at Noon" and "Passions of a Woman Loved" were both recorded at the same sessions as *The Clown*, but remained in the can for several years. They were eventually included on *Tonight at Noon*, issued by Atlantic Records in 1964, along with material from the *Oh Yeah* session in 1961. Both *Tonight at Noon* and *Oh Yeah* will be addressed in due course, as we progress chronologically through Mingus' catalog.

*   *   *

Charles got back to the Third Stream that summer, when he was invited to take part in a series of new-music performances at Brandeis University. Gunther Schuller had recently recorded an album called *Music for Brass* (Columbia), which documented the jazz-classical compositions of John Lewis, trombonist J.J. Johnson, reeds player Jimmy Giuffre, and Schuller himself. That music was originally intended for a concert, under the auspices of the Jazz and Classical Music Society, that never came together. Not wanting the rehearsals to go to waste, Schuller arranged for the pieces to be recorded. Inspired by the results, he organized the "Jazz Festival of the Arts" at Brandeis and invited several composers to contribute works to the event.

Columbia issued the Brandeis performances on the album *Modern Jazz Concert* in 1958. Most of that album, and the entirety of *Music for Brass*, are available on the CD *The Birth of the Third Stream* (Columbia, 1996). The most enduring pieces to come out of the project were George Russell's "All About Rosie," based on an African-American children's song, and Milton Babbitt's "All Set" (omitted from the CD reissue, along with Harold Shapero's "On Green Mountain"). Jimmy Giuffre submitted the blues-informed "Suspensions." Mingus' contribution, the dark and ominous "Revelations," was performed at the festival on June 18, 1957. Actually, only the first movement was performed, and he apparently never completed it, as no additional manuscripts have been found. Ironically, for its first few minutes, Mingus' composition has perhaps the least palpable jazz feeling on the album. The ensemble includes John LaPorta on alto sax; Hal McCusick on tenor sax; Teo Macero, baritone sax; Robert DiDomenica, flute; Manuel Zegler, bassoon; Louis Mucci and Art Farmer on trumpets; Jimmy Knepper, trombone; Jim Buffington, French horn; Bill Evans, piano; Teddy Charles, vibraphone; Barry Galbraith, guitar; Mingus, pizzicato (plucked) bass; Fred Zimmerman, arco (bowed) bass; Teddy Sommer, drums and percussion; and Margaret Ross, harp.

"Revelations" is a forbidding composition, inspired by the last book of the Bible, and heavy on the low brass. Buffington, Mucci, and Knepper are the featured brassmen. The theme is composed of slow, long tones, and Sommer adds accents with triangle, timpani, and various other percussion. Variations and embellishments of the theme go on for several minutes until, at 4:11, Mingus shouts "Oh, yes, my Lord!" A swell and crash, then a gospel-jazz waltz is heard with piano and vibraphone in the lead. It morphs back to 4/4 time, slows considerably, and the French horn heralds a slow, plaintive new theme. Such changes occur throughout this twelve-minute piece, in typical Mingus fashion. At 6:05 the flute and trumpets bring in another melody in waltz-time, then Evans takes a lovely piano turn at 6:47. That, too, doesn't last long before it's overrun by the flutes and a loud crash, causing Evans to take a jazzier turn. The trumpets dig into the blues pocket just before Mingus' powerful bass takes a step forward. John LaPorta carries on a gospel dialogue with Farmer, Mucci, and Knepper; eventually the entire ensemble gets swept up in the holy-roller fervor. A long, slow denouement toward silence follows. At 10:10 the world goes black, and shortly thereafter we are back to the original portentous tone. The spooki-ness prevails until the end, when Zimmerman's quietly groaning bass fades out. This was one of Mingus' last full-scale attempts at Third Stream fusion, but in hindsight the performance of "Revelations" was triumphant, and prophetic of later strata like "Sue's Changes."

In the summer of 1957 Mingus joined pianist Hampton Hawes, fresh in from the West Coast, and Dannie Richmond for some trio dates around town. *Trio: Mingus Three* (Josie/Blue Note) mostly presents their novel interpretations of musty standards—"Yesterdays," "I Can't Get Started," "Summertime" and "Laura" (over which Mingus plays "Tea for Two!")—along with Hawes' "Hamp's New Blues" and a pair of new pieces by Mingus. "Back Home Blues" is a fairly generic blues line that doesn't add much to the bassist's repertoire; it's more of a showcase for the trio of musicians. Mingus' other piece, "Dizzy Moods," heralded the next phase of his progression as a composer. It is a multifaceted tune built upon honoree Dizzy Gillespie's bebop classic "Woody 'N You." Some years later, Mingus would echo "Dizzy Moods" in the introduction to his controversial "Fables of Faubus." Hawes' piano intro is as funky as it can be. Richmond gives the tambourine a brief workout before the theme statement, which swings mightily over Mingus' steady bass walk. Although this trio with Hawes does the composition justice, "Dizzy Moods" received its definitive treatment a few weeks later.

*   *   *

Distraught by the collapse of his marriage to Celia, Mingus went on a road trip to Tijuana with Dannie Richmond. Along the way, Mingus fell in love with the sounds of Mexican music. He had been exposed to plenty of it while living in Los Angeles, mind you, but hearing it in its proper context made a strong impression on Charles. Inspired, upon his return to New York he began working on a series of compositions that boasted the spicy flavors of Mexico, yet were redolent with the inimitable Mingus flair.

The sessions for *Tijuana Moods* (Bluebird) were held in July and August 1957. Richmond, Hadi, and Knepper were still on board; Bill Triglia was hired on piano, and the elusive Clarence Shaw on trumpet. Percussionist Frankie Dunlop added the Latino vibe. For various reasons this recording was not issued until 1962, and that in a heavily edited form. More familiar is *New Tijuana Moods*, which includes four alternate takes that retain some formerly excised solos. A 2001 CD reissue included twenty-two (!) tracks, basically everything that the original album was cobbled from along with every alternate take from the two sessions. It leans toward overkill and is best for completists only.

"Dizzy Moods" was the first stone in the Latin foundation Mingus envisioned for the album. Dizzy Gillespie had pioneered the fusion of jazz and Latin music in the 1940s by performing with Cuban musicians such as Machito and Chano Pozo, so it was only appropriate that it be included in this Latin adventure. However, it still doesn't bear any palpable Latin feeling in this arrangement; it qualifies merely by its association with Dizzy. On the alternate take there are some fine solos by Shaw (who is almost completely unknown aside from this date and Mingus' next two albums), Knepper, and Hadi, and the group improvisation before the drum solo is wonderful.

"Ysabel's Table Dance" was inspired by the flamenco dancer Ysabel Morel, who is heard here playing machine-gun-rapid castanets and exhorting the band. Mingus bows his frenetic bassline over a cycling Spanish piano theme, and Shaw offers up a perfect Latin flourish on trumpet. As the pace builds, the horns spread out into separate improvisations and Mingus plays flamenco staccatos with his bow. At 2:32 a new unison horn line pops out. The Spanish flavor surges over everything and builds to unbearable intensity until 3:33, when everyone drops out except for Triglia and his brocaded, flowing piano. Next, the Latin beats are replaced by a hot swing rhythm that underscores an excellent alto sax solo by Hadi. At 5:18 (on the original track) everyone drops out to let Hadi carry on solo. Soon thereafter Mingus' flamenco bass returns, then the bustling rhythm section. At 6:16 another new bop melody emerges, this one exultant and buoyed by Shaw's mellifluous trumpet. Thirty seconds later the Latin rhythm returns on castanets and bass, swelling and swelling until 7:40 when another drop-out occurs. Hadi and Knepper play another variation on the theme before returning to the long tones heard early on. Around the nine-minute mark, Triglia's solo piano signals the castanets and bass, then the second theme's reemergence. As the piece fades out, Hadi blows blue as Morel's castanets and stomps circle around Mingus' chafing bass.

The construction of "Tijuana Gift Shop" is unusual, inspired by a tapestry that the bassist bought in Mexico. The odd initial theme sounds as if it came from the pen of free-jazz altoist Ornette Coleman. It is staccato and high-pitched, moving into a more Mingusian mode at 0:33 though the choppy lines recur in different voicings throughout the tune. The Latin drum beats conjured by Dannie Richmond are ideal. Knepper's short solo was the only one to escape the editor's knife the first time; those by Triglia, Shaw, and Hadi were all hacked out but are present on the alternate take.

"Los Mariachis" was inspired by Tijuana's itinerant street musicians, walking the *mercado* and playing for tips. Unlike the traditional *mariachi* repertoire that we might be familiar with today, these performers would play whatever style was requested or what they thought a particular tourist might enjoy. Hence the wide vacillation of styles heard in this track, from bop to blues to Mexican and back again. Mingus' funky Latin bass lines at the three-minute mark, answered first by Shaw and then the whole ensemble, highlight this marvelous track. During Hadi's frenzied alto solo, Mingus begins to shout the blues in the manner of his past gospel-jazz masterpieces. Triglia does a nice approximation of the cheery Mexican folk music before Shaw drags the band back into the hard blues.

"Flamingo" is not a Mingus original, but a ballad written by Edmund Anderson and Ted Grouya for Duke Ellington in about 1940. Here it serves as a beautiful vehicle for Clarence Shaw's trumpet playing, accentuated by harmonies from the other horns. Shaw, Knepper, and Triglia really sell the tune, by far the album's loveliest moment. Mingus was able, once again, to profess his eternal love for Ellington without breaking the record's flow.

*   *   *

Barely a week after the second *Tijuana Moods* session, Mingus abandoned all his Latin pretenses and went back to advancing the cause of bebop. *East Coasting*, the first of his albums made for the Bethlehem label, tends to be underrated in the Mingus discography. Recorded on August 16, 1957, it isn't as immediately distinctive as either *Pithecanthropus* and *The Clown*, his most recent releases at the time. The take numbers suggest that this must have been a difficult session; we hear take six of "West Coast Ghost," take seven of "Memories of You," and take sixteen of "Conversation." However, the playing across the board is more mature, perhaps, than on those earlier sessions. It sounds as if the ensemble was given time to congeal and relate to one another. Hadi, Knepper, Shaw, and Richmond blend wonderfully, and young pianist Bill Evans shines on one of his earliest recordings. Evans had come up in the nascent Third Stream at the hands of composer and theorist George Russell and clarinetist Tony Scott, and in 1956 he had debuted on Riverside Records with *New Jazz Conceptions*. Already he was becoming a master of sensitivity, particularly on ballad material.

It is easy to imagine that Mingus was still lamenting the breakup of his marriage, as *East Coasting* begins on a rather solemn note. "Memories of You," a venerable old chestnut by Eubie Blake and Andy Razaf, features Clarence Shaw's bittersweet muted trumpet in the lead voice, quietly wailing above the lonely bass before Hadi and Knepper come in to console. This is an absolutely gorgeous arrangement, and the dignified majesty of the trombonist's solo melodic passage is just one of the inspired features. Mingus' dissonant harmonic touches, like the angular piano chord that ends the piece, add the barest tint of frustration and anger to the music. Take three of "Memories of You" is added onto the 1992 CD reissue; on that one, Shaw and Hadi have a hard time uniting on the initial melody.

Next up, Mingus pays dues to the geographical halves of his career. "East Coasting" is kicked off by a driving, funky piano vamp from Evans that is echoed by all the horns before the stairstepping bebop melody is played. After the second visit to the vamp, the theme briefly takes a jagged, Monkish turn before getting back to the original bop flavor. Knepper, Evans, Shaw, and Hadi (on tenor) solo in turn, and all the while Mingus keeps up glorious walking rhythms alongside Richmond. The 1992 CD includes an alternate version (take three) of "East Coasting" that is even more spiritedly ragged.

"West Coast Ghost," clearly a self-reference, is longer and freer in spirit. This one harks back to the early influence of Ellington on Mingus' musical mindframe, with Shaw cranking out some audacious plunger-muted trumpet. With a firm left hand, Evans leads the band in grooving on a repetitive but very funky ostinato. The tune builds up in layers as the horns call, respond, and cycle through a number of hot, sweaty blues figures. Around 2:50 the pace drops to a slow ballad; Shaw is the lead voice, with Knepper and Hadi's horns singing softly around him. At 3:38 the faster blues lope is back, inspiring a short burst of solo trumpet. Then—bam!— the tempo halves again, coaxing Shaw to shift his mood. Hadi, Evans, and Knepper endure the same vacillations, quick-slow-quick, in their powerful solos. It's surprising that Mingus never returned to this piece, given that its tension and drive are reminiscent of classics such as "Pithecanthropus Erectus."

"Celia" is, of course, dedicated to Mingus' ex-wife and was no doubt composed at a happier time in their lives. Evans' minor-key piano intro suggests disharmony itself, however. The full melody is tender and pretty, but is broken up by returns to that almost bitter piano vamp. Shaw plays muted trumpet over Evans for a bit, then after a little piano cascade the melodic line comes back. The tune cycles through this pattern, tenderness to acrimony, time and again. Now and then some sections of the theme are varied, as with the longer tones at 2:14. The liner notes say that Mingus' tune reflected "the way I like feeling about her." Given the most unusual fluctuations of mood here, one might imagine that their relationship had some difficult dynamics. A fascinating piece of work.

Hearing "Conversation" for the first time makes it understandable that it took at least sixteen takes in the studio. It is a complicated piece that moves from a rather mild-mannered, positive blues feeling into hastily ascending sixteenth notes, angular bop, and back again. The horns respond to one another in beautiful harmony, building up to a nice crescendo. The call-and-response mutates into trading fours, then twos, then into single bars and fragments of measures, culminating in a brief frenzy of group improvisation. A hard-hitting piano solo follows, with Evans picking up on the heavy blues mood of those horn exchanges.

Aside from "Celia," "Fifty-First Street Blues" is the only tune here that Mingus significantly returned to later in his career: in 1960 he interwove this blues with Monk's "Straight No Chaser" and Ellington's "Main Stem" to create the tune he called "MDM" (Monk/Duke/Mingus). On *East Coasting* we hear a fuller realization of this fine piece, which would almost be a lazy plod if it weren't for the speed-ups scattered throughout the theme. Hadi's tenor sax solo is a marvelous achievement, and Shaw perfectly picks up on the vibes set up by his bandmate. Knepper and Evans also deliver some first-rate solos, and the pianist's subtle, creative accompaniment, as always, holds everything together nicely.

Mingus himself is understated on this session, rarely stepping to the fore. It may be that he was concentrating more on his development as a composer and less on his prodigious bass-playing skills. This phase was leading up to some of the freshest, most adventurous, and sometimes unsuccessful writing of his career. In the summer of 1957, Mingus was less than two years away from permanently joining the jazz pantheon.

The Poetic Blues of Mingus

As suggested earlier, Mingus always had the heart of a poet, even if its expression in words and music was not always as successful as he might have hoped. Early songs such as "Weird Nightmare" and "Eclipse" were compelling but ungainly despite their odd beauty, and his more poetic works such as "The Chill of Death" were aloof and bordered on pretentious. Nonetheless, Mingus explored the confluence of jazz and poetry on and off during his career, with varying degrees of success. He fared best when he stuck close to the blues, the quintessential African-American expression of musical poesy.

*   *   *

Mingus' next release for Bethlehem, recorded in October 1957, was yet another departure from where he had been. *A Modern Jazz Symposium of Music and Poetry* is not the most ingenuous title: "symposium" implies a sort of academic formality that is hardly present, and the only thing close to poetry is the narrative on "Scenes in the City." This album has a number of nice moments, but it tends to be overshadowed by many others in Mingus' discography. Perhaps its greatest distinction is in presenting the rudimentary material for Mingus' later composition, "Open Letter to Duke." In 2001, Avenue Jazz reissued the album on CD with three previously unreleased tracks.

The "Scenes in the City" narrative was written by Lonnie Elders III, with some assistance from Langston Hughes. Elders had a cut version called "A Colloquial Dream" at the Tijuana Moods date (expected on some CDs). The narrative is presented here by an African-American stage actor, Melvin

Stewart. According to Nat Hentoff's liner notes, Stewart explained that the piece "is an examination of a guy from Harlem and his relationship to jazz. It shows what jazz can mean to someone who's not basically a musician but who 'lives in the music' a lot." It has a number of very humorous moments, right from the intro: "Well, here I am. Right back where I was yesterday. And the day before, and the day before..." Stewart's character tries desperately to be a hipster, at one point begging, "*Please* let me be cool!" His love of jazz is the unifying thread, and there is plenty of it woven throughout by Clarence Shaw, Shafi Hadi, Jimmy Knepper, pianist Bob Hammer, and the driving force of Mingus. There are so many scenes in "Scenes" that it would take pages and pages to break them down. Suffice it to say that this is a track that needs to be listened to intently, deliberately and fully.

"Nouroog," "Duke's Choice," and "Slippers" from this session were reassembled by Mingus the following year to create "Open Letter to Duke" (on *Mingus Ah Um*, which became his most popular album). The title of the first selection is, according to Mingus, the nickname of an Armenian woman he knew. Within the context of this three-song suite, Nouroog is a woman who acts upon her desires but may not have put enough thought into those actions. The strangely compelling theme of "Nouroog" reflects a bittersweet sense of longing, not to mention the spirit of Ellington. Hadi's tenor and Bill Hardman's muted trumpet assay the lush theme for a moment, then Shaw yanks out the mute to blow short two- and three-note figures behind Hadi on the up-tempo sections. Richmond hammers out a frantic sort of Brazilian feel in these fast passages, then lays back into some light cymbal touches and brushwork in the quieter times. Hadi's solo contains genius-level reflections on the thematic material; this is one of his finest improvisations on record. Trumpeter Bill Hardman only performs on this track, strong but relegated to an ensemble role.

"New York Sketchbook" had initially been debuted at Newport in 1957, under the title "Tourist in Manhattan." (It's been said that the Newport set was recorded, but no tapes are known to exist at this time.) It echoes the "Nouroog" theme, among others, and is a philosophical extension of "A Foggy Day" on *Pithecanthropus Erectus*. The horns conjure the same kind of urban sound effects within this expansive creation. Both Bob Hammer and newcomer pianist Horace Parlan are featured on "Sketchbook," with Parlan taking only the last solo. (Actually, it's only with the left hand, for reasons that will be explained in a moment.) Hammer's playing is very impressive, and it's a shame that he is so little known outside of this session. He meshes seamlessly with Richmond's tapping, pounding and thundering all through the suite. There are plenty of typical Mingus touches in the "Sketchbook," exemplified in the last melodic passage at 8:21 fast, zipping runs that almost immediately slow to a snail's pace, classic jazz harmonies over increasingly dissonant piano, and a single hard-hit note to close.

Horace Parlan seemed an odd candidate for a bebop pianist, particularly one who would dare to tackle Mingus' daunting music. Due to childhood polio, Parlan had lost the use of three fingers of his right hand, which led him to concentrate on his left hand once he took up the piano. He first met Charles when the bassist took part in a Pittsburgh jam session, and one year later Parlan ran into Mingus right after moving to New York. The match was made in heaven, as Parlan's concentration on the lower end of the keyboard freed Mingus up to move higher on the bass fingerboard more regularly. Parlan's unique approach adds much character to "Nouroog," "Duke's Choice," and "Slippers" from this session. His introduction on "Duke's Choice" is as gentle and dignified as its subject, the perfect setup for Mingus' slow melody, layered in the sumptuous Ellington manner. One minor quibble is that Clarence Shaw seems to blow too hard during the ensemble sections. That strength is more appropriate when used sparingly, as in his stunning solo. The unaccompanied cadenza at the end is just breathtaking.

"Slippers" is an abrupt change of pace, a fluid bebop line taken at breakneck speed. This tune in particular deserves more attention in the Mingus repertoire. Jimmy Knepper's solo demonstrates how technically brilliant he could be at faster paces; there's not a missed note in the bunch. Hadi offers up an equally powerful tenor improvisation, then the horns trade a bit with Richmond and one another before the theme wraps up. An alternate take is included on the Avenue Jazz CD. On that one Knepper sounds sloppy, as though he's not quite ready to tackle such a speedy tune.

Mingus revisited one recent inspiration by recording Dizzy Gillespie's "Woody 'N You" (here titled "Wouldn't You"), which had been the foundation of "Dizzy Moods" on *Tijuana Moods*. This is one of the three unreleased tracks on the Avenue Jazz reissue of *Modern Jazz Symposium*, and it's a gem. The bassist plays the theme on solo bass before the horns come in with an unusual, triplet-based rhythm. There's a little too much echo on Hadi's tenor, perhaps the reason why the track was cut. But the solos and ensemble work are as tight as Richmond's drums. At one point during his solo, Hadi breaks out into some funky staccato blowing that is atypical of his normal style and closer to the R&B bar-walker school of tenor playing. Hammer and Knepper veritably burn through their solos, then Mingus puts them all to shame with an astonishing display of pinpoint-perfect bass technique. Richmond tumbles and pounds through his improv, then the horns trade off four-bar phrases before taking it out.

"Bounce," credited here to Mingus, is instantly familiar to any fan of bebop. It is, in fact, *not* a Mingus tune but "Billie's Bounce" by Charlie Parker. This is a previously unreleased take that simmers deliciously, one of the outstanding versions of Bird's classic tune. Once again Hadi is impaired by too much echo on his horn, but Hammer's slightly abstract piano solo is much fun. Mingus' solo again nods to the sliding double-stops he favored on

"Blue Cee" and the later "E's Flat, Ah's Flat Too/Hora Decubitus." After all the solo turns, the trombone and tenor sax absolutely sizzle as they trade off.

*   *   *

In March 1958, a special opportunity arose for Mingus to expand upon his poetic inclinations. Langston Hughes, the great African-American poet, would be recording an album of his writings for Verve Records, and Mingus was asked to score half of the LP. The other half would be written by Leonard Feather, a white pianist who was already becoming better known as a jazz critic and author. *Weary Blues* was a landmark in the jazz/poetry confluence, yet it was rarely available between the time of its recording and Polygram's 1991 CD reissue.

Feather's band included some of the top names among the older echelon of jazz players: Henry "Red" Allen on trumpet; Vic Dickenson on trombone; Sam "The Man" Taylor on tenor sax and clarinet; Milt Hinton bass; Al Williams piano; and Osie Johnson drums. That band performs on the first half, up through "Testament" (ending at about 23:30 on the CD reissue). Starting with "Consider Me," Mingus' group represented the younger crowd: himself, Hadi, Knepper, Parlan, and drummer Kenny Dennis (apparently Dannie Richmond was unavailable). Parlan, in fact, was the titular leader of the second half of the session, although Mingus was surely in charge of the affair. His score included some original material and some prior themes: "Jump Monk," "Weird Nightmare," and "Double G Train," the last of which would be recorded (but unreleased until the CD era) at the legendary *Mingus Ah Um* sessions in May 1959. The pace and arrangements are altered to suit the environment. The last run-through of "Jump Monk," in particular, is significantly slower than it was played at the Café Bohemia, though the portion included in "Dream Montage" is extremely fast. Hadi gets an opportunity for some lovely ballad playing on this date, and Knepper is a beautiful complement to him. And, of course, there is plenty of Mingus' tremendous bass to be heard. But artistically, perhaps the greatest reward is being able to hear one of America's greatest poets reciting his works in the manner he envisioned.

It is unfortunate that Polygram chose to spread all of the material out on a single CD track, making it impossible to play individual sections and poems separately. Although this material works well as a seamless suite, and the scores by Feather and Mingus were specifically intended to flow into one another, it's become a natural inclination in the CD era to want to take things track-by-track. Despite the inconvenience, and the datedness of the album's sound, this is very interesting as a meeting of three great minds.

*   *   *

In December 1958, Mingus met a young alto saxophonist named John Handy at a Five Spot jam session. Handy had arrived from San Francisco a few months earlier and was looking for a way to fit into the New York scene. Mingus recognized the twenty-five-year-old man's exceptional talents and hired him to replace the departing Shafi Hadi. Hadi had already brought in a Berklee-trained Texas tenorman named Booker Ervin, who had also impressed the bassist. These two saxophonists would play major roles in Mingus' groups for the next few years.

Mingus signed on with United Artists just long enough to cut one album for the label. *Jazz Portraits* (previously reissued as *Wonderland* or *Mingus in Wonderland*) has often been overlooked in his catalog, chiefly because of the impact of the albums which immediately followed it. But this is a marvelously enjoyable session in its own right, and it deserves more attention.

Jazz Portraits was recorded live at the Nonagon Art Center on January 16, 1959. The lineup was basically new: besides Richmond, we hear John Handy on alto, Booker Ervin on tenor, and a brilliant young pianist named Richard Wyands, who had worked with Mingus in California ten years prior. There are only four tracks on *Jazz Portraits*, each with excellent moments. The first and last tunes were composed by Mingus for an experimental film by John Cassavetes, entitled *Shadows*. This was one of his first tries at composing for the media, and both pieces would endure in his repertoire for some time.

"Nostalgia in Times Square" is one of Mingus' most ear-catching compositions, a bouncy and infectious blues. In later years he would slow down the tempo, add some lyrics and rename the tune "Strollin," but those affectations ruined the pure joy of it all as documented on this United Artists album. It's impossible not to bob in one's seat while enjoying the tight groove held down by Mingus and Richmond. The bridge section is quite interesting, a few groupings of three quarter-notes that grabs our attention with their utter simplicity. Richmond's drum roll ushers in a charming, swinging alto solo by Handy. His debut in the Mingus band is an impressive one indeed, especially the way he handles himself as the tempo doubles. If you listen closely during the fast section of Handy's improvisation, you can hear Mingus playing those sliding double-stops yet again. Richard Wyands also possesses an outstanding technique, sounding as if he has more than two hands. He pours out fast single-note lines, tinkling arpeggios and nearly orchestral chords. Next up is the redoubtable Booker Ervin, articulately reminding us that bebop has its roots in the blues. Mingus' bass solo initially has an unusual vibration to it, like an Indian tambura, then it straightens out into glorious boppishness. His trading with Richmond demonstrates how tightly the two friends had learned to mesh in the span of two short years. Mingus' sense of humor emerges as he quotes "Dixie" amidst all the trade-offs. The last statement of the theme is perfectly concise and to the point.

"I Can't Get Started" is a classic jazz tune by Vernon Duke and Ira Gershwin, made most famous by the tragic trumpeter Bunny Berigan in

1937. Handy's glorious alto sax interpretation reveals his deep appreciation and gift for ballad playing. Mingus takes over the melody after Handy's solo statement, embellishing with tremolos and deft variations as only he could. This is one of the most powerful solo improvisations he had conjured in years, a testament to his love of great compositions and timeless jazz. He and Handy give an affectionate nod to Duke Ellington by wrapping up with the theme of "Solitude."

"No Private Income Blues" is full-on improvisation, no composed theme, just the standard blues chord changes. After Mingus gets things started, Booker Ervin rips out of the gate with an edgy R&B tone and jumps headlong into the fray. Dannie Richmond is the secret weapon here, deviously keeping up a consistent hi-hat tap while his hands work minor miracles to make the energy level ebb and flow. Wyands and Handy contribute hot and heavy solos. At about 5:52 Mingus briefly halves his time, making it seem as if the tempo has dropped considerably behind Handy's solo. But soon enough, he edges back into the abrupt tempo and cooks some more. About seven minutes in, Handy's playing takes on a squealy attitude that prophetically points toward the arrival of Eric Dolphy a couple of years later. After a quick drum solo, Ervin comes back in to begin the trading of eights with Handy. These are gradually reduced to fours, then twos, then single bars and half-bars for a long stretch. Toward the end, Wyands and Mingus begin their own trades in the background. Suddenly the saxophonists burst into a joyful simultaneous duo improv that practically rips the roof off the Nonagon. Thirteen minutes of pure, unfettered jazz rapture.

"Alice's Wonderland" was also composed for Cassavetes' *Shadows* but not used in the film. It was subtitled "Diane" in honor of Mingus' girlfriend, writer Diane Dorr-Dorynek. He later recorded it simply as "Diane" with a larger ensemble, but in this small configuration it possesses a different character. It's a beautiful ballad statement, and the saxophones flow together with palpable tenderness. The melody ends with surprisingly tense trills, as if something upsetting had occurred to the lady in question. Wyands' dark piano, underscored by dissonance in the bass, carries us to an unknown place, as if we'd gone down the rabbit hole. But the positive new melody at 2:10 lets us know that things will be better from now on. Handy's alto solo leads warmly from the theme, and at 3:40 the rhythm changes only briefly to a subtle bossa-nova. Mingus' bass solo is ebullient, rich with idea streams and technical flourishes: tremolos, slides, bending, and so forth. The principal theme returns, and concludes with the fall down the rabbit-hole once more.

*   *   *

A year after *Wonderland*, Mingus immersed himself more fully in his gospel and blues roots, hence the recording of *Blues and Roots*. It is one of the most enduring items in the Mingus discography, with most of its tracks getting consistent jazz radio airplay to this day. The praise is surely well earned. It is a hallmark of Mingus' arranging talents, for one thing, harkening back to the multiple lines of New Orleans style jazz. The fact that Mingus and his men weren't entirely prepared for the session gave it a looseness and anticipatory energy that probably fueled the excellent performances.

Mingus' vision for this album was more expansive than the last, despite the less complex material, so he put together an extended ensemble: Parlan and Richmond in the rhythm section, Handy and Jackie McLean on alto saxes, Ervin on tenor, Pepper Adams on baritone sax, and Jimmy Knepper and Willie Dennis on trombones. Mal Waldron was also on hand and replaced Parlan on the final track, "E's Flat, Ah's Flat Too." The 1998 Rhino CD reissue includes alternate takes of "Wednesday Night Prayer Meeting," "My Jelly Roll Soul," "Tensions" and "E's Flat."

Blues and Roots was recorded for Atlantic on February 4, 1959. As Mingus stated in the liner notes:

> A year ago, Nesuhi Ertegun suggested that I record an entire blues album in the style of "Haitian Fight Song" ... because some people, particularly critics, were saying I didn't swing enough. He wanted to give them a barrage of soul music: churchy, blues, swinging, earthy. I thought it over. I was born swinging and clapped my hands in church as a little boy, but I've grown up and I like to do things other than just swing. But blues can do more than just swing. So I agreed.

Blues and Roots starts off in church, with the exciting gospel vibe of "Wednesday Night Prayer Meeting." The tune has remained nearly as popular as its spiritual offspring, "Better Get It In Your Soul," recorded three months later. Mingus reached back into his childhood memories of the Holiness Church in crafting this humorous and addictive composition. It begins in 6/8 time with a funky throb from the bass, to which Parlan and Handy reply with deep blues. Next in are Knepper and Ervin together, then the other horns. The written phrases and improvised responses are indeed kindred with the vocal exchanges in the black church; Mingus' experiences provide an authentic feel to the music. Parlan's piano solo is of particular interest when he breaks into a heavy-handed syncopation that battles with the drums. Ervin's tenor solo is extremely fast at the onset, then he calms down for a slower blues romp. After he has carried on for a while, the other musicians drop out and begin clapping their hands to rhythmically support Ervin. His solo continues as the other horns return, shrieking with unfettered excitement as Mingus shouts "Oh, yeah!" and such behind them.

Ervin takes the reins again on "Cryin' Blues," improvising the blues from the first beat as the trombones blat long tones beneath him. Mingus takes a hard-nosed, percussive solo with only Richmond supporting at first, then

Parlan begins to subtly elbow his way into the mix. The pianist takes over for his own deep blue solo. The full band returns to wail frantically as McLean's alto sax screams high. Part of the line played by Pepper Adams toward the end is reminiscent of Thelonious Monk's "Blue Monk."

Adams kicks off "Moanin'," blasting his way through the swoops and splats of the unusual initial melody. The canon form is used again, each separate horn line adding a layer of richness to the overwhelming sound. At around 1:28 Mingus starts to shout "Yeah, I know . . . what I know . . . ," the inspiration for this book's title. Not long after that, things settle down into a unison riff by the trombones and baritone sax, picked up by the tenor. The melody returns at about 2:04, and McLean, Adams, and Ervin solo in turn. This is one of the greatest compositions from Mingus, not to mention an essential testing ground for baritone saxophonists.

"Tensions," on the other hand, tends to be overlooked in comparison to other tunes on this session. It's a shame, because the structure of the riffs here is the stuff of genius. The lines are quite simple at heart, but the way they eventually begin to speed up brings to mind several bouncing rubber balls, with the intervals between their bounces shortening each time. Fine solos are turned in by Mingus, McLean, Ervin, and Parlan, culminating in a passionate drum improv by Richmond.

"My Jelly Roll Soul" is Mingus' tribute to Ferdinand "Jelly Roll" Morton, one of the great jazz composers and pianists of the 1920s and 1930s. He had debuted the piece (then titled "Jelly Roll Jellies") at the Nonagon Art Gallery that January, though it did not find its way onto *Jazz Portraits*. Pepper Adams and Horace Parlan have a great time with the first melodic statement. A notable feature is the stiff ricky-tick rhythm played by Mingus (slapping his bass) and Richmond during the first half of Knepper's solo, which rolls into a more beboppish support during the second half and the other solos by Parlan, McLean, Richmond, and Mingus. It was recorded again a year later on *Mingus Ah Um*, more simply titled "Jelly Roll."

One distinctive feature of Mingus' bass playing during this period was his love of sliding notes and double-stops (playing two strings at once). The bass intro to "E's Flat, Ah's Flat Too" is the definitive example of his skill with these techniques. The tune is built up as a canon: after the bass-drums intro, Adams plays the rapid melodic statement by himself, then is joined by Booker Ervin. They spread out into separate phrases at the end of that run, then the trombones enter in unison before going their own directions. By the time McLean and Handy enter on alto saxes (I believe it's McLean who plays a brief snippet of "Haitian Fight Song"), the CD player is about to levitate and Mingus vocally exhorts his bandmates. Mal Waldron's piano solo is brilliantly blues-steeped; some of its rhythms clash with Richmond's solid pulse. Solo turns follow by Ervin, McLean, Handy, and Richmond, and as the frenzy dies down, the album ends on an exhausted note. Mingus rerecorded and retitled this composition later, too, as "Hora Decubitus" on *Pre-Bird/Mingus Revisited.*

This music was some of the most exciting that Mingus had yet laid down on wax, and it set the standard for things to come. His next album upped the ante again, earning him the greatest accolades of his career.

Triumph: Columbia Records, 1959

If there was one golden year in Mingus' career, it would have to be 1959. He cut two more albums that year, following *Blues and Roots*. The first would become his most enduringly popular record ever, and the second, although usually overshadowed by the success of the first, was no dog itself.

Charles left Atlantic after *Blues and Roots*, switching his allegiance to Columbia Records this time. On May 5 and 12, 1959, he brought the band into the studio to lay down what would become *Mingus Ah Um*. The album title has caused many a non-Latin-scholar to scratch his head in confusion, wondering if it had to do with some primal blues groan or something. In actuality, it's kind of a silly pun on Latin conjugation, and we will take no more time on that subject before diving into the record itself.

Mingus was rarely able to match the fullness of scope and conceptual continuity found here, which made the high-water mark of *Ah Um* both a blessing and a curse. The first two tracks, "Better Git It In Your Soul" and "Goodbye Porkpie Hat," were to be Mingus' most popular hits, and receive consistent airplay on jazz radio to this day. The personnel and instrumentation on these sessions were rather mixed, and the liner notes of the 1998 CD reissue are contradictory, so here is the best approximation that this writer can make. All of the tracks include Ervin on tenor sax, Parlan on piano, Mingus on bass, and Richmond on drums. Mingus also plays piano on "Pedal Point Blues." Handy plays clarinet on "Pussy Cat Dues," tenor sax on "Goodbye Porkpie Hat" and the first solo of "Better Git It In Your Soul," and alto sax on everything else. Hadi plays alto on "Better Git It," "Bird Calls," "Jelly Roll," "Open Letter to Duke," and "Girl of My Dreams," but is absent from "Pussy Cat Dues" and "Goodbye Porkpie Hat," and plays tenor sax on all other tracks. Jimmy Knepper was only present on May 5 and plays trombone on "Better Git It In Your Soul," "Fables of Faubus," "Pussy Cat Dues," "Jelly Roll," and "Pedal Point Blues." He lays out on "Bird Calls" during that session. On May 12 Knepper was replaced by Willie Dennis, who plays trombone on "Boogie Stop Shuffle," "Self-Portrait in Three Colors," "Open Letter to Duke," "GG Train," and "Girl of My Dreams" but lays out on "Goodbye Porkpie Hat."

Due to the space limitations of the LP record, the original issue of *Mingus Ah Um*, and most of the reissues, contained severely edited versions of "Goodbye Porkpie Hat," "Boogie Stop Shuffle," "Open Letter to Duke," and "Bird Calls." Three other tracks—"Pedal Point Blues," "GG Train," and "Girl of My Dreams"—were omitted altogether. The 1998 Columbia/Legacy CD edition presents all twelve tracks from these sessions in their original, unedited form, giving us a clearer look at Mingus' thematic and musical vision for this special project.

"Better Git It In Your Soul" (the spelling would change over time) is definitely Mingus' most popular composition. A rollicking gospel/jazz hybrid in 6/8 time, it is cut from the same cloth as "Wednesday Night Prayer Meeting," right down to the hand-claps during Ervin's titanic sermon of a tenor solo. After the introductory bass and trombone solos, the bassist carries on like the Holiness preachers of his childhood, shouting exhortations to the musicians as they burn through the catchy melody. Mingus arranged the piece so that horn riffs emerge to support the soloists partway through their improvisations. Sometimes the riffs hammer on a single note, building tension; at other times there is an upsweep at the end of each phrase, echoing the bass solo at the very beginning of the track. Richmond's drum solo is a blissful mess of tumbling, twisting sound that roars right up to the finish.

"Goodbye Porkpie Hat" is a tender ballad dedicated to the memory of tenorman Lester "Prez" Young, Mingus' old friend who had died two months before this session. Young's hat of choice was the flat porkpie, and thanks to this recording it became a lasting symbol of his style and contributions to jazz. The tune lays a mutant blues theme upon a beautiful, very un-bluesy chord structure. The expansive initial chords are rich with 9ths and 13ths, and during the solo sections every chord is a 7th or minor 7th, which creates a notable harmonic density. Appropriately, the tenors of Handy and Ervin are the only horns to be heard, and the blending of sound is gorgeous. Partway through his solo, Handy begins to flutter-tongue, which Mingus quickly picks up on by rapidly strumming the strings of his bass. The ways that Mingus responds to each phrase of the solo indicate how deep his intuitive link with Handy had already become.

In the 1940s on the West Coast, Mingus had written and recorded a tune called "Shuffle Bass Boogie." Though there is little thematic similarity, it is a spiritual father to the more aggressive "Boogie Stop Shuffle" on *Ah Um*. This is a basic twelve-bar blues with four separate themes woven together in

Mingus' common fashion. Parlan's facility with his left hand is perfectly realized here, as he plays the choppy eighth-note melody in unison with the horns. The repetitive, off-rhythm waves he plays before his solo two minutes along is a wonderful contrast to the horns' rhythms. One distinctive feature of the tune is the way the saxes emulate the wah-wah sound of Duke Ellington's plunger-muted trumpets in the B section. Mingus was a master at making his ensembles sound larger than they were, and pulling faux trumpets out of the ether was one example of his genius in this regard. Breaking down the title: the "boogie" is the eighth-note piano rhythm, the "stop" comes in the form of a quarter-rest at the end of each phrase, and the "shuffle" is the driving rhythm maintained by Mingus and Richmond.

The quiet, unison ballad theme of "Self-Portrait in Three Colors" is reminiscent of "Goodbye Porkpie Hat" in some ways, although all four horns are used this time. This piece was composed by Mingus for John Cassavetes' experimental film *Shadows* but was not used in the soundtrack. Everything here is composed, but the streams of melody and harmony are composed and arranged in such a way as to suggest improvisation, another hallmark of the Mingus style.

In another self-reference, Mingus took portions of three selections from 1958's *A Modern Jazz Symposium of Music and Poetry* and created a new composition from them. "Open Letter to Duke" draws thematic material from "Nouroog," "Duke's Choice," and "Slippers." A series of saxophone improvisations is followed by an eight-bar drum solo, then the arrival of the "Nouroog" theme (actually, its B section). "Duke's Choice" is the next section of the ballad portion, then just when "Slippers" should be arriving, Mingus opts for a calypso section that brings to mind Sonny Rollins' experiments with the fun Caribbean style in a jazz context.

"Bird Calls" is an homage to Charlie Parker, but unlike the funereal atmosphere of "Goodbye Porkpie Hat," this is an up-tempo and energetic validation of Bird's gifts to jazz. Hadi and Handy both play alto saxes here, mirroring the dual tenors of the Lester Young tribute. The introduction briefly leans toward the direction of free jazz as Ornette Coleman had been playing it around town, then comes a fast bebop theme ending in an exultantly high, long tone from the altos. Solos follow by Ervin, Parlan, then Handy, who vows to boldly carry Parker's innovations into new territory. The track ends with high, sharp squeaks from the altos and Mingus' bowed bass.

Mingus wanted to make a profound political statement on this recording, but the folks at Columbia Records would have none of it. "Fables of Faubus" was originally conceived with lyrics that bashed Orval Faubus, the racist governor of Arkansas who had fought against integrating the schools in Little Rock. Columbia refused to let Mingus and Richmond sing the lyrics, so the tune was recorded for *Ah Um* as an instrumental. Mingus had to wait until he switched to Candid Records to cut the version he desired. The piece still works brilliantly in this fashion, despite the reduction of impact. The theme skulks like a villainous film noir soundtrack, and Mingus' bass playing is often as percussive as the drums. He and Richmond act and react like a single creature on all of the tune's odd syncopations and twists. Note that the first couple of bars of "Fables" are very close to "Dizzy Moods" on *Tijuana Moods*.

"Pussy Cat Dues" swings slow and sweet like an old-time blues, an effect buoyed by Handy's clarinet, Parlan's rolling barrelhouse piano, and Knepper's muted trombone. This was the only time Handy ever recorded on clarinet, but it is perfectly effective in conveying the mood of a smoky speakeasy. Knepper's solo is characteristically suave and unpredictable, smooth as silk one moment, bristly the next. The nostalgic spirit is carried over to "Jelly Roll," a mere retitling of the tune called "My Jelly Roll Soul" on *Blues and Roots*. This version is tighter and more swinging than the first, indicating that several months of working on the tune paid good dividends. Handy's alto solo is excellent.

The title of "Pedal Point Blues," the first of three previously unreleased tunes included on the 1998 CD reissue, refers to the maintenance of a continuous bass figure instead of a walking progression. Parlan and Mingus, sharing the piano duties, keep up a vamp in a single key while the tenor repeats one riff and the other horns spontaneously improvise. It's effective in the sense that Mingus often uses such devices to build up tension in his works, but it's not the most successful composition from these sessions.

Mingus had used "GG Train" as a section of his background music for Langston Hughes' poetry on *Weary Blues* (where it was called "Double G Train"). It was better filled-out for the *Ah Um* date. Surprisingly, given his love for emulating Duke Ellington, there is nothing in the way of a palpable link to "Take the 'A' Train." The track is mostly a vehicle for Handy, whose alto sax improvisation takes up the first three-and-a-half minutes. At about 2:40 Handy trades fours with Richmond for a while. The theme isn't heard until 3:26, and soon thereafter the tempo is slowed dramatically. At 4:15 the fast melody returns, and the track ends about twenty seconds later.

The last track was composed not by Mingus, but by Jimmy Clapp in the mid-1920s. However, the initial melody of "Girl of My Dreams" as heard here is a Mingus creation built upon the standard's chords. The original theme as written by Clapp appears about forty-two seconds into the track. The rhythm section plays in 6/8 while the horns blow 4/4, a juxtaposition that recalls "Better Git It In Your Soul" and brings the CD full circle thematically.

*   *   *

So, how does one follow up after such a masterpiece? By making a record that is almost as brilliant in its own ways, of course. *Mingus Dynasty* was his second album for Columbia, laid down in November 1959 and titled with a pun only slightly less chafing than *Ah Um*. The label even went so far as to dress Mingus in what looks to be Chinese imperial finery for the cover photo. But since Mingus had a measure of Chinese blood in him, he probably went along with the gag in good spirits.

Dynasty boasted an extended cast as well: trumpeters Richard Williams and Don Ellis; tenor saxophonist Benny Golson; baritone saxophonist Jerome Richardson; pianist Roland Hanna (before his knighting by the nation of Liberia added "Sir" to his name); vibraphonist Teddy Charles; and cameos by pianist Nico Bunink, singer Honey Gordon, and two studio cellists, Seymour Barab and Maurice Brown. As had been the case with *Ah Um*, certain tracks were hacked down to fit on the original LP. The 1998 CD reissue from Columbia/Legacy restores "Slop," "Song With Orange," "Gunslinging Bird," and "Things Ain't What They Used To Be" to their entirety, and also includes "Strollin'" which had been omitted from all prior releases.

Some of the *Dynasty* material had originated in Mingus' soundtracks for the TV teleplay "A Song with Orange In It," John Cassavetes' experimental film *Shadows*, and a TV ballet called "Frankie and Johnny." The latter was the source of "Slop," the third part of the gospel-soul-jazz trilogy including "Wednesday Night Prayer Meeting" and "Better Git It In Your Soul." The show's producers, in fact, specifically asked Mingus to come up with a new composition in that churchy vein. Thanks to this relationship, it is probably the most frequently aired tune from *Dynasty*. "Slop" is, as its title hints, a looser-limbed approach to the style. Tinkling piano, wah-wah mutes and countermelodies abound, and "Better Git It" is directly quoted (listen at about 0:37). Mingus' vocal exhortations are still effective, and once again Ervin's solo is backed for a time by hand-claps, as is Hanna's. The two cellists are supposed to be included on this track, although they are not audible at all if they are truly there.

When Mingus had recorded *Jazz Portraits* at the Nonagon Art Gallery back in January 1959, he included one of his compositions for Cassavetes' film. It had then been titled "Alice's Wonderland," but by the end of the year he had retitled it "Diane" in honor of his girlfriend and liner-note writer, Diane Dorr-Dorynek. The new arrangement for a tentet makes this sound like a completely different composition, more avant-garde in its tonality. Instead of the alto and tenor saxes, the lead voices in this version are piano, flute (the liner notes do not say who plays it, possibly Richardson), and bass. Around 2:40 the horns step back and Hanna takes control with a beautiful, wide-scoped piano solo. The mood shifts when the drum tempo briefly doubles (3:30 to 3:45), one of Mingus' favorite devices to kill predictability. The same thing happens with a few seconds of Latin time at about 4:33. In the hands of a lesser composer, such rapid switches might seem confused or even schizophrenic. But Mingus was almost always able to make such collages work.

"Song With Orange" is often confused with its cousin, "Orange Was the Color of Her Dress, Then Blue Silk." Both stem from the CBS teleplay about a girl who asks her composer friend to write a song with the word "orange" in it, knowing that the word has no rhyme. The tune has a fascinating structure, beginning with repeated phrases on piano that lead up to the slow horn melody. The theme unexpectedly speeds up through further repetitive snippets until an entirely new swing feel is in place. Hot solos follow by Ervin, Knepper, and Williams. At 4:23 the riffs begin a slow pile-up under Williams' improv, which builds to a scream, and soon Mingus is singing falsetto riffs off the top of his head.

The full title of the next piece is "If Charlie Parker Were a Gunslinger, There'd Be A Whole Lot of Dead Copycats." Thankfully, it was reduced to "Gunslinging Bird" for public consumption. It's a 6/8, twelve-bar blues at a fast pace, with bucketloads of sixteenth-note rips that make it one of Mingus' most difficult tunes to play. Mingus had a great deal of fun on this session. He enjoys Handy's alto solo so much that he sings his own cadenza, and keeps singing as the song winds down later. There was a set of tympani handy in the studio, and Richmond makes use of them both in this solo and on "Far Wells, Mill Valley."

Mingus included two pieces from the Ellington songbook on this album. The first is "Things Ain't What They Used To Be," composed by Duke's son, Mercer. After a nod to Duke in Hanna's cascading piano intro, Mingus plays the first phrase of the melody on bass, then is joined by the rest of the ensemble. He makes rhythmic alterations from the original, but the Ellington spirit is always present in Hanna's piano and certain aspects of the orchestration.

The most ambitious composition here is "Far Wells, Mill Valley," a dedication to Mingus' old Californian friend, Farwell Taylor. It begins as a disjointed waltz with flute and vibraphone in the lead, then spreads out into a more Mingusian theme in 4/4 with strategic triplets keeping up the 3/4 feeling. At around 1:10 a chugging sort of Native American rhythm appears, underscoring the flute, alto sax, and Charles' "unzipping" of the vibraphone. It seamlessly morphs into a more Asian spirit. At 2:32 everything but the piano drops out for a few seconds, then it's back to a swing beat with unusual scattered accents. Judging from the liner notes, Mingus wasn't especially pleased with the solid bop solos by Handy and Williams because they didn't use the open chord structure in the way he had intended. This is one indicator of just how seriously Mingus was taking his compositional processes at the time.

Twenty-three-year-old Dutch pianist Nico Bunink, who had impressed Mingus when the bassist heard him on the New York club scene, takes Hanna's place on "New Now Know How." The band is pared down to a sextet of Mingus, Richmond, Bunink, Knepper, Handy, and Ervin. Bunink's fine brand of syncopated support suits the melody, which is very fast in the spirit of Parker but not one of Mingus' most memorable. Most interesting is the structure of the arrangement, which renders the A section as eight-and-a-half bars long and begins not with the chorus but the bridge.

The second Ellington piece on *Dynasty* is "Mood Indigo," a slow and bubbly tune that Mingus treats with the utmost reverence. He did add one new touch, a single tone played by trumpeter Don Ellis which acts almost as a pedal point and changes the mood to a different hue of blue. The Ducal vibe is intact: Handy matches the wide vibrato of Johnny Hodges to a T, and Knepper's use of the plunger mute is fully appropriate despite the modernistic clattering and twanging of Mingus' bass in the background. Hanna's solo isn't very Ellingtonian, but neither is the doubling of tempo which accompanies it. This track was, at some point, subjected to an unfortunate studio hack job, with four bars trimmed off the end of the tenor solo at 7:09. The version present on the 1998 CD is as complete a take as is known to exist, and it's a marvel nonetheless.

"Put Me In That Dungeon" is an excerpt from the "Frankie and Johnny" ballet on CBS, and the two cellists who can't be heard on "Slop" are gloriously audible here as a textural element. It is an interesting piece with a sense of *film noir*, but unlike the other soundtrack gleanings here, it sounds like it was drawn from some other context instead of being a stand alone composition.

After the live *Jazz Portraits* session, Mingus asked his friend Nat Gordon to pen lyrics for "Nostalgia in Times Square" (also from the *Shadows* soundtrack). Mingus then slowed the pace considerably and retitled it "Strollin." It is heard on the *Mingus Dynasty* CD as sung by Nat's daughter, Honey Gordon. The languid pace and her dusky delivery completely alter the flavor of the piece, which had been as infectiously bouncy as an instrumental. Unlike the dull "comeback" version recorded by Mingus and Gordon in 1972, this one is mostly effective and pleasing. A neat touch is Gordon's introduction of Booker Ervin's tenor solo.

Because *Ah Um* was such a hard act to follow, *Dynasty* has never gotten its due as an almost-equal triumph. It did, however, lend its name to the Mingus "ghost band" led by Jimmy Knepper after the bassist's death in 1979. And indeed, some of the personnel represented here—Knepper, Ervin, Handy, Richmond—could be considered a dynasty sprung forth from his creative loins. Certainly the reputations of Knepper and Richmond were indelibly, almost exclusively connected with Mingus.

*   *   *

As a companion disc for the completists out there, Sony issued an *Alternate Takes* CD in 1999, which presents other versions of "Better Git It In Your Soul," "Bird Calls," "Jelly Roll," "Song With Orange," "Diane," and "New Now Know How." Much of the time these takes reveal why they were not chosen for the full albums. Many of them are too disorganized even for the Mingus standard of tight chops, but they have interesting moments and solid solos. "Song With Orange" even boasts a couple of portions that were cut out of the arrangement appearing on *Dynasty*.

This time around, Mingus' relationship with Columbia Records only lasted long enough to produce two albums. He would return to the label again in 1971, after a series of hills and valleys that brought him to the nadir of his career. Charles still had plenty of good music left in him after *Ah Um* and *Dynasty*, but nothing that would ever match their popular appeal.

Into the Past, Into the Future

As the summer of 1960 approached, Mingus got into a nostalgic mood. Having captured the world's attention with several albums' worth of bold new compositions, he opted to reach backward to more innocent times. He thought about the impact of Duke Ellington on his artistic development, and, perhaps more importantly, he recalled some of his own earlier works before bebop had turned his ears in a new direction. *Pre-Bird* was an appropriate name for his next recording: all of the music had originated before Charlie "Bird" Parker changed the world. (In 1965 it was reissued as *Mingus Revisited*, another suitable moniker since the compositions had been written well in the past.)

On May 24 and 25, 1960, Mingus brought an expanded cast of characters into the studio to cut the record for the Limelight label. The session began with a take on Billy Strayhorn's "Take the 'A' Train," the Ducal theme that would emerge in Mingus' live sets on and off for the rest of his life. However, with a typical Mingusian twist, the melody of "Exactly Like You" was brilliantly juxtaposed onto the other theme. The group is heavy on tenors, and Yusef Lateef, young Joe Farrell, and Booker Ervin all have solo spots. The pianist is the distingué Roland Hanna, as tasteful and swinging a player as could be found in New York. Dannie Richmond, of course, anchors everything on drums next to Mingus. The tune ends rather abruptly, seemingly in the middle of Ted Curson's growl-trumpet solo. Whether it's an editing goof or an intentional photo-finish is not known.

Mingus' "Prayer for Passive Resistance" is next, featuring the same players. It is slightly in the spirit of "Work Song," with hard percussive sounds like whips striking a slave's back. The first section of the piece sounds as if it were set in 5/4 time, making it difficult to nail down the meter as Mingus churns out the vamp on his bass. The band has a hard time working it out for themselves, but Booker Ervin holds his own during his marvelously blues-soaked tenor solo. Later the horns cycle through a taut vamp while the leader plays a quick and heavy walking line in 6/8. At about 1:50 he drops that in favor of staccato quarter notes, accompanied by Richmond's spare hi-hat taps. The subsequent section with just the tenor, bass, and drums is incredibly absorbing, and as the other horns spread out with long tones the track comes to an end.

"Eclipse," the tune Charles had written in vain for Billie Holiday, is distinguished by mournful long notes, a hectic recurring pattern by tenor sax and piano, and Knepper's crystalline trombone soaring above like a wandering spirit. Mingus and Lorraine Cusson sing just a bit of the song at the beginning before the band takes over, then Ms. Cusson handles the melodic duties. She is mixed much too loudly, but manages to stick to the theme fairly well. From about 2:03, Hanna's ornate, symphonic piano builds to a heady crescendo, then softens to a cushiony accompaniment once more as the angular, dissonant horn lines return.

"Mingus Fingus No. 2" is an update of "Mingus Fingers," the tune that Charles had written for the Lionel Hampton band more than a decade earlier. The first harmonies are nowhere near as dissonant as on the original, and Don Butterfield's tuba is a perfect complement to Mingus' bass on their unison vamp. It's not clear who performs the tenor sax solo, but Yusef Lateef is the likely candidate. The high-range trumpet solo is almost certainly Clark Terry. The horn bursts that carry on behind the soloists are some of the most chaotic to be heard in any big band of the day. The staccato sax riff that evolves from 3:09 onward is of particular rhythmic interest.

On the introduction to "Weird Nightmare," Mingus achieves a strange, sitar-like sonority by pulling the strings off of the bass fingerboard with his left hand as he plucks them with his right. The flute, harp, and muted trumpet creep out from the dark like cold monsters of the subconscious. At about 0:34 a new rhythmic structure is taken up, with a repetitive, scooting riff from some of the horns underscoring the flutes and lead trumpet. Lateef, on tenor, hastily quotes the melody of the song at 1:21 before proceeding into his short improvisation. It's interrupted by another ensemble passage, then he returns to his idea-stream as the band carries on behind him, seemingly unaffected by his presence. The vocal by Lorraine Cusson is somewhat overwrought compared to the earlier versions, or even her take on "Eclipse." Neither the key nor the written melody seem to suit her, so she strays freely from them all. At 3:09 Mingus goes back to the strange, twangy tone as his mates sail into the ether.

The pendulum tips back to Ellington with "Do Nothing Till You Hear From Me," on which Mingus plucks a breakneck intro. Duke's boys probably never took this tune at such a fast pace, and the bassist has altered the harmonies to suit his own sensibilities. The tenor sax solos swing long and hard, booted along by the rhythm section's unfailing prowess. Chazz' love letter to Duke is short, sweet and to the point.

"Bemoanable Lady" presents Eric Dolphy in his first alto sax solo under Mingus' direction since he appeared on "Story of Love" in the 1940s. It's not a typical Dolphy improvisation, understated compared to the furious free excursions he would pursue just a couple of years later. This performance is more in the smooth, sinuous vein of Johnny Hodges, Duke's favorite altoist, although Dolphy's solo goes further into new territory. The melody meanders some and is not one of Mingus' most memorable by a long shot; it is more like another attempt at aping the Ellington model. That's to be expected, however, since Charles apparently wrote it in his teen years when he was first fully enveloped in all things Duke. Clark Terry's majestic trumpet work in the ensemble helps to redeem it.

The final track is "Half-Mast Inhibition," one of the very first tunes Mingus wrote while living with Farwell Taylor back in California. This one is more classical in bent, an opulent arrangement rife with cellos, flutes, and reeds. As conducted by Gunther Schuller, the chart feels more like something Gil Evans would have devised for a large ensemble to accompany Miles Davis. Those familiar with the Evans catalog might hear reflections of *Sketches of Spain* or "Where Flamingos Fly" dispersed through this work. The title is a teenaged sexual reference, appropriate for the author of the hormonally saturated *Beneath the Underdog*. There are any number of melodies and riffs built into "Inhibition"; in fact, at times it seems more like a musical collage than a composition in its own right. Some of the sections have an inarguable charm, like the disjointed, light-hearted dance at 3:23, the folksy waltz that soon follows it, and the pastoral ending. At eight minutes, it's more than twice as long as any other track on the disc and is packed with interesting moments, even if the improvisational element is lacking. It's a fitting ending for one of Mingus' most unusual albums, an enlightening appraisal of his career and influences to date.

*   *   *

Dolphy's feature on "Bemoanable Lady" was but a pale reflection of the music he was about to create with his old Watts buddy, Charles. The band spent a year in residence at the Showplace in Greenwich Village, working out new material. In July 1960 Mingus flew his band over to France to perform at the Antibes Jazz Festival in Juan-les-Pins. For some reason there was no pianist this time, only Mingus, Dolphy, Ervin, Richmond, and Ted Curson on trumpet. But the music on *Mingus at Antibes* is so animated and beguiling that those extra notes are not missed at all. The album was released by Atlantic Records some time later, after Mingus had fulfilled his contract with the Candid label.

The band begins their set with a ferocious version of "Wednesday Night Prayer Meeting," with Mingus ripping out a powerful solo introduction. The piano's absence adds an interesting suspended feel to the group, so that when Curson takes the solo spotlight he seems to be walking the tightrope. His improvisation is as masterful as anything he built under Mingus' wing, climbing higher and higher up the ladder of intensity as the saxes pelt him with their burbling riff. Ervin ups the ante with his own solo, leading Mingus to wail spiritedly along with his pained blues howl. By the time Dolphy's turn arrives, he is ready to burst at the seams. He tears through bop phrases like a mad dog, ululates through his alto like Tarzan, sounds as if he's zipping and unzipping a sleeping bag time and time again. When the claps-and-snare rhythm hits at 6:20, he whoops and skitters as if he were speaking in tongues at a Pentecostal revival. After the horn riff comes back, Mingus gives another long, loud howl of approval at Dolphy's skills. The bandleader keeps up the wild exhortations throughout the alto solo, then Richmond takes his turn with a tremendous burst of drumming creativity. The full ensemble flies into a paroxysm of joyous sound, erupting over Richmond as he continues to pour on the gas. After the last statement of the theme, Mingus sings "Oh, yes, Lawd" in time with his bowed bass, and is answered by the band in the best spirit of this gospel-jazz classic.

"Prayer for Passive Resistance" begins once more with the odd-time intro of bass and drums, then Ervin takes up the blue theme while Dolphy and Curson toss around the sharp punctuations behind him. We can hear the audience clapping along as Ervin rides the swinging rhythmic tide, which quickly shifts to a percolating 6/8 at 1:57. Richmond almost seems to spin out of control until 3:27, when he and Mingus shift down into the staccato four-beat. All the while, Ervin is avoiding cliché in that inspired blues sermon, and the gospel choir of Dolphy and Curson wails in the background. At 5:50, Mingus steps up front to duet with Ervin, playing sliding eighth-notes to egg on his bandmate. A slow drop out of hearing range, then at 6:35 Mingus gets back to the initial bass riff and ushers the other horns back in.

"What Love" is Mingus' contrafact on "What Is This Thing Called Love," and the rapport between Mingus and Dolphy makes for one of the finest duet exchanges in the annals of jazz. Dolphy and Curson play the slow, snaking introductory melody as Mingus and Richmond improvise free-spiritedly. The trumpeter's solo is painted with swashes of blue, alternately contemplative and fluttering like a moth over the bassist's flame. Eric Dolphy picks up the bass clarinet in time for Mingus to enter into a choppy Latin feeling (2:40), which leads Curson into a Spanish motif. At 3:25 he gets back into the bebop and the others follow along, charmed by his magic. Curson flirts briefly with a waltz at 3:59, but opts for some scattered bop blowing before making room for Mingus to go it alone. The bassist goes just about everyplace in his solo, even around the mulberry bush (5:35), with the barest accompaniment from Richmond. At about 6:50 he nods to the melody as if ushering Dolphy's bass clarinet into the room. Dolphy responds with smooth accuracy, and the two begin a tremendous duo dialogue that covers the extremes of dynamics and range. Around 8:15 Richmond brings himself back into the mix, gives Dolphy a bit more elbow room, then eases his way in again as Mingus counts off the next pulse. The three-man conversation continues, but at about 9:48 it becomes a humorous back-and-forth between Mingus and Dolphy. Mingus claimed that they were hurling epithets and curses at one another in the form of music, and one can certainly imagine such "playing the dozens" in between the musical quotes and vocal proddings. Dolphy plays a short piece of circus-like theme immediately before the theme returns, and before it's all over the bass clarinet ventures on his own way as Curson sticks to the theme. It ends as it began, awash in sumptuous beauty.

Antibes marked a bittersweet reunion between Mingus and pianist Bud Powell, who had taken part in the milestone Massey Hall concert several years before. Powell had descended further into mental illness by 1960, and it had begun to affect his piano chops. But when he took the Antibes stage and joined the quartet for "I'll Remember April," none of that mattered. Dolphy quotes Juan Tizol's "Perdido" during the melody (listen at 0:16). Powell's piano solo is nearly pristine, with no reflection of the troubles within his mind and soul, and he sings merrily along with himself. Curson's solo is at 5:52, and he seems inspired by what has transpired at the piano. So does Dolphy, who delivers yet another exultant improvisation before trading fours with Ervin. In a moment, the rhythm section backs out to let the saxophonists carry on with their witty conversation. They continue for some time, letting the rhythmists come back in and bow a few more times. Curson begins to weasel his way back in after the twelve-minute mark, winding up in the middle of a three-horn dialogue that overflows with humor and excitement. After the theme returns, it winds down quickly with a few solitary notes from the piano and a final drum whack.

"Folk Forms, No. 1" is essentially a blues-based group improvisation, beginning with a bass solo and expanding outward as the horns blossom and grow. Ervin is a bit too far off-mike for a while, but finds his way back into the mix as he exchanges blows with Curson and Mingus. Each player has his say as the musicians explore all the permutations of the blues, which Mingus recognized as American folk music. They rotate through solo passages, duos, and various ensemble arrangements, all spontaneously created. Only the bass line played in the beginning and middle of the track seems to be composed; the rest is conceived on the fly over a set of blues chord changes. Exhilarating.

The Antibes set concludes with a brisk run through "Better Git Hit In Your Soul." Again, the lack of a piano gives a new tension to the familiar tune. Curson's technique on his solo is simply astonishing, particularly the way he nails the extremely fast figures at 1:31. Ervin gets in another of his good-time gospel-blues solos, complete with the usual hand-clapping passage, then Dolphy and Richmond proceed to set the hall on fire with their improvisations. As expected, Mingus calls out to the musicians as they wind down the theme with unflagging energy. It's the ideal way to finish up one of the best live jazz albums in history.

*   *   *

Mingus signed with Candid Records in 1960, and made the first of several albums for the label in October of that year, three months after Antibes. The first record, *Charles Mingus Presents Charles Mingus*, is rather strange on a number of levels. For one, there are little narrations at the beginning of each track that make it seem as if this were a live nightclub recording—Mingus introducing the tunes and telling the "crowd" to not clink their glasses or talk during the set—when, in fact, it was recorded in the studio. At least this time, Mingus wouldn't get any arguments from the listener! Besides that, Candid had given Charles permission to do what Columbia would not permit the year before: he was able to record "Fables of Faubus" with its lyrics intact. Booker Ervin had left the band, and there was no pianist on hand yet, so the album was recorded by the sparse quartet of Mingus, Richmond, Dolphy, and Curson.

"Folk Forms No. 1" is the first track on the disc, and the faux patter indicates that Mingus hadn't yet decided on its official title. After the bass intro, Dolphy blows a more distinctive melody than was present in the Antibes version. The rhythmic clash between his alto and Mingus' bass is interesting, and complicated further by Curson's entrance at 1:43. The four men bounce ideas off of one another like a constant barrage of ping-pong balls, altering the intensity and volume of the music at individual will and following as they see fit. At 4:46 Dolphy and Curson end their entrancing dialogue so that their leader can spread out and have his say. Following Mingus' incisive bass solo, the horns enter and trade off short phrases. The bass and drums offer only sparse accompaniment until 7:45, when a sharp drum roll leads to a rhythm loose enough to have come out of New Orleans. The performance continues for just over thirteen minutes, sustaining interest the whole way.

In introducing "Original Faubus Fables," Mingus refers to the governor as "the first, or second or third, all-American heel." Between the trimmed-down instrumentation and the vocals, this feels like a different composition from the Columbia version. There is a definite harmonic gap left by the absent piano, and Mingus' bass playing is sometimes too scattered to fill in that chasm. But the singing is hilariously rough and makes up for the musical lags. The first refrain sung by Mingus and Richmond is, "Oh, Lord, don't let 'em shoot us / Oh, Lord, don't let 'em stab us / Oh, Lord, don't let 'em tar and feather us / Oh, Lord, no more swastikas!" Later they append, "Oh, Lord, don't call the Ku Klux Klan!," and "Two, four, six, eight / They brainwash and teach you hate!" When Mingus sings "Name me someone who's ridiculous, Dannie," the drummer responds, "Governor Faubus!" They go on to paint a side-splitting picture of the governor and others as fascist white supremacists. All the while Dolphy and Curson stick to the night-stalking theme. Curson's trumpet solo is fleet, high-toned, and gripping, and the falsetto-vocal ascents and descents add a bizarrely entertaining coloration. Dolphy's alto solo is typically askew, and he unites his thought-streams perfectly with those of the rhythm players. Mingus' unaccompanied outing on bass is like an instrumental blues manifesto against racism, passionate and far removed from the dark humor of the vocals.

The arrangement of "What Love" is basically the same as it was at Antibes, with Curson taking the first solo. A brief little circus motif marks Dolphy's move to the bass clarinet. Next is Mingus, whose improvisation contains a number of small slides, drones, and sixteenth-note phrases. At 5:51 he plays variations on the melody, breaking it down with very fast, staccato plucking and then calling in Dolphy's bass clarinet. That solo is nearly transcendent, a primal blues-gospel wail to the heavens which explores every note and facet of the cumbersome instrument. Once again his interaction with Richmond and Mingus is like an impassioned dialogue without words, and from 8:40 onward he and the bassist effectively emulate the inflections of human voices. At times, your imagination might lead you to hear one of the cursewords that Mingus claimed they were musically throwing at one another.

Now and then Mingus would come up with some very long titles for his tunes. A glaring example is the contrafact on "All the Things You Are," which he called "All the Things You Could Be By Now if Sigmund Freud's Wife Was Your Mother." He claimed that he first came up with the idea around 1940 when audience response got out of hand at a concert. Whatever the case, it's an odd one because the chord structure isn't really close to the original tune. Mingus instructed the musicians to keep "All the Things You Are" in mind as they played, so it's more of a conceptual variation than a contrafact *per se*. The melody is fast, scurrying, sliding and hiccupping along in such a complicated way that it's not even that memorable as a structure. Curson quotes a racetrack fanfare, some classical snippets, and gets in some truly beautiful jazz runs. Dolphy picks up the baton in a similar mood, but after a few seconds in the rhythm section drops out and leaves him to wail in bittersweet solitude. From there the pace keeps picking up and dying off on reflex, no prior warning of each shift. The altoist's free-jazz instincts are in firm fettle, even though it would be a few more months before he would appear on the classic *Free Jazz: A Collective Improvisation by the Ornette Coleman Double Quartet* for Atlantic. At 6:38 Curson gets back into the groove, playing a monotonous whole-step alternation, while

Dolphy blows wildly over the roiling rhythm section. The trumpet drops out at 7:17 but returns at 7:45 to carry out the theme with Dolphy. This is one of Mingus' most energetic, cathartic cuts for Candid, and the album set the pace for some most unusual explorations.

It should be noted that the 2002 King (Japan) CD release of this album adds on a forgotten track, called "Melody from the Drums," which is a nine-minute-plus feature for Dannie Richmond. It's a nice showcase for one of the more underappreciated drummers in jazz, but it doesn't add much to the session's value in the long run.

During the Candid period, Curson and Dolphy let Mingus know that they wanted to leave the band soon to concentrate on their own projects. Charles was hurt, but he didn't want to hold them back from growing as musicians. Yusef Lateef recommended two young players whom he had known back home in Detroit. Alto saxophonist Charles McPherson and trumpeter Lonnie Hillyer had grown up on the same street, and came to New York together to find work. Lateef felt that their energy level and skills would be compatible with the bassist's music, so Mingus agreed to go check them out. McPherson and Hillyer regularly took part in the afternoon jam sessions at Café Wha? and Mingus brought his bass down to the club. He sat in with them and was so impressed that he told them to be at the Showplace at 9:00 that evening.

It doubtlessly helped that McPherson was a disciple of Charlie Parker, had studied the master's playing so intently that he could hold his own on fingerbusters such as "Donna Lee" and "Anthropology." Parker has remained so engrained in McPherson's technique that he was asked to overdub the missing alto parts on the soundtrack to Clint Eastwood's *Bird*, the 1988 biopic about Parker's life. McPherson has also given concert performances of original arrangements from Bird's *Charlie Parker with Strings*. Small wonder, then, that Mingus felt the young altoist would be an appropriate fit for his music.

Curson and Dolphy stayed on with the band for a few more weeks to help their replacements learn the music. McPherson remembers that "the band's book at that time, songs that we would play on a regular basis, included 'Fables of Faubus,' 'Reincarnation of a Lovebird,' 'Portrait,' 'Pithecanthropus Erectus,' 'Wednesday Night Prayer Meeting,' 'Eat That Chicken,' 'Better Get It In Your Soul,' 'Peggy's Blue Skylight,' 'The Shoes of the Fisherman's Wife,' 'Self-Portrait in Three Colors,' and 'Eclipse'."

Mingus' compositional skills left a lasting impression on McPherson. "I was with Mingus for about twelve years, off and on, and his composing was a strong influence on me, probably more than any other aspect of his persona. I particularly liked his ballad writing. Sometimes in my own ballad writing I still hear some of his influences, some little passages, a couple of bars here and there of things that we used to do. Mingus could write ballads that were melodic in a mysterious way. He used to be able to write things that were haunting and pretty at the same time, with a real depth to them."

McPherson continues: "Mingus was a real taskmaster, very emphatic about how he wanted his music played. He was insistent on everyone giving 120 percent. Sometimes he would teach us the music from the piano, and sometimes things were written out, which could actually be harder because of the complexity of what he was doing." But despite the leader's adamant stance about how to handle the music, McPherson formed a strong and lasting bond with Mingus. "Sometimes the persona that is presented to the reading public is largely the result of what the writer wants to focus on. Too often it's just the sensational part. Unfortunately, lots of people are more interested in things that have a grabbing effect on them. Good deeds are not newsworthy, and it's always been like that in jazz. Miles turning his back on the audience and spitting onstage, what kind of suit Miles wore, if he was driving a Ferrari, Bird peeing in a phone booth, that kind of thing. If Charlie Parker wasn't such a character, I have to wonder if he would have been written about in the same manner. And it was the same with Charles."

"Mingus did have nice points," McPherson recalls. "I remember doing a benefit for a poet named Kenneth Patchen, who was a friend of Mingus. Patchen wasn't well and they were doing this benefit to raise money for him. Charles did it for nothing but he did want to pay us. So at the end of the benefit, after we performed, Mingus began doling out five-dollar bills to the players. I turned it down and told him to put it in the basket for Patchen. What's five dollars going to do for me? I can buy a couple of beers with it, but this is a benefit. Then Mingus looked at me and his eyes welled up. From that point on I could do no wrong in the band. Even if I was acting silly on the bandstand he would look the other way because he had me pegged as a nice young man. He thought I had a heart that these other guys who took the money didn't have; he thought my level of conscience was differ-ent...Mingus could be moved by things, and he seemed to have a good sense of what's right and wrong, but that hasn't always been reported. Ideologically, on a moral level Mingus might not have even been wrong, but it would be, 'I wouldn't handle it that way, so Mingus is a jerk.' Sometimes the better part of discretion eluded Mingus; he just wouldn't edit what he was doing or saying."

*   *   *

Recorded in November 1960, the Candid album simply entitled *Mingus* contains three compositions, including two with an expanded ensemble. "MDM (Monk, Duke and Me)," which runs nearly twenty minutes, is a brilliant medley of Duke Ellington's "Main Stem," Monk's "Straight No Chaser," and the bassist's own "Fifty-First Street Blues" (previously recorded on *East Coasting*), layered on top of one another. Mingus starts off playing a hot walking bass intro, with Richmond fast behind.

The "Main Stem" theme is then played by all the horns, including Hillyer, McPherson, Curson, Dolphy, Ervin, Britt Woodman, and Jimmy Knepper. The solos are paired by instrument, giving us the chance to compare the approaches of different musicians on the same horn. Woodman takes the first solo, a very humorous muted venture that melds into a group horn vamp at 1:09, then keeps going in a marvelous Ellingtonian vein. Knepper takes up the reins with his own witty excursion, echoing the spirit of Woodman but with a slightly thinner tone. Next up at 3:25 is McPherson, who seems stuck for ideas but projects a sweet Parkerian sound. Dolphy follows at 4:59, with a similar tone to McPherson's but a conception that strays far from the usual bebop mode. Ted Curson finds some middle ground between free and bop, while Hillyer's character on trumpet is the very essence of sweetness. All along, the hard-hitting horn vamp recurs at regular intervals. At 8:53 everyone drops out and leaves Hillyer to sail alone; then, with a few sporadic tom-hits, Richmond sidles back into the groove and carries Hillyer out. Ervin takes the band to church, as per his usual style, and is followed by Dolphy again, this time with his whooping, moaning bass clarinet. He punches the energy level up to untold levels, making way for the final horn exchanges: trading of fours and twos by Knepper and Woodman, then McPherson and Dolphy (back on alto), Curson and Hillyer, and finally the "odd couple" of Ervin's tenor and Dolphy's bass clarinet. At 17:58 the rhythm section takes over, beginning with a beautiful linear solo by pianist Nico Bunink. You will remember that Mingus had discovered him a few years prior, and invited him to play on "New Now Know How" (on *Mingus Dynasty*). Unfortunately Bunink's spot here is a short-lived showcase; within a couple of choruses, the horns reenter to take out the melody.

Mingus had already reinvented "Stormy Weather" with the Jazz Work-shop band in 1955, but cast it in another new light on this session. Dolphy plays the melody straight to begin with, backed only by the soulful bass. On the second melodic phrase the altoist begins to hold notes out longer, building the emotional impact. He repeats the final line of the chorus several times, then gets rhythmically freer on the bridge. Next, Ted Curson enters with a warm muted obbligato, harmonizing in a wonderful jazz lament. The alto sax solo is full of signature Dolphyisms—high interval leaps, pulsing tongued rhythms, humanoid wails, and rapid runs up and down the scale—but the emotionality is kept in check and comes off as authentically blue. Mingus follows through with a quiet, heartfelt bass improvisation. Richmond's accompaniment is subtle for a time, then moves into a loose swing feel at around 8:45. Mingus responds cheerfully to the new setup, his hands sliding up the fingerboard for some sweet high-range figures and variations.

"Lock 'Em Up (Hellview of Bellevue)" is the most personal piece here, a bitter yet humorous recollection of the time that Mingus had gone to

Bellevue Mental Hospital in search of some counseling, and ended up being admitted as a patient and held against his will. The melody is frenetic and fragmented, jumping headlong into free-jazz tonality as a reflection of the mania going on inside Bellevue. Everything is played at extremes of volume, speed and timbre, from the wild opening bass line to the layered horn phrases and the solo turns by McPherson, Curson, guest pianist Paul Bley, and Ervin. Right at the break in the tenor solo, Mingus (or maybe Richmond) gives a shout of joy that keeps the saxophonist burning. While the drummer struts his stuff, the horns occasionally peek out with a short, crazed vamp. The melody rushes back in and dissolves in a gooey puddle of sound. One fun note for the astute listener: the little horn vamp just before the one-minute mark draws extremely close to Neal Hefti's "Batman" theme, which, of course, had not even been conceived in 1960. We can only speculate about what Hefti listened to for his inspiration!

*   *   *

Following the success of the 1960 Newport Rebel Festival, Mingus, Max Roach, and some other friends formed the Jazz Artists Guild to try and organize future events. The Guild didn't last more than a year because of dissent and a lack of direction, but one of its better accomplishments was the album *Newport Rebels* (Candid, 1961), which brought many of the Rebel Festival's artists into the studio. The disc features several different ensembles, with Mingus included in three of them.

Of principal interest on *Newport Rebels* is the first track, Mingus' "Mysterious Blues." The ensemble includes Jimmy Knepper, Eric Dolphy, pianist Tommy Flanagan, trumpet legend Roy Eldridge, and drummer Jo Jones, the man who literally invented the hi-hat cymbal ride that is so central to the feeling of swing. Flanagan introduces the tune with a crisply swinging piano intro. The melody is bone-simple, nothing more than six repetitions of the same eight-note pattern over a basic blues chord pattern, but the swing is almighty. Eldridge, like Jones, is an elder statesman who influenced Dizzy Gillespie during his service with the bands of Teddy Hill, Fletcher Henderson, and Gene Krupa. His pair of solos (muted at 0:51, open at 6:29) bring the real essence of swing into the 1960s, meshing perfectly well with the more outward vision of the younger players. In between Eldridge's improvisations come fine turns by Dolphy, Knepper (muted and lush), and an unaccompanied Mingus.

Next is trumpeter Booker Little's moody, busy "Cliff Walk," named for the hotel where Mingus and friends conducted the Newport Rebel Festival. His band includes Max Roach on drums, bassist Peck Morrison, tenorman Walter Benton, and trombonist Julian Priester. Mingus returns to the bandstand in a quartet with Eldridge, Flanagan, and Jones, assaying the dusty chestnut "Wrap Your Troubles in Dreams (And Dream Your Troubles Away)." This is the home turf for the elder players, with Eldridge commanding the lead, but Mingus is an impeccably suitable accompanist. His too-brief solo at 3:08 is the most advanced thing here, yet it is a magnificent complement to Eldridge's return for the last few bars.

Powerful vocalist Abbey Lincoln (Roach's wife) joins Dolphy, Jones, trumpeter Benny Bailey, bassist Peck Morrison, and pianist Kenny Dorham (best known as a hard bop trumpeter) for a convincing, bluesy treatment of "Ain't Nobody's Bizness If I Do." The last track features the Mingus/ Eldridge/Flanagan/Jones quartet once more, this time on a totally impro- vised blues called "Me and You." Mingus' vibrant bass tone and deep, soulful probing set the pace, Eldridge summons up bright new wells of energy, and Jones whacks ideal accents when he can pull himself away from that inborn cymbal ride. The true spirit of jazz, summed up in just under ten minutes.

*   *   *

Some of Candid's subsequent repackages have made Mingus' catalog during this period rather confusing. In 1988 the label issued a CD called *Reincarnation of a Lovebird* (not to be confused with the 1970 Prestige album by the same title) composed of material from the 1960 and 1961 Candid sessions. It features a septet version of the title track, first carried aloft by Eric Dolphy's phoenix-like flute. He switches quickly to bass clarinet and grants the lead to Hillyer and McPherson; Ted Curson keeps time with Dolphy on the whole-note backing line, sometimes using a plunger mute for added effect. McPherson's tone on the melody is as sweet as candy. Hillyer's exuberant trumpet solo starts out with a thin tone but fills out well as he progresses. Dolphy's turn on flute flutters like a happy skylark, invigorating and brilliant, and McPherson follows up with similar exultation.

Next up is an alternate take of "Wrap Your Troubles in Dreams," from *Newport Rebels*. After Mingus plays the theme solo, Flanagan politely takes over command only to surrender it to the bassist again. Roy Eldridge's trumpet carries the melody out fully, supported by Flanagan's pinpoint- precise accompaniment. Following a charming muted trumpet solo Jo Jones makes like a tap-dancer, hoofing it smoothly across the drum kit with his brushes flailing. He keeps up his firm accents for a moment after Eldridge gets back to the melody, then everyone makes way for Mingus. The trumpeter's solo break is warm and swinging, and he and Mingus practically stroll out hand-in-hand.

Eldridge is also the featured guest artist on "R&R" and "Body and Soul." Mingus begins the former with a walking bass line composed of note-pairs that descend. Over a hip, swinging but subdued drumbeat, Eldridge plays the relatively simple bebop head with a muted trumpet. On the repeat he is joined by Ervin and Knepper; then, after a second solo break, McPherson joins the other horns for the melodic statement. The trumpeter bursts into his solo with a low-to-high rip before the theme is even done. He seems to run out of breath before he runs out of ideas. McPherson is fiery and quick in his thought-streams, tasteful Knepper and Flanagan take it nice and slow in their separate spotlights, and Mingus covers most of the bass' range while Richmond maintains a quiet little cymbal ride. Eldridge then takes one more solo turn, blowing sixteenth-note runs, sinuously exotic lines, and a mighty squeal. The theme returns as it had before: Eldridge alone, then McPherson and the others alongside him.

On "Body and Soul," Eldridge's trumpet playing is full of vibrato and old-time swing, leaning closer to the spirit of Coleman Hawkins than to Dizzy. At exactly the two-minute mark he blows a brilliant solo break, doubling the tempo and setting the stage for McPherson to tear out of the gate on alto. On one occasion he breaks away from the Parker mold to echo Dolphy's freer approach. Knepper performs with his usual rubbery aplomb, negotiating the long horn as if it were a kid's plaything. He is one of the smoothest bebop trombonists since J.J. Johnson laid the foundation. Tommy Flanagan is all goodness and light, the most traditional man here besides Eldridge, and Mingus' long solo turn is rich with perky eighth-note runs and motivic variations. The trumpeter takes a solo, reaching up into the exciting higher range of the horn to elicit groans of approval from the bassist. When the tempo slows again, Eldridge really carries home the ballad feel.

"Bugs" is a bright, cheery bebop line, not unlike something Bird and Dizzy might have crafted in the late 1940s. It certainly bears little resemblance to Mingus' other compositions from this period. McPherson, of course, has a marvelous time soloing on this Parkeresque tune. He loses the beat a couple of times, which may be a reason that this track went unreleased for a while. Tommy Flanagan careens through the changes like Bud Powell, pounding a kicky bass line with his left hand, and Booker Ervin's tone is almost abrasive as he blasts through his boppish improvisation. Hillyer's solo begins on rough ground—he sounds starved for ideas—but quickly finds his groove. Eventually his phrasing and tone approach those of Dizzy himself. Richmond bounces all over the kit for his too-short solo turn, then it's back to the theme.

* * *

The 1990 Candid CD *Mysterious Blues* includes the three *Newport Rebels* tracks on which Mingus had played, along with some unissued and alternate takes. "Vassarlean" is another retitling of "Weird Nightmare," this time inspired by Charles' experiences with Tijuana's prostitutes back in 1957 (or, he alternately claimed, it was inspired by a student at Vassar College). Hillyer takes the lead voice while McPherson, Curson, and Dolphy, on bass clarinet, harmonize in deep shades of blue. At about 3:12, things take on an almost hopeful tone when the rhythm section's spirit perks up behind Hillyer's elegant solo. That positive motif recurs a couple of other times in this version, altering the normally somber mood.

Alternate takes of "Body and Soul" and "Reincarnation of a Lovebird" are on tap here. Roy Eldridge is a bit more creative with the melody on this take of "Body," tossing in more smears and growls. This arrangement is structured similarly: McPherson's alto sax solo, then Knepper, Flanagan (more up-tempo and boppish this time), but no Mingus improv. Eldridge takes the last turn, reaching just as high and with more spirit than the prior reading.

Whereas the prior version of "Reincarnation" began with piano and flute, this one kicks off with a drum roll and then some pensive, old-fashioned piano from Flanagan. As the theme kicks off at 0:52, Charles McPherson is notably more subdued on the front line. Ervin and Hillyer handle the melody this time around, with the other horns tackling the backup line. The trumpet solo sounds infinitely more confident. Also found on this disc is "Melody from the Drums," the Richmond feature which was tacked onto the *Presents Charles Mingus* CD reissue.

In actuality, the best reference for the Candid days is the Mosaic three-disc boxed set, *The Complete Candid Recordings of Charles Mingus*. It collects all of the primary tracks from this period of Mingus' career in a concise, well-presented format. One big complication: Mosaic's issues are limited editions, and by now this collection would be scarce. At any rate, the track breakdown is as follows for those willing to hunt it down:

Disc 1: Folk Forms No. 1; Original Faubus Fables; What Love; All the Things You Could Be if Sigmund Freud's Wife Was Your Mother; Stormy Weather; Melody From the Drums
Disc 2: Reincarnation of a Lovebird No. 1; Vassarlean; MDM; Bugs; Reincarnation of a Lovebird No. 2; Lock 'Em Up (Hellview of Bellevue)
Disc 3: Mysterious Blues; Body and Soul; Body and Soul (alternate); R&R; Wrap Your Troubles in Dreams; Wrap Your Troubles in Dreams (alternate take), Me and You

The next step in the great bassist's recording career was the setting aside of the bass altogether to concentrate on the piano. Mingus was nothing if not unpredictable, and *Oh Yeah*, which marked his return to Atlantic Records, was full of surprises. All of the blues and gospel ideas Mingus nurtured on *Blues and Roots* are brought into full, crazy bloom on this session from November 6, 1961. Mingus sticks to playing the piano, singing, and shouting exhortations to his sidemen, which include Richmond, Knepper, Ervin, reeds player Roland Kirk, and sitting-in bassist Doug Watkins. For the first time in years there was no trumpeter in this group, which changed the texture significantly.

A native of Columbus, Ohio, Kirk was blinded as a child but learned to play the trumpet, clarinet, saxophones, flute, and several other instruments.

His unusual arsenal of horns included the stritch, a straight-bodied alto saxophone, and the manzello, a curving soprano sax variant. One of Kirk's most distinctive abilities was playing two or three horns at the same time, cramming them all into his mouth and using alternate fingerings to produce remarkable harmonies. It's unfortunate that he was barely with the bassist's band for three months because there is so much potential heard on this one session. The reedman went on to establish an utterly unique career as a leader in his own right.

Although he is a noticeably different bass stylist from Mingus, Doug Watkins firmly holds the low end together on this singular record. Almost three months to the day after this session was taped, Watkins was killed in a car accident. His bass playing here can't really compare to the sheer power and creative force of Mingus', but then, no one else's ever could, either. Still, Watkins serves as a substantial rudder, particularly since Mingus' rhythmic sensibilities on the piano left something to be desired and necessitated a firmer foundation.

Mingus scats the introduction to "Hog Callin' Blues," which is an altered "Haitian Fight Song." The same urgent, recurrent sixteenth-note line is played by the trombone, and the pacing and rhythm are exactly the same. Kirk blows a siren-whistle before going off on a slurred, rough-edged tenor sax solo that builds to great intensity. At 2:00 Kirk screeches out a loud series of goose honks, goading the other horns into a hot ensemble response. By 3:27 he's getting into a deeply funky groove, wailing high and dropping low again; one minute later he trades off low-end skronks with Knepper, then poots out some short, flatulent snorts and flaps. Mingus verbally prods the band to switch gears, ending the tenor solo and moving on to collective improvisation. The tune devolves until all of the men are playing at the absolute peak of intensity. Shortly before the ending, Knepper brings back the sixteenth-note riff and escorts the band out.

Next up, Mingus sings "Devil Woman," a very slow, intense blues that recalls some of the later work by the Jazz Crusaders. The leader moans, pounds, and tinkles on the piano while several separate horn lines sashay around him. It's an appropriate showcase for Mingus' view on blues, an essential component of jazz' lifeblood. Kirk's tenor solo is all shades of indigo, more focused and traditional than he was on "Hog Callin' Blues." The leader takes a percussive, evolving piano solo that contains some beautiful touches, then Booker Ervin steps up to preach his gospel-informed take on the blues. He and Mingus meld together like water and ice, and the bassist-on-piano offers similar encouragement to Knepper on his mournful improvisation. Mingus briefly resumes his soulful singing as the horns provide a silken choir of support. At exactly the nine-minute mark, we can hear Kirk in self-harmony, playing tenor sax and stritch at the same time.

Titled after one of Max Roach's habitual exclamations, "Wham Bam Thank You Ma'am" has a somewhat unusual opening, with Mingus playing very Monkish, dissonant lines over the steady walk of Watkins and Richmond. The melody is also odd: a couple of ascending triplets followed by a long note, the same pattern again, then a staggered low-high figure, the triplets and long notes again, another series of low-high variation, then a descent back to the beginning. Ervin's slightly angular tenor solo is followed by Kirk on manzello (the liner notes say it's stritch, but it definitely sounds like the soprano variant instead). He takes an unaccompanied break; at 3:08 the rhythm section comes back, drops out once more, and returns with a funky, staccato quarter-note line in the piano.

"Ecclusiastics," a mangling of one of the Old Testament books, is Mingus' finest move toward gospel since "Better Get Hit In Your Soul." Drawing from the inspiration of his childhood church experiences, it moves from strong hammered chords on the piano to a slow and soulful line, featuring one long, ascending stretch, a few unexpected eighth-note figures, and an exquisite harmonization that ends with Mingus shouting, "Oh yeah, Jesus, I know!" At times the tempo jumps up to a Holiness Church rollick, bringing more shouts from the leader, who settles down at 1:54 to play some respectable blues piano. His improvisation takes a lovely turn away from the blues at 2:55, becoming a cheerful line reminiscent of *Peanuts* pianist Vince Guaraldi's creations. Roland Kirk steps up for a tenor solo, hinting at "Down by the Riverside" before sailing off into a gospel reverie that soon finds him playing the tenor and stritch simultaneously. The passion builds to a huge climax, with Mingus wailing at the top of his voice. Then suddenly, at 4:52, the bottom drops out and the theme(s) return. The leader carries everyone out with continual vocal exhortations, hollering the album's title over and over again.

Mingus sticks to the gospel-blues mode for "Oh Lord, Don't Let Them Drop That Atomic Bomb On Me," which he introduces over a piano tremolo that expands into a hot melodic line. The horns enter quietly as Mingus sings, "Mm-hm, uh-huh, don't let them drop that atomic bomb on me/Oh Lord, oh Lord, don't let 'em drop it/stop it/bebop it!" Kirk blows a forceful, holy-rolling manzello solo filled with wails and long, snaking notes, while the other horns continue their sluggish riffing. Mingus sings one final, short chorus, pounds out one last piano line, and finishes up.

"Eat That Chicken" is one of the most humorous tunes in the bassist's catalog, a good-spirited romp with the whole band singing "Oh Lord, I wanna eat that chicken, eat that chicken pie" complete with scatting. The composition is a tribute to Fats Waller, and it hews close to his exuberance as Kirk (on manzello), Ervin, and Knepper carry on in the Dixieland tradition. Mingus' piano positively thunders as the trombonist blasts out one of his finest plunger-muted solos. Ervin's tenor improvisation boosts the energy further, and Mingus keeps shouting "Oh yeah!" time and again in support. At 3:15 the tenorman and pianist lock together unexpectedly on the melody, then Ervin breaks away. At 3:42 the leader says, "We're goin' home now" and leads the band back into the sung chorus with occasional horn accents. The track ends with a final hungry statement from Mingus.

From those few moments of good humor we move into something completely strange: "Passions of a Man," easily the most bizarre thing Mingus ever came up with. Eerie bowed bass, Kirk's blown siren, spoken lines in made-up languages, and a slowly emerging tribal line in the horns are all patched together in a sonic crazy-quilt. Mingus' voices are overdubbed several times, and he carries on unintelligible conversations with himself as the musicians play odd, primitive riffs and rhythms off in the background. It continues in much the same manner for several more minutes, the offbeat energy rising and falling in a sort of free improvisation. At 4:21 the piano emerges again like the dawn, with Mingus softly speaking his last lines. It ends with a single hard drum whack.

There have been a couple of editions of *Oh Yeah* issued on CD. The 1988 version appends a twenty-four-minute interview between Mingus and Atlantic label head Nesuhi Ertegun. Mingus talks on and on about his inspirations and goals, playing bass, and the reason that he didn't play bass at all on this particular recording. He touches upon bass legend Slam Stewart, Louis Armstrong, Lionel Hampton, Bud Powell, Jelly Roll Morton, his unique compositional style, why he doesn't use written arrangements, and a criticism of John Handy's desire to lead his own sessions. Several times he illustrates points on the piano. The 1999 Rhino/Atlantic CD omits the interview in favor of including three extra tunes from the *Oh Yeah* session: " 'Old' Blues for Walt's Torin," "Peggy's Blue Skylight," and "Invisible Lady." Of the two editions, the 1988 version is more highly recommended for two reasons: because the interview provides invaluable insight into Mingus' personality and creative drive, and because the extra tracks from the 1999 CD are already available on *Tonight At Noon*.

*   *   *

Now, as we mentioned a couple of chapters ago, Mingus had recorded the tracks "Tonight at Noon" and "Passions of a Woman Loved" in 1957 during the sessions that resulted in *The Clown*. Because of their rather avant-garde nature, the tunes were left on the shelf until 1964, when they were paired with the above-mentioned outtakes from *Oh Yeah*: " 'Old' Blues for Walt's Torin," "Invisible Lady," and "Peggy's Blue Skylight." The resulting record, *Tonight at Noon* (Atlantic, 1964), does not present the smoothest track progressions, but it is a fascinating, well-recommended document of Mingus at his most creative.

For something that was recorded in 1957, "Tonight At Noon" is highly advanced and points toward the eventual development of free jazz as a viable form. The personnel is Mingus on bass, Shafi Hadi on alto sax, Jimmy Knepper trombone, Wade Legge piano, and Dannie Richmond on drums. The first thing we hear is a shaken tambourine, closely followed by

Mingus' walking bass and Richmond's cymbal taps. The bassist moves into the sliding double-stops that he favored on tunes such as "E's Flat, Ah's Flat Too"; Legge begins a percolating line; Knepper blows a tentative blues wail that is answered by the piano. Legge pounds hard note clusters when Hadi emerges, and soon everyone is taken up in the free-association dialogue. At 1:35 the piano dies out and Mingus is left to play his slides all alone for a moment. Fourteen seconds later Legge is back, and soon the horn section is playing the theme: three repetitions of a fast bebop phrase, followed by seven exactly repeated note-pairs. On the last repeat the note-pairs are played thirteen times, a lead-in for Hadi's superbly executed, too-short alto sax solo. Legge solo at 2:57 features a left-hand bass drone underneath his amazingly fleet right-hand runs. Knepper then blows trombone about as fast as it's ever been played, an astonishing display of technique that is accompanied by melodic brilliance. Richmond doesn't miss a beat as he rushes into his drum improvisation, which is gradually overtaken by Middle Eastern sounds on the alto sax and piano, high muezzin wails from Mingus, and free trombone blasts. Precisely at 5:15, Mingus brings the theme back and the band carries it out to a pinpoint ending.

The personnel shifts for "Invisible Lady"; as you recall, it's the *Oh Yeah* lineup of Mingus (on piano), Richmond, Knepper, Ervin, Kirk, and Doug Watkins on bass. We're led from one of Mingus' wildest compositions to one of his most beautiful ballads. And who better for the lead voice than the pristine Jimmy Knepper? Following a lush intro on piano, the trombonist plays the crystalline melody in the high range of the horn, moving the listener like no slideman has, perhaps, since Tommy Dorsey cut "Sleepy Lagoon" in the 1930s. The band offers the subtlest backup as the gorgeous theme continues to wend its way from the speakers. Knepper's improvisation is just as lovely, an organic extension of Mingus' melody. It seems that the only other horn here is Ervin, blowing soft support lines all the way. Absolutely exquisite.

Perhaps Kirk was saving his wind for " 'Old' Blues for Walt's Torin," the title of which remains one of Mingus' unsolvable mysteries. He blows both tenor and stritch on this multilayered theme, carrying on a reed-trio dialogue between himself and Ervin. An initial wave of tremulous sound from Kirk's horns and the piano leads into the melody, part of which is answered by Ervin while Knepper conjures up his own responses. Kirk's virtuosity causes the band to sound significantly larger than it is, filling this outstanding arrangement with a tactile richness. Certain elements like the bridge at 1:21 have a sort of vintage, pre-Ellington feel, perhaps inspiring the "old blues" title. Ervin's tenor sax solo is quite powerful, not as edgy as Kirk can sometimes be. At 3:14 Kirk grabs onto Ervin's last falling note. The two horns tear off on a masterful, double-time unison chorus before Ervin returns to the solo spotlight. Another unison line comes at 4:14; Kirk is a bit more out of tune this time, but it's still effective. Mingus' stentorian left-hand descent on the piano ushers the horns out, and he takes an interesting, blues-flecked solo that ventures into some unexpected tonal areas. The stratified themes come back, lushly sauntering all about until the final chord.

This session includes the first recorded version of "Peggy's Blue Sky-light," which would become one of Mingus' most enduring and often-interpreted compositions. Here, the piano states the theme in free time with plenty of embellishments, much in the spirit of Art Tatum. Kirk enters on manzello, continuing the free mood with a note held very long just a few beats into the theme. It's a captivating excursion that, in some ways, nods to what John Coltrane was doing with the soprano sax around the same time. The rhythm section comes in at 1:34, punctuating Kirk's phrases with quiet three-note hits. Knepper joins in on the next chorus, Ervin right afterwards with an intriguing octave-jumping riff. The pace slows considerably at 2:50, with Knepper's trombone high in the rafters and the saxes in concordant harmony, then picks up about a half-minute later. Ervin's tenor solo is an unhindered flow of pure melody with charming rhythmic accents; Richmond and Watkins maintain the most subtle of swing pulses. The piano improv by Mingus streams logically from Ervin's ideas, and the two finally come together, at 6:37, with a marvelous exchange of thought. All the players restate the theme and end in beautiful accord.

"Passions of a Woman Loved," the final track, takes us back to the 1957 session with Hadi, Knepper, Legge, and Richmond. This is absolutely nothing like the similarly titled "Passions of a Man"; the present track is an attractive ballad with an unexpected, drawn-out speedup halfway through the first melodic statement. It's as if the band were so caught up in playing their triplets, they tripped down the stairs. The second section is broken up by rhythmic and tempo roadblocks: a measure or so of melody, then tap-tap-tap and a break, that same motif repeated, then a drastic slowdown wherein the horns sail off with their own free-flowing lines. Legge is almost heavy-handed on his piano feature, drawing out rich chords that part to make room for a circus-waltz theme at 1:55. The bowed bass is an excellent textural addition. At 2:27 they shift back to the hard-swinging motifs, which last only a moment before Legge gets into piano ripples that are answered by Mingus plucking an ostinato high on the bass fingerboard. The band continues cycling through all these different themes until Knepper's·attractive trombone solo at 4:49. The quick waltz returns in time for Legge's piano improvisation, bright and cheerful for the most part, even after an angular Latin motif threatens to take over. Again, the piano style is reminiscent of Vince Guaraldi. Hadi flits and floats in a cathartic reverie from 7:03, an uplifting experience that is complemented well by another try at the waltz section, then a cycle back through the various themes. This is an amazing construction, and it's a shame that it never got more attention.

                                        *   *   *

Between October 1961 and October 1962, Mingus brought his band to the fabled Birdland to play a number of gigs. Many of these were recorded, and there exists a *very* rare four-CD set of all of the available Birdland concerts (*Charles Mingus at Birdland—The Complete Sessions*, BAT [Italy]). Many of the dates have been bootlegged over the years in various formats, some of which I will touch upon quickly. Bear with me because these get confusing and are scattered over multiple discs besides the BAT set. (Thanks to Esa Onttonen for his outstanding online discography, which kept this section from being even more befuddling.)

On October 21, 1961, Mingus played piano alongside Kirk, Knepper, Richmond, Yusef Lateef, and Doug Watkins. The set included "Hog Callin' Blues," "Ecclusiastics," and a tune that Mingus announced as "Blue Cee" but which bears no resemblance to the studio track known by that name. The last two tracks are on *Vital Savage Horizons* (Alto [Italy]), the first track only in the BAT set.

By March 24, 1962, the ensemble was significantly different: Mingus (back on bass), Richmond, Charles McPherson on alto, Booker Ervin on tenor, Richard Williams on trumpet, and a talented Japanese lady named Toshiko Akiyoshi on piano. The set list had also changed, now including "Take the 'A' Train," "Fables of Faubus," and "Eat That Chicken." These are available on *Hooray for Charles Mingus* (Session Disc [Italy]) and *Live at Birdland 1962* (Jazz View [Italy]), although the latter disc's version of "Eat That Chicken" is just a few seconds long. One week later, on March 31, the same lineup played a set including "Oh Lord, Don't Let Them...," "Eat That Chicken," and "Monk, Funk [*sic*] and Vice Versa" (the last-named is on *Vital Savage Horizons*).

On May 5 the band was augmented by a couple of bassists so that Mingus could get in some piano time; Herman Wright plays bass on the first run-through of "Eat That Chicken"; Henry Grimes plays on "Reets and I," "Devil Woman," and the closing reprise of "Eat That Chicken." Mingus only plays bass on "Monk, Funk or Vice Versa," lays out on "Reets and I" and plays piano on the rest. Akiyoshi only plays on "Monk, Funk..." and "Reets and I." The following week, on May 12, Grimes stuck around and played bass alongside Mingus on "Peggy's Blue Skylight," "Tijuana Table Dance" and another "Eat That Chicken." Both of the May dates are combined on both *In Concert* (Jazzman [Italy]) and *Charles Mingus* (Tempo di Jazz [Italy]).

Two more Birdland dates followed the Town Hall concert, which we will get to in a moment. For the sake of consistency over continuity, I will include those last Birdland shows here. On October 19, Mingus came in with Richmond, McPherson, Jaki Byard, Pepper Adams on baritone sax, tubaist Don Butterfield, and trumpeter Eddie Armour. The band played "Eat That Chicken," "Monk, Funk . . . ," and two tunes from the Town Hall set, "My Search" and "Please Don't Come Back From the Moon." These, too, are included on the aforementioned *Hooray for Charles Mingus* and *Live at Birdland 1962*, and once again the latter disc has only a short fadeout on "Eat That Chicken." Both discs also have incorrect titles for "My Search" (here titled "The Search"), "Please Don't Come Back . . . " ("Moonboy") and "Monk, Bunk . . . " ("King Fish").

On October 26, the same band minus Butterfield returned for one last Birdland gig. This time the set was "Monk, Funk . . . ," a new tune called "O.P.," "My Search," and "Eat That Chicken." *A Night in Birdland, Live Volume 2* (Yadeon) includes all of these tracks; the unusual compilation *Charles Mingus and Cecil Taylor* (Ozone) omits "Eat." It should be noted that this version of "O.P." includes an exceptional stop-time section that was left out of some subsequent versions, including the massive *Epitaph* (Columbia) set recorded by Gunther Schuller a decade after Mingus' death.

*　*　*

As Mingus' profile in the jazz business grew, so did his ambitions. First came a reunion with Duke Ellington and Max Roach on the phenomenal trio album *Money Jungle* (United Artists/Blue Note), made in September 1962. The disc featured hot, cutting-edge performances of all-Ellington material. Next Charles desired to conduct a large-scale concert which would bring the kind of dignity and respectability to jazz that had been the sole province of classical music. With the help of Newport Festival head George Wein, Mingus arranged for a performance at Town Hall in New York. He began composing an extended suite of music which reflected the African-American experience, uniting jazz and social protest. Some of the compositions were so special to him that he wove them into a suite he entitled "Epitaph," which he said was intended for his tombstone.

Charles intended this special concert to be an open-door recording session with a live audience, so that the listeners could experience first-hand how a jazz record date came together. But his poor organizational skills and a bevy of other problems conspired to throw a wrench into the works. The one available time slot at Town Hall (October 12, 1962) was weeks earlier than he had planned for, and the arrangements were not coming together as quickly as needed. It was brave enough for Mingus to talk United Artists into hiring a thirty-piece orchestra for the concert. It was something again when he realized that his usual method of dictating charts by voice was not going to work in this situation. He hired a slew of arrangers who labored round the clock and were still writing out the charts as the concert took place. As there were no on-stage monitors in place, the musicians couldn't hear one another very well. And to top it all off, there were a number of difficulties in the recording process itself, from distorted LP masters to the engineer's flat failure to record the last rehearsal. It is nothing short of a miracle, then, that *Town Hall Concert* was ever issued. An even greater triumph is the 1994 Blue Note CD issue, *The Complete Town Hall Concert*, which appends some unedited and alternate takes and corrects the song titles which were botched on the original release.

The complete personnel of this session was unknown for many years and seemed lost to the ages, but was finally pieced together through extensive research. The ensemble includes saxophonists Charlie Mariano, Charles McPherson, Jerome Richardson, George Berg, Buddy Collette, Eric Dolphy, Pepper Adams, and Zoot Sims; oboist Romeo Penque; contrabass clarinetist Danny Bank; trumpeters Richard Williams, Snooky Young, Ernie Royal, Clark Terry, Eddie Armour, Rolf Ericson, and Lonnie Hillyer; trombonists Quentin "Butter" Jackson, Britt Woodman, Jimmy Cleveland, Eddie Bert, Willie Dennis, and Paul Faulise; guitarist Les Spann; Mingus and Milt Hinton on bass; pianists Jaki Byard and Toshiko Akiyoshi (then Mariano's wife); Dannie Richmond on drums; and Warren Smith and Grady Tate as percussionists. The arrangers on the date included Gene Roland, Melba Liston, and Bob Hammer.

The concert begins with "Freedom," a blues lament with a hummed theme that is punctuated by hand-claps from the band. Over this Mingus recites a poem that is partially self-referential and partially a stab at the Communist "witch hunts" of the era:

> This mule ain't from Moscow
> This mule ain't from the South
> This mule's had some learning
> Mostly mouth to mouth
> This mule could be called stubborn and lazy
> But in a clever sort of way
> This mule could be working, waiting
> And learning and planning for a sacred kind of day
> A day when burning sticks and crosses
> Is not mere child's play
> But a madman in his most incandescent bloom
> Whose lover's soul is imperfection in its most lustrous groom

After the recitation, Mingus and the musicians sing a blues stanza about freedom, ending with " but no freedom for me." As the chant of "Freedom" continues, the horns play sweeps in the background and the baritone sax blows up-front accentuations. A hard tom-tom rhythm heralds a loud, shrill series of horn riffs, then the band cycles back to the humming, claps, and recitation. The track closes with Mingus encouraging his people to "stand fast."

The second portion was originally titled "Clark in the Dark," acknowledging the lead role of trumpeter Clark Terry but, according to biographer Brian Priestley's liner notes, it is actually a continuation of "Freedom." The baritone sax burbles sporadic riffs as the other horns blow long blasts. Terry is up front as the solo trumpeter, screeching in the highest range, which Ellington trumpeter Cat Anderson was also known for. The drummer keeps up a light swing pulse on the hi-hat, even when the horns rocket out into crushing dissonances.

"Osmotin'" is a variation of "Monk, Bunk and Vice Versa," and its theme is obviously built upon Thelonious Monk's "Well You Needn't" with an additional nod to old-time cornetist Bunk Johnson. The B section consists of a series of descending eighth-note groups, with "Tea for Two" laid underneath. The band plays a mutated Charleston rhythm behind Charles McPherson's upbeat alto sax solo, growing ever louder and higher until the next multilayered section at 1:15. After further solo space for McPherson, the band resumes the upward surge, then comes a short piano feature that is probably played by Toshiko Akiyoshi. The track ends abruptly; it is speculated that Mingus might have hoped for a second take that was never recorded.

The first part of "Epitaph" is clearly "Pithecanthropus Erectus," but it is botched horribly by the ensemble. Lack of rehearsal time is the most likely culprit, as with most of the blatant errors here. The theme collapses into a bit of collective improvisation, then Eric Dolphy and Mingus begin one of their compelling duo conversations, in the spirit of "What Love." At 2:05 a vibraphonist leads the band into the next section behind Dolphy, a fascinating passage that balances lovely melody and harsh dissonance. The high-end trumpets quote a couple of Ellington tunes, "Carnegie Blues," and "Just Squeeze Me," as the track rolls on. The pace speeds up before the four-minute mark, and an earth-shaking plunger-muted duet between Clark Terry and Britt Woodman ensues. After a moment the trumpeter bows out and leaves the trombonist to wail at his Ellingtonian best. Some of the other horns echo the rhythmic structure of Woodman's solo. What would seem to be a solo drum break starts up, but once again the band is cut off mid-stream.

A new, clangorous introduction calls in "Peggy's Blue Skylight," which is played more smoothly than the version on *Tonight At Noon*. The sax section handles the melody this time, an alluring arrangement by Melba Liston. The saxes are poked at playfully by the somewhat dissonant trumpets. This is one of the most successful performances of the concert, and even the hard, angular intro passage is nailed almost perfectly. A baritone sax solo of lush beauty is turned in by the undersung Jerome Richardson, followed by an equally adept statement from McPherson that is carried out to the track's end.

"Epitaph, Part 2" is not related in any definitive way to the first section. It bears a minor-key, almost Oriental theme led by Penque's oboe, with Spann's boinging guitar, tympani, and various horns peeking in and out of the mix. Trumpeter Ernie Royal is the featured soloist, but is so poorly miked that he sounds quite distant. Inevitably, it moves in a slow crescendo that peaks at around 3:08, then drops back off to eeriness. Around 4:20 the volume and activity level begin to increase again, culminating in a devastating drum flourish by Richmond.

"My Search" is mostly a rhythmic variation of "I Can't Get Started," one of the leader's favorite standards. The underscoring harmonies are so strong and dissonant that they almost obliterate the melody at times. A relatively short solo by McPherson precedes Mingus' exceptional improvisation, which dances around the thematic material with a low-key joy. As he winds up, the band shoots skyward in a big crash of energy, then the marvelous Akiyoshi presents a cascade of piano beauty. Later in the decade, the emigré pianist would form an acclaimed big band with her second husband, saxophonist Lew Tabackin; at this point, however, she was still somewhat of an unknown quantity. After the piano solo, McPherson returns to deliver another, more extensive, and luscious solo. The harmonies in the ensemble are most unharmonious, often obliterating any real sense of beauty that McPherson is trying to convey. The track seems to end hastily. Still, this is probably one of the most fully realized arrangements on the album.

During the concert's intermission a set was performed by saxman Fess Williams, Mingus' uncle (his son was the subject of Charles' 1954 composition, "Eulogy for Rudy Williams"). When the band returned, McPherson took the lead on "Portrait," the chart of which was based on the arrangement Thad Jones recorded in 1954. The alto sax melody is warm and inviting, but once again the ensemble backing is over-loud, technically inept and too dissonant for the theme it's built around. Jaki Byard's piano interlude is every bit as gorgeous as McPherson's offering, and by the three-minute mark the other performers seem to have settled better into their roles. The flutes are used pleasantly in the ensemble, and the coda is as smooth as satin.

On the original LP release, "Duke's Choice" was mistitled "Don't Come Back"; this is clarified on the CD issue. Buddy Collette has the distinguished alto lead this time, with swanky, Ellingtonian backup from Byard and the band. Bob Hammer's arrangement cuts out some of the orchestral instruments, sticking to a standard big-band lineup. The track is wrapped up by a letter-perfect trumpet cadenza by Richard Williams.

Early on, the infrequently heard "Please Don't Come Back From the Moon" is reminiscent of Mingus' older, Jazz Workshop-era compositions, but apparently it was of recent vintage. Once the arrangement moves past the melody, at about 1:04, it becomes one of the most devilishly complicated pieces in the set. The trombones set up a herky-jerky vamp that is countered by the screaming trumpets. Richard Williams begins a good muted trumpet solo in the heart of all this, but the chart is so animated and loud that it's difficult to hear him until the brass drops out at 1:43. He loses the mute at 2:14 and takes firmer command of the situation, scoring high points for his skillful improvising. The band seems to lose momentum between the end of his solo and the beginning of Byard's. The pianist performs as well as always, then settles into Dukish chording behind one of the more unexpected performers: Zoot Sims, a white tenorman from the West Coast who, like many of his counterparts there, idolized and emulated Lester Young. Again, the sax is undermiked which reduces the impact of his solo. Charlie Mariano suffers much the same fate, though he is slightly more audible. This track, too, ends on a heartbeat instead of a firm sense of resolution. This time, it's because the union reps signaled to Mingus that the curtain had to go down.

Mingus offered the last of his many apologies to the audience, and some players started to pack up and go. However, the jocular Clark Terry blew the opening to Duke's "In a Mellotone," many of the other players picked up on the vibe, and the rest is history. Warren Smith's vibes are an especially nice touch on this chaotic arrangement, which is most likely not a pre-planned chart from the set as much as a spontaneous creation. At 0:49 one of the trumpeters plays the traditional closing figure from Ellington's version, as if he thought things would end there. Instead, Jerome Richardson tears off into a powerful solo on baritone sax. He rouses the audience and band members to a furor, with whistles, claps and stomps resounding through the hall. Pepper Adams follows on a second bari sax turn, at about 2:30, then at 4:05 Clark Terry does what he does best. His trumpet solo is bright, bubbly, and infectious, bringing another crash of applause. At 5:45 Eric Dolphy dashes off a line as if he were claiming the next solo, but he is overridden by Britt Woodman. Partway through his trombone solo, the stagehands begin to lower the curtain and shut out the musicians. Once Woodman finishes, the band goes back to the theme while some of their mates continue to improvise. With the curtains shut, the trumpets blow a little bit of circus music (7:32), Dolphy races through "52nd Street Theme" in continued defiance, and someone in the brass section emulates a police siren coming to close the joint down.

The CD reissue includes another excellent take of "Epitaph, Part One" that was recorded after the hall had been cleared. (Obviously, given the applause, there were still listeners present.) This one runs more smoothly, although some horns still have trouble with the section right after the crescendo (0:18). Not long after that mark everyone drops out but Dolphy, whose free-ranging improvisation is soon backed up by Mingus. Around 1:10, the rest of the ensemble emerges with a combination of slow, plodding staccato notes by the lower horns, screeching trumpets, and a static drum pulse that almost defies swing. At 2:48 the mood shifts, becoming steadily louder and more forceful. All along Dolphy continues to wail, ululate, and groan with his distinctive alto sound. Woodman is the next soloist, blasting out the same kind of plungered, humorous lines as he had on the first take. Dannie Richmond, who was pretty well cheated out of his drum highlights for most of the concert, gets a chance to shine for a few moments, roaring from downstage before settling back and letting Charlie Mariano have some. A Bostonian of Italian blood, Mariano was a pioneer of jazz-rock and world-music fusions later in his career. Giving him the final solo of this ill-fated evening was prophetic, as he would next play a key role in one of Mingus' finest hours.

Resurgence: The Impulse Albums

Reeling from the negative impact of the Town Hall experience, Mingus plunged into another period of depression and psychoanalysis. It was the start of a long descent into self-doubt, economic collapse, and emotional anguish. Ironically, these difficult times did not prevent him from recording what would be considered the triumph of his career.

On January 20, 1963, barely three months after the Town Hall disaster, Mingus and his expanded ensemble recorded *The Black Saint and the Sinner Lady* for Impulse. It is a suite of dances—or it was intended to be, despite the difficulty of actually dancing to the end product—a ballet inspired by the African-American experience. It is universally said to be Mingus' finest hour, surpassing even *Ah Um* and *Blues and Roots* in the canon. It is an odd distinction for a performance so unique that, unlike most of Mingus' other works, it has almost never been performed again by him or anyone else. Little wonder, though; it's one of the most complex compositions ever attempted in a jazz framework.

For some time Mingus had maintained that jazz was part of America's folk music, created by blacks out of their own heritage and experience as much as any other native folk art. In "Folk Forms" he had analyzed the status of blues as an authentic folk music. And, when *Black Saint* was released, he insisted that Impulse Records replace the word "jazz" in their current motto so that it read, "The new wave of *folk* is on Impulse!" He was trying to recast and dignify jazz' place in the arts, as much as his own place within the music. And this unique African-American dance suite was a fine place to start. The band rehearsed and refined much of the material during a long engagement at the Village Vanguard, tweaking the composition until Mingus had it where he wanted it.

Mingus wrote a good portion of the liner notes for the album, speaking informally about the music and his sidemen, whom he praised with uncharacteristic, almost effusive kindness. He left the remaining liner note space for observations by his psychologist, Dr. Edmund Pollock. The doctor talks about Mingus' painful childhood, prior setbacks, and the indomitable spirit that led him to rise above adversity time and again, to keep creating music that was fresher and more challenging than any he had made before. He also offers his own bystander's insights on the music and the forces which inspired it.

The personnel on *Black Saint* are Rolf Ericson and Richard Williams, trumpets; Quentin Jackson, trombone; Don Butterfield, tuba; Jerome Richardson, Charlie Mariano, and Dick Hafer, reeds; Jaki Byard, piano; Jay Berliner, guitar; and, of course, Mingus and Richmond in their usual roles. What the liner notes don't reveal is that Mariano's alto sax solos were all overdubbed after the fact. Mariano was present at the recording session but had only played ensemble parts at the time. In the end, it doesn't matter when his solos were cut; they stand as some of the most awe-inspiring moments of his career, and of the substantial Mingus discography.

"Track A—Solo Dancer (Stop! Look! and Listen, Sinner Jim Whitney!)" begins with an almost martial drum pattern. Soon we hear low blats coming from Butterfield's contrabass trombone, a recurring whole-note alternation in the saxophones, and finally Mariano's poignant alto. A general sense of suspension gives way to brisk waltz-time at 0:49, just before Richardson's anguished baritone sax solo. The band's volume gradually increases, and at 2:29 Dannie Richmond suddenly drops the waltz pulse. A roll, a tumble, and then a quiet 4/4 feeling pervades as the melody returns. We come slowly back to the waltz beginning at 3:16, as the trumpets and saxes harmonize on the melody. Richardson takes a soprano sax solo at 4:11, one of the very few times that the straight horn had been heard in Mingus' music up until then. It's a tremendous improvisation that sets the band ablaze. It's evident that Richardson was well aware of what John Coltrane had been doing with the soprano sax lately. The track ends rather suddenly, with no exit theme.

Byard invokes a sincere spirit of Ellington on his introduction to "Track B—Duet Solo Dancers (Hearts' Beat and Shades in Physical Embraces)." The piano is absolutely orchestral, setting the tone for the most Ducal section of the suite. A few fragments of the horn passages hint at Ellington's "Solitude." Mariano hints gently at Johnny Hodges but mostly maintains his own personality, focused on pure beauty of tone and conception. Just before the two-minute mark the theme takes a dark turn, shifting into a minor key. Very low pulses from the tuba are answered by the baritone sax; Jackson and one of the trumpeters carry on an anguished battle using their plunger mutes. The tempo speeds up frantically, then drops off at 4:18. Everyone slinks back but Jackson and Richmond, who keep striking at one another musically. The ensemble returns at 4:47 to the original form: splatting contrabass trombone, sax sweeps, and the irresistible 6/8 drive of the drums as Jackson wah-wahs his way along. He drops the plunger mute a bit later, swaying into a short, pretty passage alongside the saxophones at 5:49. Mariano carries the band aloft on a final run through the melody.

"Track C—Group Dancers ((Soul Fusion) Freewoman and Oh, This Freedom's Slave Cries)" is also introduced by the piano, but this time it's Mingus playing in quite a different mode. No faux Ellington here, rather more of a contemporary-classical feeling. He breaks out into a waltz, spins wildly off tempo, then pirouettes and flops. At 0:38 the horns begin popping up here and there behind his hall-filling reverie, then fade back once more to let Mingus continue his marvelous exposition. He invents bright new variations on the basic theme over and over, some dark, some glittering. At 1:35 the waltz melody arrives, borne on the flutes of Richardson and Hafer with buoyant responses from the low brass. It only lasts for a few moments before Mingus' piano takes over again. But at 2:37 the waltz reappears, this time led by the trumpets. Two run-throughs, then we shift gears to a Spanish motif featuring Mariano's poignant alto sax and Jay Berliner's magnificent acoustic guitar. The band spirals into almost a free-jazz mode, with Richmond barreling to insane speeds. In his section of the liner notes, Dr. Pollock reveals Mingus' inspiration for this passage: the Inquisition, a country cousin of slavery, and the somber artworks of El Greco. As the slower theme returns at 4:30, Mariano is still on the front line, digging deeply into the blues as his bandmates play long tones of agreement. Mingus steps forth to join in a dialogue with the altoist. Somewhere around 5:45 the tempo begins to pick up very gradually. The trumpets and saxes move into their higher range, and at 6:24 a quick 6/8 pace is started by Richmond. The backing horns keep up their long notes even as the speed continues to increase. Precisely at 7:00 the band stops on a dime, leaving Mariano to rip through an exemplary solo cadenza.

The last three "modes" of the composition are combined onto a single CD track. It was clearly Mingus' intention to have these modes unified—throughout this section we hear reflections of prior movements, tying it all together thematically—but it would have been nice to have some digital hints tossed in. "Mode D—Trio and Group Dancers (Stop! Look! And Sing Songs of Revolutions!)" begins with a drum roll, a solemn piano figure, a quick burst of wah trombone and flutes, then Mingus plays a solo bass passage which ushers in an Ellingtonian flow of vibrato-heavy saxophones and muted brass. Actually, the brass passages are more Mingus than Duke, rich with more modernistic harmonies. They are interrupted unexpectedly at 1:40 by Berliner's guitar, which moves us back to an Iberian mode. Berliner is a phenomenal player whose talents were similarly utilized by arranger Gil Evans. His Spanish guitar chops might seem out of place in this setting, but let us keep in mind that this is a Mingus project and therefore subject to any spontaneous shift of mood or genre. Berliner eggs on the ensemble to the point that the horns end up in a frenetic exchange of Spanish flourishes; of particular interest is the three-way brass dialogue between Richard Williams, Rolf Ericson, and Quentin Jackson.

At 4:29 a sudden, hard four-beat figure parts the curtains and introduces "Mode E—Single Solos and Group Dance (Saint and Sinner Join in Merriment on Battle Front)." The same introductory piano figure is heard, answered in the same way by the flutes and trombone. After the piano cadenza, the fleeting waltz theme from "Track C" is presented by the flutes at 5:00, then quickly dropped. We're treated to more plaintive, astonishingly beautiful piano; a bit heavy-handed, perhaps, but very compelling. It is interrupted by the flute theme again, but Mingus continues undeterred with another solo that spreads out in low-end pounds and shimmers. At 6:32 a brand new theme is presented by the ensemble, a modern jazz ballad in which Mariano and one trumpeter take the lead roles. The altoist begins his improvisation in a milieu of warm encouragement from the others (including himself in the sax section; remember, Mariano's solos are overdubbed). Berliner jumps in almost rudely at 8:18, trying to nudge the altoist back into a Spanish mood; the ensemble strikes back for a moment, but inevitably the alto and guitar return to their vibrant Latin conversation. As happened before, they suck in the other players so that a chaotic group improvisation results.

Since this is three movements combined into one track, we can take 11:33 as the likely starting point for "Mode F—Group and Solo Dance (Of Love, Pain and Passionate Revolt, then Farewell, My Beloved, 'til It's Freedom Day)." (Gotta love those Mingus titles.) Mariano leads a Ducal melody that is briefly whacked by an out-of-context blare from Ericson. Richmond conjures a hard swing rhythm as a base for wonderful plunger-muted brass dialogues. The band follows dutifully as the drummer radically kicks up the pace again, a very slow increase spread out over more than a minute. The musicians are running breakneck by the time Richmond suddenly drops back to a snail's pace at 13:31. Then the speeding-up process starts all over again, no doubt wearing the hornmen to a frazzle. One hopes there weren't too many takes required of this section in the studio. A return to the slow pace comes at 15:17, with Jackson's world-weary trombone belting out the blues. Then, sure enough, around 15:40 Richmond begins to kick the tempo up yet again. Butterfield, Hafer, and Richardson on baritone sax keep up the foundation of long tones while Mariano, the rhythm players, and the other brass soar off on another collective improvisation. That, too, dies away, and at 17:15 we are brought full circle: the original structure of the first section, with Mariano's poignant melody laid over the base of low brass and swooping reeds. Finally everything drops off except for the alto, which delivers a masterful solo coda and fades into the night.

*   *   *

Having completed his difficult masterwork, Mingus did something that was most out of character for him: he devoted most of his next album to reinterpreting past works. *Mingus, Mingus, Mingus, Mingus, Mingus* (Impulse, 1963) is a consistent favorite among fans and radio personalities. (Just for the sake of convenience, we will refer to this album as *Mingus x 5* from now on, please, no shouts from the purists.)

Not only did Mingus try new things with old compositions, he even changed their titles. "II B.S." (perhaps a nod to one of the bassist's favorite activities) is a restructured "Haitian Fight Song." "I X Love" (which could be interpreted as "I Kiss Love," "I Cross Out Love," or any number of other codes; this is the same Bob Hammer arrangement as that played at Town Hall) is a significant revision of "Nouroog," from *A Modern Jazz Symposium*. "Goodbye Porkpie Hat" becomes the less obfuscatory "Theme for Lester Young." "E's Flat, Ah's Flat Too" is retitled as "Hora Decibitus," meaning "the hour of bedtime." This is especially ironic; who could sleep amidst such high-energy music? The album also includes the 1957 composition "Celia" and Ellington's "Mood Indigo."

It should be noted that "I X Love" and "Celia" were recorded on the same day as *Black Saint*: January 20, 1963. The personnel is also exactly the same. The other tracks of *Mingus x 5* were taped precisely eight months later, on September 20, 1963. The band is a blend of old, recent, and new sidemen: Richard Williams and Eddie Preston, trumpets; Britt Woodman, trombone; Don Butterfield, tuba; Jerome Richardson, Dick Hafer, Eric Dolphy, and Booker Ervin, reeds; Jaki Byard, piano; Mingus, bass; and Walter Perkins on drums, subbing for Dannie Richmond, who may have been jailed on drug charges.

Mingus is in fine, powerful form on the intro of "II B.S.," his dynamic pluckings accentuated with unusual percussive strikes by Perkins. Mingus strikes the basic groove, the drummer follows, then the band leaps in eagerly. This larger ensemble gives the tune a different sound than the prior versions of "Haitian Fight Song." The staccato sixteenth-note passage in particular has a refreshing fullness to it compared to the stabbing texture of Jimmy Knepper's solo delivery. Booker Ervin seems happy to be back in the band; his tenor sax solo has a wild-eyed urgency that exceeds his usual temperament. Perkins is a gem here, whacking rimshots during Byard's jagged piano solo. Dannie Richmond would always be the ideal drummer for Mingus, but it's interesting to hear someone else tackle the job now and then. Mingus responds well to the challenge, locking in perfectly with the drums. The energy level of "II B.S." is so infectious that the track seems to end before it has been satisfactorily resolved.

"I X Love" brings us more of the lush Mariano alto saxophone, elevated by that wondrous *Black Saint* ensemble. Mingus' arrangement is letter-perfect, a fine realization of the potential of "Nouroog." It's not mentioned whether the trumpet soloist is Ericson or Williams, but the muted improvisation is fabulously smooth and sensuous. The oboe of Dick Hafer is an ideal textural touch in this impeccable chart. Mariano's solo is one of his best ever, alternating between tenderness and heartbroken anguish.

"Celia" begins in a similar mood, another brocaded ballad with Mariano on the front line. But before the thirty-second mark hits, the groove shifts into a medium-tempo swing feel. Mariano makes a seamless transition from mournful ballad style to an edgy blues disposition. These change-ups occur throughout the piece. Whenever Mingus wrote compositions with a woman in mind, he habitually structured the tunes to reflect all of the different layers of the women's personalities and his relationships with them. Sometimes they could get overbearing—"Sue's Changes," written a decade after "Celia," is almost too complicated to sustain interest—but this one bears a particular multifaceted charm.

"Mood Indigo" is another heartfelt homage to Ellington, handled with the proper sense of nostalgia. The muted horns, slow pace, and tinkling piano are ideal nods to the Ellington aesthetic. Mingus' bass is prominent during the theme, and he steps up at 1:17 for an exceptional solo that continually acknowledges Duke's original intent while stating his love for the maestro in a distinctly modern fashion. That's pretty much what the track is: a love letter from Mingus to Ellington, framed in one of his hero's most timeless compositions. The bassist respects "Mood Indigo" enough to leave it where it stands, no tempo changes or drastic harmonic alterations.

Despite its inarguable gospel foundation, and his prior statements about it, "Better Get Hit In Yo' Soul" is written off in the liner notes as having no religious significance. Nat Hentoff states that Mingus denied the church-music inspiration: "I just enjoyed the challenge of playing in 6/8 time faster than anybody had ever tried before. And I wanted to show that a band can swing as deeply in 6/8 as in the more usual time signatures." All that aside, this is a pretty good performance. Britt Woodman isn't as strong a technician as Jimmy Knepper, turning some formerly tongued lines into slurs. The trumpets don't quite achieve the holy-rolling feel of the original versions, either, but the saxophones are spot-on and Mingus works minor miracles with Walter Perkins. Jerome Richardson is the keystone of this whole performance, blurting out his baritone sax riffs with panache and taking a tremendous solo in the hand-clap-backed slot normally held by Booker Ervin. At 3:09 we can hear a more rigid ensemble passage that's new to the piece, subverting the 6/8 pulse in favor of a stiff, ironic 4/4. It is gone after a single chorus, and we're back to a more familiar throb that leads back to the melody. Usually the tune would finish up at the five-minute mark, but Mingus appends an entirely new section. This is a bright, upbeat blues romp in 4/4, complete with hammering horn riffs and trade-offs between players. A new step in the evolution of one of his most enduring compositions.

"Theme for Lester Young" is beautifully handled by the saxophones, with Mingus plucking forceful complements on his bass. Around 1:10 the rest of the band creeps in; a haunting muted trumpet wafts overhead as the melody continues. Ervin's tenor sax solo is the essence of bluesy longing, and ironically it bears little or none of the character of Young's playing. No matter; the recognition and affection are clearly present. The tuba might be a little oppressive at times, but in general the ensemble support is excellent. At 5:24, after the final theme statement, an ominous, low rumbling takes over and changes the mood of the track.

Mingus' bass on the introduction of "Hora Decubitus" delivers those trademark sliding double-stops that he had favored for the past few years. Jerome Richardson gets the first try at the melody, and the other horns join in before he's done with the first pass. The layers here are marvelous: wah trumpets, trombone scribblings, a hot-and-heavy 4/4 rhythm, and plenty of sizzling blues from Booker Ervin. After the tenor solo, Eric Dolphy crashes in with furious blowing on his alto sax. Little has been heard from Dolphy in this session up until now, and he finally announces his presence with the usual wild flair. His tonality, or actually his avoidance of tonality, changes the spirit of the piece and inspires Richard Williams' own flight of fancy. His high-range explorations, in turn, encourage the whole ensemble to figuratively rise up and dance. The all-in conclusion is purest Mingus.

The 1995 CD reissue of *Mingus x 5* includes a bonus take of "Freedom," the chant with which Mingus had opened the Town Hall concert. This is a great find, much clearer and better-executed than the live version that no one had quite been ready for. Mingus recites the poem with righteous specificity while his bandmates hum, clap, and whack the tambourine in support. Then several of the men sing "Freedom, for your daddy's daddy" and the like while the horns pop in one by one. After a dissonant instrumental break, we are treated to another fiery blues solo from Booker Ervin. As the band swells around the tenorman, Richard Williams blurts out plungered responses to Ervin's sweaty sermon. At about 3:20 the pace starts to slow dramatically, and ten seconds later we're into a slow blues with hard drum punctuations and mighty walking bass. Mingus wails vocally along with Ervin when the brass vamp enters, then the tempo slows even more to get back to the sung chorus. One mystery: there is one voice in the final passage that is inarguably female, yet there is no woman listed in the personnel.

As with *Pre-Bird*, Mingus had paid a visit to where he had gone in his career thus far. The next phase of Mingus' experimentation took another crucial turn. He returned to the piano, but instead of playing a supporting role as he had on *Oh Yeah* and *Black Saint,* this time Charles recorded an entire album of solo piano musings. *Mingus Plays Piano* (Impulse), taped on July 30, 1963 (between the sessions represented on *Mingus x 5*), presents a new face of his unhindered creativity. He is no Horowitz, not even a Tatum nor a Powell, but Mingus uses the piano to flesh out his ideas in a different manner than his bass and ensembles could accomplish.

The first selection on the album, "Myself, When I Am Real," is a masterpiece of introspection. From the first tremolo Mingus develops a breathtakingly beautiful theme, more classical by far than anything resembling jazz. In this it seems a valid display of his heart's affection, this man who always aspired to transcend the restrictive label of jazz to become a composer of world-class status. In this one piano piece, perhaps, Mingus came closest to achieving that distinction. From the slow, thoughtful section it progresses into a slightly warped ballet, with a bass pedal-point as the foundation for a spinning, twirling exploration of pure melody. At 2:40 it slows and quietens, small variations coming as if he were thinking about the implications of what he just said. Following another visceral extrapolation, Mingus settles back into calmness at 4:32. This performance was simply magnificent, so much so that Jaki Byard saw fit to write a full orchestration several years later. One version was recorded on *Let My Children Hear Music* (1972, Columbia) under the title "Adagio Ma Non Troppo." Most astonishingly, Mingus claimed that this track was completely improvised in the studio.

Next, Mingus interprets some of his favorite standards. "I Can't Get Started" is a tune he had revisited time and again during his career, and he treats it with kid gloves on this album. Sometimes he paints it in tints of blue, as with the final note of the chorus at 0:48. At 1:47 he moves into a bit of a stride feeling, albeit much slower than traditional for the form. "Body and Soul" is treated with similar reverence, yet Mingus is freer with the theme. Coleman Hawkins had reinvented the tune at the end of the 1930s, barely sticking to the melody at all, so Mingus has few qualms about stirring in his own variations. This, too, is a timeless performance. The later take on "Memories of You" alters the mood of the piece a bit more, keeping some spirit of nostalgia but modernizing the harmonies. He stretches out the tempo like Monk would, but without all the dissonance. He also takes on "I'm Getting Sentimental Over You," drawing out the melody well beyond anything that Duke might have done with the piece.

Mingus shifts gears entirely on "Roland Kirk's Message," pounding out a vital, hard blues theme inspired by the renegade blind saxophonist. It's a pity that this track is less than three minutes long; it would be nice to hear Mingus dig further into this blues bag. He self-harmonizes as Kirk did with his multiple horns, crafting a clever tribute to a most unusual musician. "She's Just Miss Popular Hybrid," another Mingus original, is a well-built song to which one can imagine him setting words.

The next track was mistitled as "Orange Was the Color of Her Dress, Then Silk Blues." This is actually "Song With Orange," related but significantly different. Mingus plays the theme at much the same pace as the full ensemble used to, widening the palette a bit more for expressiveness. The melody is instantly recognizable and performed well, although his left-hand work is a bit clunky at times. It is interesting to hear this kind of reductionism performed on Mingus' music, especially by the master himself as he boils his compositions and inspirations down to their barest essence.

"Meditations for Moses" is not related to the "Meditations" that would be part of Mingus' sets for the next couple of years. This piece is certainly meditative, with a slight Middle Eastern flavor to it, and it's perhaps the most Mingus-sounding piece on the disc. He utilizes a lot of heavy tremolos (0:42) and his signature dissonances (1:15) to strong effect, along with frequent shifts of mood, from pastoral to restive to ominous.

Mingus' vintage composition "Portrait" is revisited here as "Old Portrait." This is a loving, bittersweet rendition of an old favorite, given perhaps the kind of treatment it should have always received. Mingus was always one to give his sidemen the leeway to interpret the music in their own fashion, and it's refreshing to hear a fine composition like this one reevaluated by its creator.

The album's final selection is "Compositional Theme Story: Medleys, Anthems and Folklore." It's a long, consistently beautiful string of attractive themes held together by the warmth and tenderness of Mingus' interpretations. Some of the melodies might be familiar, some not, but the pianist wraps us up in a comfy blanket of musical beauty and bids us to just listen.

*   *   *

From this matchless point in his artistic development, Mingus would soon embark upon the busiest, most tumultuous period of his career. The pastoral beauty he revealed on the piano album would become a scarce commodity by the time this frantic era came to a close.

The 1964 Tour

In the spring of 1964, Mingus embarked upon a tour of Europe that would result in one of the largest bodies of bootlegged recordings in jazz history, not to mention some of the most creative live music of its kind. The multiple versions of tunes such as "Fables of Faubus," "Meditations," and "So Long Eric" give listeners the chance to see how these compositions were developed and altered on the road. Mingus didn't bother with singing the lyrics to "Faubus," most likely because they would be lost on non-American listeners. But he and his sidemen had great fun on the tour, particularly when it came to the grand bebop tradition of quoting other songs during the improvisations. One could make a party game out of identifying all the different tunes dredged up from the players' minds during this remarkable string of concerts.

Prior to the tour Mingus rehired Eric Dolphy, who was happy to be on board but made it clear that he would leave the band afterwards to concentrate on his own advanced ideas. Mingus accepted that, and even composed an altered blues called "So Long Eric" to honor his longtime friend. Sadly, that tribute turned into an epitaph mere weeks after the tour's end.

* * *

Before heading to Europe, the sextet—Mingus, Dolphy, Richmond, pianist Jaki Byard, tenor saxophonist Clifford Jordan, and trumpeter Johnny Coles—performed for an NAACP benefit at Town Hall on April 4, 1964. It must have been difficult for Mingus to return to the site of what he perceived as his greatest failure, but the concert went on nonetheless.

The recorded *Town Hall Concert* (Jazz Workshop, reissued Fantasy/Original Jazz Classics) was dedicated to Mrs. Dupree White, the NAACP coordinator who had organized the gig, and to the departing Dolphy.

Two long pieces were performed at the NAACP show. "So Long Eric," nearly eighteen minutes long, begins with an excellent, blues-rich bass solo by the leader. The quick, triplet-centered melodic phrases are rhythmically similar to "Wednesday Night Prayer Meeting" but are teamed here with repeated note pairs and twelve-note trills that spread over nearly four full measures. On the third measure of those trills, Jordan breaks off and blows a strong, descending quarter-note figure, providing an excellent contrast. Johnny Coles' trumpet solo is relaxed, perhaps a bit tentative. A couple of choruses in, the tempo doubles and prods the trumpeter to a second wind. Dolphy and Jordan add more depth with their quavering figures behind the soloist, calling the tune's tonality into question. The tempo doubles halfway through Coles' improvisation and slows again after he's finished. The next solo turn is for Byard, who shows an excellent feel for bop and stride piano styles, tinted with gospel accents. As the tune progresses, Byard bangs out huge tremolos which kick up the tension and volume. After his solo is done, the pianist settles into playing choppy chords behind Jordan, who digs into a passionate blues vein. The other horns blow some counterpoint that heightens the tune's energy before another doubling of tempo. A while into that fast section, another barrage of strangely keyed riffs bursts out from Dolphy and Coles, changing the flavor of the piece once more. Mingus' solo bubbles at times like a kettle threatening to boil over, then he tones down to spar with Byard on a quieter level. He vehemently trades four-bar stretches with Richmond, who does everything possible to throw the boss off track. Finally the bassist backs away and lets the master drummer have his say. Dolphy's improvisation is like a drunken ice-cream truck, constantly teetering back and forth between tonality and freedom. Byard is happy to jump on the free-jazz bandwagon, toying playfully with the altoist with an utter disregard for the intended key. The melody returns, more loosely strung together now. Just as it seems about to wind down, the band slides into a completely different feel as Dolphy reclaims the lead for more improvised mayhem.

The second piece of the session is a very unusual tune that has been called many things: "Meditations," "Meditations on Integration," and "Meditation (on a Pair of Wire Cutters)." Mingus announces the piece under that last title, although in the liner notes it is posthumously titled "Praying with Eric" in honor of the reedman's passing. It's a highly unusual piece, with the piano, tenor, and trumpet burbling and jumping beneath Dolphy's eerie minor-key flute line and Mingus' bowed-bass unison. For a time it seems as if every member of the band is playing in a different meter, so disjointed is the structure of the piece. Dolphy is awe-inspiring on both flute and bass clarinet, which he takes up after the initial melody statement.

This is another multi-layered composition, moving from modal jazz to pastoral beauty. Byard is responsible for the latter, turning in a breathtakingly gorgeous piano solo that would do Bill Evans (and Debussy) proud. Dolphy follows that tender thread when he returns with his flute, hovering and fluttering about like a tiger swallowtail. The pianist's lines slowly become more abstract, straying slightly from the original tempo and tonal center. At around 8:45 the flautist starts to bend his notes like runny watercolors, heralding the arrival of a Spanish motif in the piano. About a minute later the horns come back in with an urgent riff; forty-five seconds after that, a typically Mingusian bop melody takes center stage. The bass clarinet is back as Dolphy rips and puffs through another dynamic improvisation. Byard continues his piano explorations—this tune really belongs to the pianist and Dolphy—spreading out fine new textures for our perusal. Coles' solo comes in at 15:35, followed by another strong bass outing by Mingus. Jordan improvises heatedly from 18:31 onward, analyzing repetitive figures in the manner of Joe Henderson, with Byard and Richmond in hot pursuit. After exhaustive exposition, the original melody finally returns at about the twenty-four-minute mark.

*   *   *

A few days after the Town Hall concert, Mingus and his friends were on their way to Europe. The first stop was Amsterdam, where they played a marathon set at the famous Concertgebouw on April 10. The concert is available on *Mingus in Amsterdam 1964* (DIW/Japan, one disc) and also on *Concertgebouw Amsterdam, Volumes 1 and 2* (Ulysse AROC/France, two discs) in the same order.

Mingus introduces "Parkeriana," his medley of fragments from Charlie Parker's compositions, by its original title, "Dedication to a Genius." It obviously wasn't the first thing performed that night, as the bassist calls it "the next thing we'd like to play." After a powerfully swinging bass intro, the horns get going on the theme of "Ow!," then cycle through a number of other melodies ("Anthropology," "Billie's Bounce," and so on) that were close to Parker's heart. At times Dolphy gives an uncanny emulation of Bird's alto sax style, an influence that wasn't usually up front in the younger man's playing. Johnny Coles' solo is cheerful and vibrant, drawing from the inspirations of Dizzy Gillespie and Miles Davis in a further homage to Parker's heyday. Jaki Byard's piano solo vacillates between Dixieland and 52nd Street with liberty, exciting the hell out of the Dutch audience. His expansive knowledge of jazz piano's full history made him a vital asset to the band at this stage of Mingus' career. Richmond keeps up the pace set by the pianist in his drum solo, a short crash-boom-bang affair before Clifford Jordan claims the stage at 10:19. The tenor saxophonist is a hard-core bopper at heart, with a good understanding of R&B and swing forms to temper his brusque approach to the horn. His unaccompanied breaks, at 12:30, 12:56, and 13:23, are among Jordan's many high points on this tour. The last such break literally stops the show with applause, then Richmond gets a better shot at his solo turn. Dolphy's alto saxophone solo isn't as outlandish as some of his offerings; he sticks closer than usual to the Parker model but doesn't—perhaps can't—adhere to it outright. Around 16:45, Coles begins to blow on Dizzy Gillespie's "A Night in Tunisia" behind Dolphy, another bow to the bebop canon celebrated in this animated medley.

Mingus plays the melody, alone, to introduce "So Long Eric." Piano and drums back him up on the next statement, then the horns enter. Coles' trumpet solo is poised in comparison to the Town Hall concert, and he blows some Miles Davis-like warbles via half-valve techniques (holding the trumpet's valves part-way down to alter the quality of the notes) and alternate fingerings. Jaki Byard concentrates more specifically on the blues feeling in his solo than he does on any other selections played during this tour, and the tighter focus helps maintain a unified feeling in this particular piece. Mingus' bass riffing behind Clifford Jordan's tenor sax solo is so loud it's almost distracting, but the leader backs off after the first chorus to let his pupil shine. The horn riff behind Jordan, starting at 8:52, is played in a different key that drastically clashes with the basic chord changes. The next round of riffs, at 10:07, is not only discordant but rhythmically off-kilter, too. Jordan ends his improvisation with a sweet blues line, ushering in the leader to trade off four-measure stretches (called "trading fours") with Dannie Richmond. The drummer's solo comes at 12:09, ranging between scatterations across the drum kit, light cymbal rides and hot swing pulses. Eric Dolphy then improvises freely, avoiding downbeats and key with searing jumps into the high register of the saxophone. Any resemblance to Charlie Parker, aside from pacing, is down the drain; this is the future of jazz alto. At 18:20 the rhythm section drops out, adding mere drops of color for several moments as Dolphy is left to speak his mind. Once again, toward the end the pace slows significantly, only to be driven upward again before the finale.

Byard is responsible for "AT-FW-YOU-USA," his finger-busting solo feature. The "AT" is for Art Tatum, "FW" is Fats Waller, "YOU" draws the listener into the equation, and "USA" heralds a salute to the great American art form of jazz. Usually one or the other segments of the full title was missing from the liner notes or announcements on stage; this particular version is just called "AT-FW-YOU." As Mingus states, Byard takes us through "the traditions of so-called jazz piano" in this piece.

*   *   *

On April 12, the band stopped in Oslo, Norway for a concert at University Aula. The set included "So Long Eric," "Parkeriana" (a 2½-minute false start, often mistitled as "Ow!," and an 18½-minute full rendition), "Orange

Was the Color of Her Dress," and "Take the 'A' Train." Over the years the tracks have been spread across several albums, mostly bootlegs, in different arrangements. The Oslo concert is also partially documented on the Green Line/Jazz and Jazz VHS video, *Charles Mingus: Live in Norway 1964*. The commentary in this book will consider the CD recording and video, both of which should be in the hands of interested collectors.

Although the Green Line video is missing the full take of "Parkeriana," it gives an enjoyable, if grainy, look at how the sextet operated at this time. Probably for filming purposes, the bass, drums, and horns are clustered together in a tight semicircle, with the piano behind Clifford Jordan and Mingus. The bassist begins with Mingus attempting to play an introduction to "So Long Eric." The wooden stage floor is slippery and the bass peg keeps sliding, so Charles has to stop and request that the technician cut the false start from the tape. After stabbing the peg into the floor, which brings startled guffaws from the audience, Mingus begins the tune again and the band falls into line right behind him.

Coles, with shaven head, takes the first solo on "So Long Eric" with his eyes shut tightly. He plays behind the beat with such an odd tonality that the piece takes on a modal feeling. Coles makes effective use of long tones, setting up dissonance as they clash with the emerging chords. Byard's piano solo is in much the same mode as at Town Hall, lots of spirituality and bluesiness.

Coolly clad in tiny oblong sunglasses, Jordan shows a bit of Dolphy's influence in his solo, playing tremulous lines and bop passages in the tenor's highest range. After a few minutes the band begins playing at a furious pace, with Dolphy and Coles blowing a hard three-note riff to egg Jordan on. The tenorman explores some repetitive motifs, then settles into a deep blues mode. When Mingus claims his solo turn, he makes playing the "doghouse" seem as easy as dialing the phone. His bass is not especially well recorded on either the album or video, but the VHS provides a good exposition of his fleet-fingered technique. A couple of minutes along, Mingus drops out suddenly, opening the floor to drum commentary by Richmond. They exchange phrases for a while before the drummer goes into a characteristic off-tempo solo on his small kit. (Anyone who thinks that a good drummer needs five toms and ten cymbals need only see Richmond in action here.) Eric Dolphy, the tune's namesake, jumps in with a frenetic, free alto sax solo. He must have possessed one of the fastest tongues in the business, given the rate at which he honks out flurries of sixteenth notes all over the horn's range. In the corner of the video screen we can see Jordan hand-signaling Coles, counting down the cue for their horn riffs. At other times in this concert there are no visible signs of direction, suggesting that the band must have put immense rehearsal time into this complicated material. Dolphy keeps returning to altissimo (very high-range) squeals and short figures. He finally assumes a pattern of descending triplets ending in high notes, cuing the band's return to the melody. The long twelve-note repetitions slow down over time, then quicken again as Dolphy continues to improvise until the end.

"Orange Was the Color of Her Dress, Then Blue Silk" was composed by Mingus for the same teleplay that gave us its kissing cousin, "Song With Orange." This is a more ambitious, very distinctive work. It begins with Byard playing the initial figure as a fast rip, soon complemented by Dolphy's bass clarinet. The tempo unexpectedly doubles for about four bars, during which the reeds play a certain repeated figure. That motif is kept up at the same tempo while the rest of the band drops back into slow time behind Coles' melody, and everyone ends on a quarter-note triplet that recurs as a signature throughout the tune. Byard's solo is thoughtful and unhurried. After a fashion he gets more heavy-handed, hammering out high right-hand chords and burbles. The horns state the signature triplet to end each cycle through the chord changes. The piece eases back into a ballad feel before Coles' well-executed, melodic solo. Dolphy responds with visible joy to some of the trumpeter's phrases. It's interesting to watch Richmond's buggy eyes on the video, darting between the players as he watches for cues and reacts to Cole's solo ideas. The bassist follows with another effortless solo, concentrating on the middle and high ranges of the instrument. After one of the horn triplets he reaches way up on the fingerboard and builds from a tremolo into some beautiful statements. The final run through the melody is pretty loose, especially when Jordan takes the lead.

What is titled on the video as "Ow!" is actually "Parkeriana." This is not a full-on reading, but rather a 2½-minute false start. Mingus' rapid bass intro brings on the bop melody, which dissolves into long, smeary notes blown out of tempo. Dolphy continues to roll out the various Parker melodies as Richmond grabs onto a new pace, whacking the kit with phenomenal speed as Coles prepares for his solo. A few notes later Mingus cuts off the band, dissatisfied with the way the piece is coming together. The editing of the videotape makes it seem as if he instantly counts off "Take the 'A' Train," which was not actually the case. At any rate, the Ellington theme is handled fairly straight except for some harmonic modernization. During another tonally ambiguous solo by Coles, Dolphy picks up the bass clarinet to play horn accents with Jordan.

Byard shows a good sense of Ellington's nuances, paying homage to the master's piano style without copying it outright. When the band drops out, as they do during each solo turn, Byard dramatically holds a bass note before sliding into a hot stride style that inspires enthusiastic responses from his bandmates. Dolphy's bass clarinet solo is just as extreme as usual, with interesting hard blats and staccato riffs spraying more color onto his performance. He handles the unwieldy horn with incomparable smoothness, and in fact set the standard by which all other bass clarinetists in jazz have been measured. The unaccompanied section of his solo is almost transcendent as he comes up with creative new percolations and wide interval jumps. As he approaches a lofty finish, Dolphy gets into some fun trading with Coles and Jordan. The tenorman solos next, with a beefy tone that lies somewhere between Ben Webster and Sonny Rollins. The riff set up behind him by Dolphy and Coles is harmonically unlike anything Ellington probably ever considered for this tune, but in the Mingus microcosm it works well. Jordan kicks things up a notch with altissimo riffing once the band drops out. The video and CD recording both end as Jordan's solo is just winding down.

*   *   *

On April 13 the band was in Stockholm, Sweden, where both the rehearsals and concert takes were recorded. Unfortunately, this session has not been the subject of legit CD release as of yet. An Italian CD, *Meditations on Integration* (Bandstand), presents three pieces from the Stockholm set, as well as a slightly shortened take of "Meditations on Integration," taped in Copenhagen the following day. (That last track will be looked at in a few moments, in the context of the full Danish concert recording.)

The disc begins with a loose-limbed eleven-minute rendition of "Peggy's Blue Skylight," which had first been recorded at *The Clown* sessions (that version appears on *Tonight at Noon*) and was presented at the ill-fated Town Hall concert. Clifford Jordan improvises with vigor as the other musicians play the mournful, painfully slow melody. At about 1:28 Jaki Byard begins to hint at a faster tempo while the horns melt like butter all around him. The real tempo shift comes with the melody's emergence at 1:40. Now the horns are all in one accord, articulating together like a well-oiled machine through the difficult tune. It takes a few seconds for Johnny Coles to get his act together, but his solo finally begins at 3:03. As is typical for the trumpeter, his ideas are understated and more quietly expressed than those of his bandmates. The applause is polite but sparse as he makes way for the leader's vibrant improvisation. Mingus explores some motifs from the tune's melody as he settles in with Byard and Dannie Richmond. At 7:27, Dolphy's alto sax rips through the veil of comfort and soon becomes a fountain of screeches, wails, and blats. The tempo increases in a heartbeat, practically before the listener can realize it, but within a few bars we're back to the original pace. Dolphy doesn't seem ready to relinquish the spotlight by the time the melody cuts him off at 9:23.

The Swedish take on "Fables of Faubus" is perhaps one of the most disorganized on record. Dolphy rushes some of his bass clarinet blasts during the theme, and the basic pulse seems uncomfortably fast overall. Two minutes in, when Coles begins soloing over the manic Latin motifs, the band seems to better settle into the groove. The trumpeter is audibly confident this time around, wittily quoting Nat Adderley's "Work Song" at the moment when the rhythm section backs off from supporting him.

At about 3:45 he gets into some great smeary blues, bouncing ideas off Mingus and Richmond. It's one of Coles' most satisfying improvisations, despite the rough start of the track. At 6:43 the band rips back in before Byard's solo turn, a festival of bebop prowess. A set of burbling repetitions precedes the hilariously staid, fragmented quoting of "Yankee Doodle," which ends with Byard hunting for the right note. When Byard takes it to church, then to the concert hall, Mingus gives out a wild yell of approval. At 9:53 the bass clarinet and tenor sax skulk softly outward, then start carrying on like a Holiness congregation behind the pianist. A stilted boogie beat about eleven minutes along dissolves into nothingness, just to be kicked aside by a new riff. Clifford Jordan's solo screams with intense heat, turning to molten lava as the bass clarinet buzzes ominously and Byard and Richmond pound out smashing beats. The final thematic statement is ripped to shreds halfway through by the searing group improvisation.

Mingus' bass on "Orange Was the Color of Her Dress" is more audible than the Oslo session, giving power to his fast plucked parabolas during the first several bars. The arrangement and solo order are much the same as before although, after the sped-up bars in the theme, Coles opts to play the next line at a slower pace than in some versions.

*   *   *

Next, on April 14, the band performed at Old Fellow Palaet's in Copenhagen, Denmark. The concert has been issued on European CDs as *Astral Weeks* (Moon), *Live in Copenhagen: The Complete Concert* (Landscape) and perhaps other titles as well. As of this writing, all of these releases are unauthorized bootlegs, although in time the Mingus estate might issue legitimate versions.

The quality of the Copenhagen tapes is horribly muddy at the beginning, when Byard and Mingus bang out the intro to "Orange Was the Color," but improves slightly as the hour-plus of music wears on. At times Richmond is totally inaudible. "Orange" is changed slightly from the Oslo set. During the bridge here, Dolphy's bass clarinet lands significantly behind the beat; after the bridge, the repeated riff from the double-time bars is used where it hadn't been before (listen for it at about 1:47 into the CD track). This must have been intentional as it occurs at the end of the track as well. Byard's is the first solo again, longer, more confident, and looser than in Oslo. Coles, too, sounds sharper and more energetic despite the digestive troubles that were plaguing him during the tour. Mingus' bass improvisation is strong, fluid, and clear, with amazing high-range tremolos and bluesy figures in the third chorus. Later Dolphy strolls in unhurriedly with the bass clarinet, engaging in a wild dialogue with Mingus that recalls their tradeoffs at Antibes.

The flute-bass unison on "Meditations" is given a sense of urgency by the bustle of the horns behind them. Dolphy switches to bass clarinet at 1:35.

The brief doubling of tempo happens at about 1:43, and again at 2:04 as Dolphy's solo takes off with almost a singing quality. He croons, screams and hints at "London Bridge" as the rhythm players thunder and the other horns float in suspended time. When they pass the four-minute mark, Richmond briefly adds a Latin cymbal ride now and then as Dolphy's manic opera roars on. A hard-hitting four-beat rhythm underscores Coles' trumpet solo. At about 6:30 the tempo doubles again, becoming a sheer jazz avalanche that culminates in Richmond's snare roll to signal a reshift of time. A ballad feel is attained just before the eight-minute line, giving Coles a chance to show his pretty side before Jordan takes off again atop the fast four-beat. The tenor saxophonist plays it safe for the first chorus or two, but when the band begins to push him with dissonant sounds and broken rhythms, he goes off into left field. Ten minutes in, Byard seems about to push Jordan off the bandstand, but the tenor continues for a couple of more choruses. Another period of slow balladry, then an odd, angular series of ensemble lines emerges to be pounded down fiercely by Richmond. At 12:35 the mania starts all over again, with Dolphy channeling a maimed chicken through his horn while urgent, dissonant traffic buzzes about him. Mingus has trouble with his intonation when he picks up the bow again for the dire out-chorus.

The pianist positively burns for the first minute and a half of the track, paying due homage to Waller, Tatum, and other past masters of jazz piano. He briefly calms down for a lush, gorgeously harmonized passage, then picks up the anxious pace again. Byard is a completely different kind of player than Horace Parlan or Mal Waldron, but ideal in this setting. The fact that Mingus gave such a feature to a sideman speaks to his appreciation for Byard's artistry.

"Fables of Faubus" is delivered as an instrumental, as it was all during the tour, and at a faster pace than usual. Although this track is over half an hour long, the band is able to keep up the level of interest admirably. It is actually one of the most entertaining, wide-ranging interpretations of "Faubus," with a number of unexpected songs quoted by Mingus and the others.

Dolphy's bass clarinet can be hilarious at times, barfing out loud honks that clash deliberately with the other horns. The bridge at around 1:04 has an almost Middle Eastern feeling, and is dashed against the rocks when the band briefly move into a faster tempo. Coles' trumpet solo is less focused than usual, and almost bittersweet in its denouement. Four minutes along, Mingus starts slapping the side of his bass in rigid syncopation with Dolphy's grunts. At about 5:30 the tempo is quite insane, the level of energy unrelenting as Richmond flails and the reeds make rapid stabs at Coles. A minute later, the drummer whips out the Latin vibe again and keeps it up for several good measures before Byard takes his solo. Jazz gives way to classical formality, which just as soon falls into a minor-leaning "Yankee Doodle!" Another minute or so of lush piano, then Mingus begins to play

"Boogie Stop Shuffle," which Dolphy and then Richmond pick up on. The shuffle beat continues as a platform for Byard and Mingus to carry on grandly. Eleven minutes in, Coles adds some plunger-muted trumpet but fades back into the mist. Byard indulges in some concert-piano majesty before the track takes yet another Latin turn. Jordan's boppish solo follows, and he makes the gear-shifts from Latin to bop with aplomb. The tenor saxophonist quotes "Everything Happens To Me" as the mood shifts again, this time to a dark, brooding spirit with long tones and hard drum punctuations. Atonality becomes the norm when Coles and Dolphy blow haunting howls and lure the tenorman down that path for a moment. Next we hear a minor-key riff in the Ellington mode, with Byard plunking off-tempo responses, then another incredibly fast passage. For over a minute Jordan and Richmond battle alone, becoming freer in their exchanges until Mingus' bass returns some rude sense of order. Practically exhausted, Jordan is left to wail very high on the horn toward the end of his solo. Mingus takes over and all but burns the house down. During the unaccompanied stretch he quotes "Turkey in the Straw," "The Old Grey Mare," gives a couple of string-borne laughs, then goes "Deep in the Heart of Texas." Byard adds firm but quiet piano accents about twenty-four minutes into the track. The bass solo continues until around 26:30, when Dolphy bursts out again with his bass clarinet improv. The band resumes the usual cycle of Latin beats, dropouts, bebop, and whatnot, with a Spanish motif like "Ysabel's Table Dance" taking over at twenty-eight minutes or so. Dolphy wails and groans along with Byard's fluttering Iberian motifs for a while, moving into keening multiphonic grunts when Mingus steps forward. The theme returns behind Dolphy at 32:28 and is carried out to a collapse at the end.

*   *   *

From April 17 through April 19 the sextet was in Paris, France. On the first two nights, Mingus and company performed at Salle Wagram. Those concerts have appeared on LP and CD on several occasions, most notably on *Revenge!* (the inaugural release on Sue Mingus' Revenge Records label, two CDs, 1996). Despite the incredible quality of the music on these dates, the Paris stop was marred by the sudden illness of Johnny Coles. The trumpeter, who was suffering from a perforated ulcer, fell off the stage right after the band finished the opening tune, "So Long Eric." Coles missed the rest of the tour, but Mingus carried on confidently with the remaining quintet. Unfortunately, the liner notes of *Revenge!* provide no insight about the music at all, merely a statement by Mrs. Mingus about her battles against bootleggers of her late husband's music.

"So Long Eric" is mistitled here as "Goodbye Porkpie Hat," as it had been on all prior issues of this material. It's disappointing to see the error repeated on the Revenge release, but overall this is not a major quibble. Due to the timing logistics of CD programming, it's presented as the first track of Disc 2 of *Revenge!* But, for the sake of considering Coles' place in the session, we'll look at it first. It begins with Mingus playing the initial motif high on the bass. The drums and piano enter on the repeat, with Richmond playing the twelve-note passage on the hi-hat along with Mingus. Despite his illness, Coles delivers a well-crafted, high-range solo. He climbs dramatically during the 3/4-time ride section, pushed on by the restrained horn riffs and Richmond's escalating tension. Coles hints at Gershwin's "I'm Beginning to See the Light" before entering the most break-neck stretch of his improvisation. The applause is strong when he winds up at about 5:30, giving way to Byard's sparse but entertaining musings. Within a minute the pianist has built up to a firm, cheery swing-feel that brings audible enthusiasm from the live audience. This solo is one of Byard's least expansive on the tour, but despite the restraint he succeeds in keeping the joint hopping. Cliff Jordan is in his usual high mettle, his tenor taking on a rough, tart tone as he dives into the spirit of the blues. At times he sounds more like a bar-walking R&B saxophonist than an adventurous post-bopper. The power of his excursion sets the pace for Mingus to turn up the heat in his own solo. Richmond takes over so firmly that it doesn't seem any trading of fours will happen, but after a moment Mingus gets back into the fray. Kudos to Gene Paul, who remastered the Paris tapes for this release; otherwise, the excitement of these bass-drum exchanges might be as diminished as on all the European bootlegs. The remastering brings out every slight tap of sticks on drumheads and each squeak of fingers on taut bass strings. Their exchanges culminate in a red-hot shuffle rhythm that presents the perfect red carpet for Dolphy. His alto saxophone solo is so humorously avant-garde that it's difficult to find individual notes that actually match up with the chord changes. The cumulative effect of his virtuoso technique, blinding speed, and completely original ideas blots out any negative effects of the foreign sounds he produces. He crosses over from purest bebop to psychotic nursery rhyme to audio volcanics with idyllic ease. Before the twenty-three-minute mark Dolphy carries on like a gaggle of angry geese, nudging Richmond into a long drum solo of equal brute strength. By 26:45 the audience is on its feet, whistling for more. During the "trill" section of the final theme, Mingus plays the descending quarter-note part previously played by Cliff Jordan.

"Peggy's Blue Skylight" starts Disc 1 of *Revenge!* The first sounds on this track are group improvisations: fragments of bop lines from Jordan, wails and moans courtesy of Dolphy's alto, Byard's random tinklings, and sprays of cymbal and drum. Just before the 1:30 mark, the pianist conjures an old-time jazz feeling out of the ether, but that is abandoned within a few seconds. Dolphy calls up the melody at 1:49. This time the first solo is Byard's, beginning at about 2:55. The pianist plays swinging single lines with his right hand for the first minute, moves briefly into his signature block chords, then keeps switching between chords and flowing, spontaneous melodies. At 5:08 Jordan elbows his way into the spotlight, going into a solo before Byard has fully fleshed out his last idea. Mingus takes center stage at 7:50 with a beautifully resonant tone and percussive touch. Then, at 9:43, Dolphy tears through an abstract, stilted solo that is more reminiscent of his time with Ornette Coleman's free jazz project (*Free Jazz: A Collective Improvisation by the Ornette Coleman Double Quartet*, Atlantic, 1960) than anything he had done on the Mingus tour thus far. It's chock full of the wide interval leaps and high-range screed that also typified Dolphy's work for the Blue Note label.

Listeners might notice that the band sounds disoriented during the first minute or so of "Orange Was the Color." The ill Coles had just fallen off the bandstand and been taken to the hospital. Eric Dolphy had encouraged the others to finish the concert, and they did so, albeit with some quick mental rearrangement of the tune. Byard's playing of the melody is initially choppy and not entirely swinging, but he loosens up after the fast section. Also, the reedmen take a while to hook up during the bridge at 1:37. The leader gets things back on track with his long, masterfully conceived bass solo, giving the others time to gather their thoughts about "Orange" and the upcoming tunes. This is an ideal opportunity for listeners to focus intently on how Byard and Richmond react to Mingus and one another. This is a rhythm section at the height of its collective intuition, solidly predicting and answering each creative impulse. Dolphy's bass clarinet solo moves the band out of their quiet reverie, hooting and swinging tremendously at a very fast pace in contrast to Richmond's slow drive. Listen to all the brilliant elements contained in this single improvisation: the trumpet-like brays at 5:52; the deep, bluesy swing immediately afterwards; edgy falsetto whoops at 6:06 and 7:00; the quiet, upward stair-stepping from 6:22 to the tune's signature triplet; and the marvelous tumble downwards at 6:44. Byard has a hard act to follow when he takes over at the eight-minute pole, but as expected the pianist reminds us how he earned his place in this quintessential band.

"Meditations on Integration," as played in Paris, features some of Dolphy's most delicate, beautiful flute work as he takes off freely from the haunting melody. The band has some intonation problems on the bridge before the four fast bars and at several points afterward. In his bass clarinet solo, Dolphy explores a folk-song motif at 2:44 and leans toward "Turkey in the Straw" without fully getting there. When the pace settles down, prior to the five-minute mark and Mingus' solo, the bass clarinet is immersed in beauty and grace. The leader's three-minute improvisation is enriched by slides, tremolos, and his flawless accuracy. Next up, Jordan's tenor sax burns like wildfire and creaks like a rusty hinge while Dolphy wails long, high notes far behind. At 9:09 Jordan and Byard get into a short Middle Eastern vibe before a different hard-swing beat leaps out from the rhythm section. At 9:51 the two horns spar back and forth; Jordan plays a great descending line as if he were trying to lose Dolphy, but the bass clarinet stays on the trail. At 11:10 a pair of low tenor honks heralds the end of the swing beat in favor of sparser support. At 11:52 the horns blast three-note clusters like a modern-day car alarm, then the fast pace returns and keeps building to mind-boggling speed. The three-note motif recurs again while Jaki Byard thunders in the low end of the piano. Finally, the ensemble returns to the written themes and Dolphy picks up the flute once more. Byard subtly moves into a solo at about 15:18, playing through lovely pastoral strands tinted with Spain. Mingus gets out the bow at 16:28 and dances passionately through a captivating bass passage that offers a stunning complement to Byard's flow of ideas. Dolphy's flute solo comes at 18:18, continuing the idyllic momentum (disrupted for a second by a loud thump from Mingus' bass). Hearing the interplay between flute, bass and piano, one can easily imagine fauns dancing through an ancient forest. Around twenty-one minutes into the track, the tonality of Dolphy and Mingus is so mushy and sinuous that all sense of a key center is lost. Byard's hammered chords at 21:43 shift the mood once again. The pianist is alone in his anger for a few moments, but at 22:12 Richmond delivers a massive drum roll that leads us to the tune's bitter end.

Coles isn't missed much on "Fables of Faubus," which is handled well by the two reed players. Dolphy has a lot of fun with this rendition. He tensely holds the first note until the other players follow suit, and he plays around with his keys and tongue on the second run through the theme (listen at 0:44). It's difficult to hear Mingus and Richmond in the background as they go through some of the vocal routine. Richmond manages to squeeze in more than one "motherf***er" during the rant. Mingus takes a lengthy, fluid solo. Starting from 2:54 he is unaccompanied and free to expound on his political outrage as exemplified in the piece. At 3:56 he quotes "When Johnny Comes Marching Home," which morphs into "The Old Gray Mare." Byard and Richmond return at 4:41 with sharp hits that punctuate Mingus' nod to "It Ain't Necessarily So." The bassist plays on in an ominous minor mode with Richmond and Byard still tapping out two beats per measure. After the medium swing pulse returns at 6:33, Mingus returns briefly to "When Johnny Comes Marching Home" and "It Ain't Necessarily So." Uproarious applause is heard at 7:21; a bit premature, as Mingus still hasn't had his full say. Clifford Jordan comes in at 7:45 for his solo, which is soon subjected to battery by Dolphy's bass clarinet ululations and Richmond's momentary slide into a hot Latin rhythm. Nine minutes in, Jordan blows a bit of "Oh Susanna" as the rhythm section drops out, leaving the reedmen to wail and holler dynamically. Dolphy backs down into low three-note poots, then comes Richmond with a titanic bashing of snare to bring back the rhythm. All these switches and turns, and the track is still only half over! Still to come is Byard's solo (with yet another snippet of "Yankee Doodle"), Dolphy imitating Ellington's wah-trumpet section, a great if short Native American groove, another hellacious bass clarinet solo, even a stab at the Mexican character of "Ysabel's Table Dance!"

Mingus and Richmond kick off "Parkeriana" in quiet duo before the "Ow!" theme is played. Afterwards, Jordan's long tones provide a disconcerting contrast to Dolphy's dizzyingly fast alto lines. The tenor sax sounds almost drunk next to the burning alto, which sails off into a cuckoo-clock rhythm in between Parker riffs. Mingus' burly bebop solo is followed by a more traditional stride-piano sashay by Jaki Byard. The pianist then moves into bop territory himself before deciding upon some heavy chord pounding. An excellent tenor improv by Clifford Jordan is followed by more mania from Dolphy, and some unbelievable trading between the two saxophonists that threatens to tear the roof off the music hall. Dannie Richmond's drum solo ups the ante yet again; check out the long section where he's just working with the cymbals, about twenty minutes into the track.

*   *   *

Because of the similar set lists, there has been much confusion over whether the material issued on *Revenge!* is the same as that on *The Great Concert of Charles Mingus* (Prestige). It is not; the session issued by Prestige was recorded on April 19 at Paris' Theatre de Champs-Elysées. For some goofy reason, the version of "So Long Eric" on *Great Concert* is actually a pastiche of performances from Salle Wagram and Champs-Elysées. Johnny Coles is present on the first half of the track, but as we know, he took ill on April 17 and missed the rest of the tour.

As of this writing, a new edition of *Great Concert* is pending on CD from Verve. The author was not able to obtain a copy for review prior to press time, but I trust that the material within will be as timeless, entertaining, and innovative as expected. Of particular note on the original release were "Orange Was the Color," the Mingus/Byard duet on Duke's "Sophisticated Lady," and Dolphy's tremendous feature on "Parkeriana." This tour, by the way, seems to have gotten Parker out of Mingus' system. As enjoyable and consistent as the medley was on the band's sojourn in Europe, Mingus never recorded a studio version and rarely, if ever, returned to it again. Byard apparently started this set with "AT-FW-YOU," but it was cut for technical reasons and has never been appended to subsequent releases. It is, however, slated for inclusion on the new Verve release. Rumor has it that this new CD will also restore the original rendition of "So Long Eric," without Johnny Coles pasted on. I have few qualms about recommending it, sound unheard.

*   *   *

The band wrapped up the European tour a few weeks later. Dolphy stayed on to play his own gigs around the continent, while Mingus returned home with his sidemen. They landed a few bookings in the United States to keep up the pace, including a spot at the Jazz Workshop in San Francisco on June 3 and June 4. *Right Now: Live at the Jazz Workshop* (Debut) presents a rather unusual but dramatically energized pair of twenty-three-minute selections.

With Coles, Dolphy, and Byard all out of the band, Mingus was caught a bit short-handed. He retained Cliff Jordan and Dannie Richmond, hired a female pianist named Jane Getz, and brought John Handy back into the fold for the first piece of the set. "New Fables" is an update of "Fables of Faubus," as you might gather. Jordan is the lead voice and adds some odd flourishes to the theme, including an unexpected tremolo at certain points (0:36 and others). His playing is less exotic than Dolphy's, but still edgy and tense as needed for this gripping material. Mingus is inspired to shout along with Jordan now and then, notably during the up-tempo Latin groove at 2:00. The later stop-time section gives the tenorman another chance to shine, and he does so without hesitation. From that point on, the interaction between the musicians is nothing short of magical. Around the five-minute mark, Mingus begins to bow the "Ysabel's Table Dance" motif on his bass, prodding Jordan to change directions. The tempo speeds up a minute later, and soon the tenorman is wailing and screeching in the top register while Getz plays rich brocades on the piano. The free-time section ends at 7:04, and Jordan continues with his high screams as Richmond flails the snare and cymbals. A sudden drop at 7:40, then a new groove is pulled out. Mingus solos from 10:07, bopping fluidly along with Richmond and Getz. A minute or so later the bassist gets into a loping, countrified mode which hints at "The Old Grey Mare." He manages to squeeze Gershwin's "It Ain't Necessarily So" into the same frame before suddenly boosting the tempo. At 12:40 he sings a falsetto line to usher the band back in, finishes up his solo, and makes room for Jordan to return on the melody. At 13:45 Handy finally gets his turn, ripping into a deft solo in the fastest section of the tune. It escalates into a free-for-all that doesn't settle down until after the twenty-minute mark, at which time the band sidles into a very slow blues. Handy and Getz toss off some fine gospel vibes and wind up the tune on a downbeat tone, or so we think, until that quick Latin pace rears its head and we find ourselves back to the melody.

"Meditation on a Pair of Wire Cutters" was the title that Mingus originally gave to the "Meditation" piece, according to the taped introduction from the NAACP concert at Town Hall. Mingus plays the plaintive theme with his bow while the others jostle about on the supporting riff. It feels very strange to have only a single horn in the ensemble, as this tune was previously performed by two or three horns. Jordan seems a squeaky hinge more than part of a well-oiled machine, but he handles the lack of harmonic support well. Getz does a reasonable job of backing the tenorman on the riffs and during his solo. And an outstanding solo it is, rife with bluesy grit and leaps into the high register. Getz' piano solo is reasonably strong, considering her unfamiliarity with Mingus' performance style and compositional quirks. She has recorded comparatively little during her career, and the Jazz Workshop set is regarded as one of her best moments. Afterwards, the tempo builds to a crazed level as Jordan and Getz trade their abstracted lines and spiral toward a free jazz vein. Around 14:30 the band returns to the bowed-bass theme and bustling backup, from which Mingus and Getz dance out with a marvelous duet cadenza. Mingus has a bit of trouble with his intonation but still turns in a touching bowed improvisation. Sometime along the line Jordan switches to flute, changing the texture of the ensemble. This weird, suspended-time passage ends with Mingus bowing what sounds like evil laughter, then a short burst of final melody, a trill, and the set concludes with a loud drum whack.

*   *   *

On June 29, 1964, just two months after Mingus left him on his own in Europe, Eric Dolphy died from complications of diabetes, a condition he didn't even know he had until it was too late. Dolphy had made some triumphant strides in his career: a major jazz accomplishment in his album *Out To Lunch* (Blue Note), and that magnificent European tour that concluded with *Last Date* (Fontana), a live album he made with a pan-European rhythm section. An era had ended, and Mingus was crestfallen at the passing of his dear old friend.

Falling Away

After the flurry of touring Europe and America in 1964, Mingus took some time to relax a bit in 1965. It was a year that held little palpable reward and more frustrations for the bassist, and it wouldn't be long before Mingus' life took some dire turns.

Eric Dolphy's death had hit Mingus hard, but the bassist was still able to close out the year on a positive note. On September 20, 1964, he made a triumphant appearance at the seventh annual Monterey Jazz Festival, on California's beautiful Central Coast. The resultant album, *Mingus at Monterey*, was issued on Mingus' brand-new label, this time simply called Charles Mingus. Despite a long period of unavailability, it remains one of the finest live albums in his catalog.

Mingus was given the opportunity to assemble a larger band for the festival, and he responded with a fresh eruption of creativity. He crafted a masterful arrangement of "Meditations on Integration" for twelve players including Dannie Richmond, Jaki Byard, John Handy, old friends Buddy Collette (alto sax, flute, and piccolo) and Red Callender (tuba), and six other hornmen: Charles McPherson on alto sax, Jack Nimitz on baritone sax and bass clarinet, Lou Blackburn on trombone, and Melvin Moore, Lonnie Hillyer, and Bobby Bryant on trumpets.

The Monterey concert began with a twenty-five-minute medley of Duke Ellington compositions, drawn from the bassist's favorite harvesting ground. Following a gushing introduction by festival head Jimmy Lyons, Mingus and Byard begin a duo improvisation on "I've Got It Bad (And That Ain't Good)." It's virtuosic and low-key at the same time, a beautiful achievement. After a couple of minutes, McPherson's alto sax emerges on the theme of "In A Sentimental Mood." His style is very much in the vein of Charlie Parker, resulting in a gorgeous rendition of one of Ellington's most perfect ballads. Byard then dives into the lesser-known "All Too Soon," embellishing the melody with his expected twists, flutters, and cascades. The mostly unknown Lou Blackburn is given a minute to deliver "Mood Indigo," with a bit of support from John Handy's tenor, then Mingus gets back into the lead for a vibrant, staccato reading of "Sophisticated Lady."

After all this lush beauty, the sudden arrival of "Take the 'A' Train" takes us by total surprise. At nearly fourteen minutes, it takes up the bulk of the medley. McPherson is practically on fire during his solo turn, blazing with the energy of Dolphy though less abstract. The solos by Hillyer and Handy are equally deft, and Richmond's drums prod the soloists ever higher. The drummer winds up the solo turns with a titanic display of his prowess, ushering in the others for one final romp through the theme.

"Orange Was the Color..." begins as it did during the European tour, with Byard stating the initial theme and Mingus rapidly running up and down the bass fingerboard in response. The horns begin the theme at a slightly faster pace than normal, then the second run-through is done more slowly and flexibly. Something strange now happens with the bridge, starting at about 1:35 into the track: the horns stretch out their notes to extreme lengths while the rhythm section improvises freely. This is an unexpected, almost surreal turn that ends up being pretty effective as a mood change. McPherson takes another fine alto solo, sinking down into the blues a time or two. Byard's intuitive responses to the saxophonist at about 5:08 and 5:23 result in warm cascades of sound. The pianist's solo comes at around 6:25 as he works in fistfuls of Monk and Fats Waller before settling into a deeply impressionistic mode. The pulse jumps instantly when Lonnie Hillyer begins a hot, boppish solo that is a highlight of the show. When the theme returns, it's back to the rhythmic and temporal flexibility that made this such a special rendition of the tune. It is especially impressive that McPherson and Hillyer were able to achieve such unity of pace while bending the rhythm every which way.

Mingus' lamenting, almost melodramatic bowed bass is the first voice heard on "Meditations," performed by the full twelve-piece band. Buddy Collette's flute doubles the theme with the arco bass, tearing off for a couple of passionate measures between the melody lines. The bridge crescendo at 2:17 is especially effective with this larger group, although the recording quality dims as the volume increases. McPherson's alto solo is his most manic yet, exploding with unfettered energy as the tempo and rhythm continue to shift all around him. The more dissonant harmonies arranged by Mingus for the big band are remarkably effective in conveying the piece's sense of anger and urgency. This fury sets the pace as Collette's flute and Byard's piano spar with one another. The piano stalks off with the other horns, leaving Collette fluttering in the forefront; then Byard thunders back in with hard-hammered figures across several octaves. The next theme roars out of the horn section, slows a bit, then we're back to the dire portents of the initial melody. Byard returns later with a quieter, more orchestral approach, making the one piano sound as full as two or three played in unison. Mingus' bass groans in the background as the leader frets and worries with his bow. He moves to the front later, exchanging musical commentary with Byard and Collette in a lovely, almost classical manner. But, as usual, this idyll doesn't last very long before it's overwhelmed in a crush of improvised sound from the full ensemble.

*   *   *

It is unfortunate that Charles McPherson's contributions to the band in this period are so poorly represented on CD today. *Mingus at Monterey* was long absent from the market until King Records in Japan finally reissued it on CD. The other two albums on which McPherson is featured were issued on the Charles Mingus/Jazz Workshop imprint, and consigned to near-oblivion after the bassist's business skills proved inadequate to keep the label alive.

My Favorite Quintet was recorded live on May 13, 1965, at the Tyrone Guthrie Theater in Minneapolis, Minnesota. The band is McPherson on alto; Lonnie Hillyer on trumpet; Jaki Byard, piano; Dannie Richmond, drums; and, of course, the leader on bass. A heightened sense of excitement permeates the three long tracks, beginning with a lively version of "So Long Eric" that motors on for nearly twenty minutes. It is followed by an even longer medley of standards: "She's Funny That Way," "Embraceable You," "I Can't Get Started," and "Ghost of a Chance." As if Mingus were trying to place himself within the annals of the great standard composers, he completes the medley with his own "Old Portrait," one of the most venerable tunes in his book. The album closes with a funny and inimitably creative look at "Cocktails for Two," one of the most frequently abused pieces of American music.

My Favorite Quintet was reissued twice after its initial appearance in the market. Prestige Records released it in 1980 as part of a two-LP set, in combination with the later *Town Hall Concert*. Some time later, the French label America Records issued it as one LP, but with the *Town Hall* album cover mistakenly used. As of this writing it has never been issued on CD, a gross oversight that will hopefully be corrected in the near future. It is significant to note that the album cover indicates this as "Volume One." No subsequent volume was ever released, although in 2005 Sue Mingus did indicate that there was further material from this concert which would be issued on her new label, Sue Mingus Music.

*   *   *

More familiar to Mingus' fans, but nearly as scarce on the market, is the recording with the cumbersome title *Music Written for Monterey 1965, Not*

Heard . . . Played in its Entirety at UCLA, Volumes 1 and 2 (Jazz Workshop, reissued in 1984 by Sue's old label, East Coasting, and finally due for CD reissue in 2006). Its genesis lies in one of the uglier incidents at this time in Mingus' career.

As he had for the doomed Town Hall concert, Mingus had written a large suite of new material for the 1965 Monterey Jazz Festival. He had hoped to up the ante after his triumphant appearance there in 1964. The band worked on this new material during a two-week stint at the Village Gate and hacked their way through a few rehearsals at Mingus' apartment. It didn't help that Mingus kept changing his mind about the way tunes should be played, not to mention that McPherson literally learned his parts over the phone, with Mingus singing the lines, because the altoist couldn't make it to any of the rehearsals.

On the day of the festival everything dragged on without relief, each act playing well beyond their appointed time. By the time Mingus' turn on stage arrived, much of the audience had left the grounds. The bassist was perturbed that the boxes full of *Mingus at Monterey* he had planned to sell at the gig never showed up. As expected, he was in high dudgeon onstage. The band—the same lineup as on *My Favorite Quintet*—premiered three of his ambitious new works: "The Arts of Tatum and Freddie Webster," "Don't Let It Happen Here," and "They Trespass the Land of the Sacred Sioux." But the heat and sparse acknowledgment were distasteful to Mingus, and after barely half an hour he led the band off stage with a sarcastic "When the Saints Go Marching In." It was a saddening experience for the leader, made more ironic by the fact that his former sideman, altoist John Handy, had been the smash hit of Monterey 1965 leading his own band.

One week later, on September 25, 1965, Mingus took his expanded ensemble into Royce Hall at UCLA. This octet included McPherson, Richmond, and Hillyer along with trumpeters Hobart Dotson and Jimmy Owens, French hornist Julius Watkins (who first recorded with Mingus on Oscar Pettiford's 1953 session for Debut), and tubaist Howard Johnson. Byard wasn't available, so there was no pianist present until Mingus took to the keyboard himself. He brought along the book of new material and presented it in a heavy, turbulent program of more than an hour's length.

"Meditation on Inner Peace" (*not* the same as the usual "Meditations") kicks off the set with an extended introduction by Mingus on bowed bass. Howard Johnson offers a steady pulse on tuba, and Lonnie Hillyer's trumpet figures team wonderfully with the leader's mournful musings. It's a very long, rather static piece without all the expected tempo shifts. Everything is quite slow, but there are surges of energy when Watkins and Dotson scream up in the high registers of their horns.

As Side 4 of the LP actually comes on the reverse of Side 1, let's consider "Don't Be Afraid, The Clown's Afraid Too" next. This is a rather plodding tune with a recurring, if oppressed, feeling of circus music. It's an analogue to "The Clown," if you will, coming from the same spirit of hopelessness behind the mask of joy. Hobart Dotson begins the piece and is featured as the first soloist. The ensemble doesn't seem all that comfortable with this tune; even Dannie Richmond sounds out of sorts. Johnson's tuba is astonishing, though, as he tears out of his rhythm seat on an impressive solo.

Mingus' fragmented piano is the first sound on "Don't Let It Happen Here," then a high trumpet note before the leader begins his haunting, politically fiery recitation:

> One day they came and they took the Communists
> And I said nothing because I was not a Communist
> Then one day they came and they took the people of the Jewish faith
> And I said nothing because I had no faith left
> One day they came and they took the Unionists
> And I said nothing because I was not a Unionist
> One day they burned the Catholic churches
> And I said nothing because I was born a Protestant
> Then one day they came and they took me
> And I could say nothing because I was as guilty as they were
> For not speaking out and saying
> That all men have a right to freedom on any land
> I was as guilty of genocide as you, all of you
> For you know when a man is free
> And when to set him free from his slavery
> So I charge you all with genocide

He ends the recitation with a feral falsetto wail, which is followed by a break of instrumental searching, then a series of trumpet trade-offs between Dotson and Hillyer. After Dotson's long solo feature, the pace slows again to its original snail-drag.

Next comes "Once Upon a Time There Was a Holding Corporation Called Old America." (Mingus would later replace that awkward title with the equally clunky "The Shoes of the Fisherman's Wife Are Some Jive-Ass Slippers.") This is an extremely hard piece to work through, and clearly the musicians weren't given enough time to learn it properly. We hear a false start, then Mingus stops the band and explains the tune to them. Another false start, and Mingus sends Dotson, Johnson, Owens, and Watkins offstage to figure out their parts. The liner notes humorously indicate, "Expel large group from band for mental tardyness *(sic)*." In the meantime, the remaining quartet play "Ode to Bird and Dizzy," a bebop festival which weaves together tunes by Charlie Parker, Dizzy Gillespie, Tadd Dameron, Fats Navarro, Oscar Pettiford, and others. McPherson and Hillyer sizzle on this one, and the solos by Richmond and Mingus are phenomenal. Too bad the end of Richmond's turn is marred by a loud microphone whistle.

When the other players are summoned back to the stage, "Once Upon a Time" is left on hold for a while. Instead, the band moves into "They Trespass the Land of the Sacred Sioux," which begins as a slow dirge with stridently clashing tonalities among the different horns. Watkins' French horn heralds the arrival of the cavalry to slaughter the Native Americans of the title. The horns and slashing piano serve to further emphasize the conflict, and a mournful aura pervades the piece.

Hobart Dotson is featured on "The Arts of Tatum and Freddie Webster," wailing and straying far from key as the band slogs along with a slow repeated figure. It's highly uncharacteristic for there to be so much extremely sluggish material in Mingus' set list, but his depression had been affecting him more severely and might well have come out in his compositions from this period. This particular tune might be a suitable homage to the trumpeter Webster, a big-band player who had profoundly influenced Dizzy Gillespie, but it certainly doesn't suit the vivacious, expansive piano jazz of Art Tatum, at least not the first half-plus of the track. All in all, though, Dotson's solo is beautiful and nicely suited to the material he was given. After an almost interminable span of down-time, the group finally picks up pace to give Tatum his due.

At long last the band decides to give "Once Upon a Time" another try. It begins with the slow, dirgelike passage that the band tripped over last time. Dotson still has a hard time with the high notes, but Mingus decides to keep going past the exultant alto sax figure blown by McPherson. Ellington's spirit pervades the tune, especially the section just prior to the increase in tempo. Some of the horns have a hellacious time keeping up with the drums and piano, and by the waltz section they've almost fallen apart again. The humorous bursts from Watkins' horn seem to keep the players' spirits uplifted, however, and things move onward. Mingus plays a dignified, stately piano solo that waves in a new slow passage. During Jimmy Owens' bone-crushing trumpet improvisation Mingus wails and sings cheerfully, seemingly satisfied that things are finally on the right track.

*   *   *

Mingus' mental troubles began to afflict him further after this point in his career. Filmmaker Thomas Reichman followed Charles through his daily routines and trials to assemble the intriguing documentary *Mingus* (released 1968, available from Rhapsody Films on VHS). Along with concert footage, poetry readings, and plenty of dialogue, Reichman captured the sad trauma of Mingus' eviction from his apartment. At one point during an on-camera rant, Charles frustratedly fires his shotgun into the ceiling of the flat. It's difficult to watch, for the rough film quality as much as the bittersweet content, but it provides a fascinating window into what was going on in the bassist's life at the time. It has been alleged that the eviction footage was a reenactment, but that is disputed by Brian Priestley and other Mingus historians.

*   *   *

In November 1966 Mingus made one of his last live appearances before taking a three-year hiatus. At the famed Lennie's-On-the-Turnpike in Peabody, Massachusetts, he performed with Richmond, McPherson, Hillyer, tenorman John Gilmore (long a fixture in Sun Ra's avant-jazz ensemble, the Arkestra), and pianist Walter Bishop, Jr. They can be heard in the soundtrack to the *Mingus* film, as the sextet plays "All the Things You Are," "Peggy's Blue Skylight," "Take the 'A' Train," "Portrait," and a rhythm-trio tune called "Secret Love." The performances are almost defiant, as if Mingus knew he would be going out with a bang. Gilmore and Bishop are seamless fits into the ensemble, and one wishes that they could have had better opportunities to keep on under Mingus' tutelage.

From the end of 1966 Mingus withdrew almost entirely from the music business. He stopped performing, wrote occasionally, and didn't bother to keep in touch with many of the friends who had offered him moral, financial, and musical support over the years. His effective disappearance became a metaphor for jazz itself, which was quickly being overtaken by rock music in the public consciousness.

A Slow Climb

It wasn't until 1969 that Mingus began performing again, having overcome some of his personal demons and financial difficulties. He worked through a number of gigs, compositions, and sidemen until he settled upon some combinations that seemed to be lucrative and inspirational. It took time for Charles to regain his footing in the jazz business, and it was not the best era for him to attempt a comeback. Rock music had elbowed jazz completely off the charts in the past few years, and more and more clubs in the United States were dumping their jazz bookings in favor of bigger draws from the rock and pop fields.

*   *   *

One of Mingus' working groups played some gigs at Slug's in New York City in March of 1970. The Jazz View label has issued two sets from March 31 on CD: *Dizzy Atmosphere: Live at Historic Slug's, Volume 1* and *Fables of Faubus: Live at Historic Slug's, Volume 2*. The ensemble includes the faithful Dannie Richmond and Charles McPherson, trumpeter Bill Hardman (whom, you might recall, had made an appearance on *Modern Jazz Symposium of Music and Poetry* in 1957, before joining Art Blakey's Jazz Messengers), and altoist Jimmy Vass, who was early into a career that embraced free jazz with Sunny Murray and Rashied Ali, and soul-jazz with organist Charles Earland. The set lists are strong enough: "Ray's Idea" by bassist Ray Brown, "So Long Eric," "If I Should Lose You," "I Can't Get Started," "Dizzy Atmosphere," "Peggy's Blue Skylight," "Better Get Hit In Your Soul," and "Orange Was the Color" on the first volume; "Fables of Faubus," "In A Sentimental Mood," "Take the 'A' Train," Charlie Parker's

"Billie's Bounce" and "Ko-Ko" in medley, "O.P." and "Greensleeves" on the second. However, the performances reveal an ensemble and leader who are still rather unsure of themselves. It can be safely said, on the other hand, that few people beyond Mingus could have fared so well in a comeback after three years of virtual silence.

* * *

In October of 1970 Mingus went to Europe with a more stable lineup. Richmond and McPherson remained, and Jaki Byard came back to the fold. The trumpet chair was resumed by Eddie Preston, who had graced *Mingus, Mingus, Mingus, Mingus, Mingus* in 1963. The last slot was filled by new-comer Bobby Jones, a long-haired blond who turned out to be a wizard on tenor sax. He was a completely different kind of player than Booker Ervin, coming from the bands of Jack Teagarden and Woody Herman. Jones had many personal clashes with Mingus during the two years he was in the band, but his tone and creativity more than earned him his chair.

The French release *Charles Mingus in Paris* (Ulysse) is one of the scarce albums to document this era in the bassist's life. Recorded in Paris during the fall 1970 tour, it includes stronger renditions of "O.P.," "Orange Was the Color," "Fables of Faubus," and an Ellington medley of "In A Sentimental Mood," "Sophisticated Lady," "Mood Indigo," and "Take the 'A' Train." All of the players are featured well, and the ensemble is more cohesive than the prior grouping with Vass and Hardman. Jones and Preston prove to be truly capable musicians, transcending any doubts about their suitability.

Of the most interest is a new composition called "The Man Who Never Sleeps," probably a self-reference. The slow ballad theme alternates long tones with sixteenth-note figures in the second and sixth bars, not to mention a good dose of the signature triplets and a second theme by the saxophones. There are nods to other Mingus works, primarily "The Shoes of the Fisherman's Wife" and "Sue's Changes." It's an interesting piece that Mingus never got around to recording in a studio setting. This bootleg live recording is about as close as we can come to appreciating his vision for that particular composition.

* * *

In Italy, the Lotus label released *Statements* on LP in 1970. It consists of three tracks recorded in Milan on October 25 of that year: "Orange Was the Color," "The Man Who Never Sleeps," and "O.P." Another Italian label, Blu Jazz, issued a live set on CD (*Charlie Mingus Sextet Live*), recorded on October 28 at Theatre National Populaire du Palais de Chaillot in Paris. That disc includes "So Long Eric," "The Man Who Never Sleeps," "Pithecanthropus Erectus," "She's Funny That Way," and an unspecified closing theme. As with everything from this transitional period in Mingus' career, these albums are very difficult to come by but well worth tracking down for the completist.

*   *   *

Also nearly forgotten now is *Reincarnation of a Lovebird*, which the Mingus band recorded for Prestige in November 1970 after returning from the tour. Obviously, this is not to be confused with the Candid album of the same name. The title track gets one of its most interesting treatments, with the young horn section adding a distinctively modern edge. A cover of "I Left My Heart in San Francisco" is the bassist's celebratory nod to his West Coast stomping ground, finding him in especially good form, and Charlie Parker's "Blue Bird" is transformed into a gigantic, seventeen-minute blues workout for the whole sextet. New takes on "Pithecanthropus Erectus" and "Peggy's Blue Skylight" are not quite as successful, sounding as if the band was running out of steam. Another new work, "Love is a Dangerous Necessity," begins with hard, ominous note pairs that successfully convey the danger aspect of the title. It then cycles through the usual set of Mingusian tempo and mood changes. This rendition is interesting, but not very fleshed-out; the expanded chart by the Mingus Big Band, recorded on *Tonight At Noon: Three or Four Shades of Love* (Dreyfus, 2002), gives a better idea of where Mingus might have taken the piece in the future.

Reincarnation marked the last hurrah (for now) of Dannie Richmond, who left the group shortly thereafter and headed for the more lucrative opportunities of rock music. Saddened but undeterred, Mingus pressed on with composing and rehearsing.

*   *   *

In the autumn of 1971, Mingus' huge autobiography, *Beneath the Underdog*, was finally published by Knopf Books. The editors had hacked away hundreds of pages of his rants and fantasies, paring it down to a surrealistic, half-lying masterpiece that reflected the author's confusion, desires, heartaches, and joys. Mingus soon returned to Columbia Records with a bold vision for the future and a bulging book of new music. Not *exactly* new, but certainly reshaped and revitalized. His next album would stand as one of the highest marks in his career, a most welcome turn of events given the past few years.

Let My Children Hear Music, brilliantly produced by old friend Teo Macero, is a timeless document of Mingus at his best. Three of the compositions are new, the rest are expanded revisions of prior art, and all are executed with passion and professional élan. That said, this project was not without its stumbling blocks. Some of Macero's edits are not exactly subtle, but that is to be expected when one is dealing with music this dense and complex. Also, a number of the musicians are not credited, some due to contractual conflicts; others, perhaps, were victims of shoddy record keeping. Those known to have participated include trumpeters Lonnie Hillyer, Joe Wilder, and Snooky Young; reedmen Bobby Jones, James Moody, and Charles McPherson; Julius Watkins on French horn; Sir Roland Hanna, piano; and Charles McCracken, cello. The arrangers included Alan Raph and Sy Johnson.

The first track, "The Shoes of the Fisherman's Wife Are Some Jive-Ass Slippers," had been previously performed at the 1965 UCLA concert under the title "Once Upon A Time There Was a Holding Corporation Called Old America," and written for Monterey 1965. This time around the band is much more attuned to the complicated piece, and for the most part it comes off without a hitch. After a sumptuous piano passage by Hanna, and a languid reverie by all the horns, McPherson takes a fast-paced, expressive alto sax solo. Listen to the complexity of the arrangement behind McPherson, and how well all of the threads fit together. Byard follows, then a second McPherson solo. The ending of that turn is picked up on quickly by Hillyer, and the two horns improvise together for a while. The trumpeter's ideas are so structurally sound and confident, and he makes his improv sound as if it were part of the written arrangement. On the free-jazz section, Jones joins in with McPherson and Hillyer. They are eventually nudged aside by the brilliance of another lushly orchestrated section, and the piece ends on a lovely note. This is one of Mingus' most memorable late-period works.

Sy Johnson (or, some claim, Jaki Byard) worked a miracle in arranging "Adagio Ma Non Troppo," which is a superb ensemble rendering of "Myself, When I Am Real" from Mingus' 1963 solo piano album. It sounds even more classical here than it did on the piano alone, with dense brass orchestrations, stately piano, vibrant clarinet, and other adornments. McCracken's cello is featured alongside as many as six bowed upright basses. He engages in a fabulous exchange with Mingus starting at around 1:30. The tune progresses through a number of significantly different sections, including a bracing outing for the flutes and French horns.

Similar to "The Shoes," "Don't Be Afraid, The Clown's Afraid Too" had its origins in the 1965 Monterey material and was played on the UCLA album. This version received a lot of studio augmentation, with surrealistic, echoey circus noises overdubbed by Macero and Mingus. Hillyer blows a shrill, high line over all the cacophony, then the French horn and tuba step out with a downright jaunty melody. The other musicians enter in stages, and at 1:53 a warped circus waltz is taken up, eventually smoothing out into a swing feel. The soloists are McPherson, Hillyer, and Jones. More circus noises enter at 4:34, evoking mayhem in the monkey cage, which spills out into an ensemble free-for-all. The piece cycles through similar events, right up to the dit-dot ending and the charge of the circus animals through the tent.

The 1992 CD reissue of *Let My Children Hear Music* includes the previously unheard "Taurus in the Arena of Life," a four-minute track which was probably cut from the original album for spatial reasons. It begins with a baroque piano introduction which lasts a few bars before being shoved aside by an expansive, Ellingtonian orchestration. We can still hear the piano carrying on behind all the horns, and soon a Spanish motif in the spirit of "Ysabel's Table Dance" emerges. It is a busy piece, even among all of this hectic company. But it has many excellent features, like the way the complementary lines of trumpet and saxophone flow together.

In "Hobo Ho" Mingus reaches back into his gospel bag, recalling the tremendous tenor sax features he used to write for Booker Ervin. The beneficiary this time is James Moody. Actually, Mingus composed this tune with Lionel Hampton's tenorman, Illinois Jacquet, in mind, but he was not available for the session. Moody acquits himself well, booting the band with low-end honks and hard-edged blues lines. Underneath it all lies Mingus' funky, unchanging bass ostinato, which keeps the tune on pace for ten minutes. The constantly tightening tension is finally broken at 3:58 with the introduction of a new riff, then the pressure continues to build. At 5:51 the tempo slows for just a second, then a blast of tuba kicks us back to the funk.

At long last, one of Mingus' oldest compositions receives its due. "The Chill of Death" was written when Charles was still a teenager, and first recorded in the 1940s but never released. It is another dark jazz narrative borne out of his deepest fears and beliefs:

> The chill of death as she clutched my hand
> I knew she was coming, so I stood like a man
> She drew up closer, close enough for me to look into her face
> And then I began to wonder, "Hadn't I seen you some other place?"
> She beckoned for me to come closer, as if to pay an old debt
> I knew what she wanted; it wasn't quite time yet
> She threw her arms around me as many women had done before
> I heard her whisper, "You'll never cheat me, never anymore."

The ensemble maintains a haunting, dangerous undercurrent. No improvisation is heard until after 4:00, when McPherson steps out with his alto for a long, tormented turn. The piece ends with a feeling of incompleteness, as if McPherson's alto were snuffed out before his time.

"The I of Hurricane Sue" was composed for his wife, Sue Graham Mingus, and it is as complex a creation as the both of them. Mingus maintained that it was a tribute but not a reflection of her personality; one might guess otherwise. Overdubbed storm sounds and whirled sound-tubes resonate through the first section, echoed by manic tinkling on the piano. The theme is principally stated by French horn and tenor sax, with the other horns in acrid harmonies. McPherson and Jones take the first solos. Watkins' horn solo is brilliant, luxurious, and a marvelous antidote to the traditional jazz sounds. This transcendent wall of sound seems to fully epitomize the fusion of jazz and classical ideas that Mingus had been aiming for since the early 1950s, a validation of his life's work.

*   *   *

The year 1972 saw a new round of adulation for Mingus within the jazz community, with increased bookings and a powerful tribute concert at Lincoln Center's Philharmonic Hall. *Charles Mingus and Friends in Concert* was recorded on February 4, 1972, with a large contingent of celebrants on hand: comedian and M.C. Bill Cosby, James Moody, Gerry Mulligan, Dizzy Gillespie, old-school tenorman Gene Ammons, Lee Konitz, and others.

Columbia put a great deal of effort into marketing the concert album, attempting to bring the honoree back into the limelight as spectacularly as possible. The cover art is reminiscent of *Bob Dylan's Greatest Hits*, with Mingus' head depicted in a blue-auraed silhouette. On the original LP's back cover (and now, the back of the CD booklet), the set list and personnel are superimposed in white over Mingus' silhouette, as had been done on the Dylan cover. Deliberate or unconscious, the symbolic comparison is interesting!

Despite all the pomp and circumstance involved in this overdue glorification, the music is not always up to the usual Mingus standards. The ensemble is overloaded, and it seems like many of the musicians have trouble finding the groove, despite most of them having direct experience of playing with Mingus. Teo Macero conducts; the band includes Konitz, George Dorsey, Richie Perri, and Charles McPherson on alto sax; Bobby Jones and Ammons on tenor; Mulligan and Howard Johnson on baritone sax; Lonnie Hillyer, Eddie Preston, Lloyd Michaels, and eighteen-year-old Jon Faddis on trumpet; Dick Berg and Sharon Moe on French horn; Eddie Bert, trombone; Bob Stewart, tuba; John Foster, piano; Milt Hinton, bass (along with Mingus, naturally); and Joe Chambers, drums. The guests included Dizzy Gillespie and Honey Gordon on vocals, Randy Weston on piano, and James Moody on flute. Mingus might not have felt that he was in good enough shape to shine, as he only takes three solos during the entire show. (And of those three, only one was issued on the original LP release!)

After an introduction by Bill Cosby, "Jump Monk" begins with a free-tempoed, abstract introduction, then an unaccompanied solo statement by Gene Ammons. Once the band jumps in, Ammons takes off in his signature rough-edged blues mode. One expects that he was an influence on Booker Ervin, who shared that love of and talent for blues. At 1:59 Eddie Bert's plungered trombone starts to prod Ammons after a couple of choruses, and Bert takes the lead before the ensemble jumps onto the melody at 2:17. One minute later Ammons is back in the solo spot, tearing through some gut-bucket choruses. Lonnie Hillyer and Charles McPherson then improvise in duet, their long history and friendship providing inspiration in the span of a few dozen bars. In the ensemble, the presence of tuba and French horns adds an amazing fullness of sound.

"E.S.P." dates from the early days of Debut Records, where it was known fully as "Extrasensory Perception." Lee Konitz is a featured soloist, as he had been when he cut the track with Mingus and a handful of Lennie Tristano disciples in 1952. His tone is now brighter and his ideas better articulated. The piece is still ambitious, but this interpretation doesn't come off as avant-garde as the one twenty years prior. Hillyer, Ammons, and the always distinctive Gerry Mulligan turn in thoroughly swinging improvisations, too. The ensemble passages following the solo turns seem overdone.

Cosby jokes for a moment about "Fables of Faubus" being cut from the set, and about Mingus actually wearing a tie at a gig. Then he announces "Ecclusiastics," getting the name wrong, and the stately introduction is played. The band really nails the moods of this one, from the up-tempo sections with wah trumpet to the slow stripper grooves. Ammons is a completely different player than Roland Kirk, but he knows his gospel as much as his blues, and he delivers an ecstatic solo turn. Ammons' style of early R&B sax playing was largely considered "old hat" by the 1970s, so this was as much his chance to verify his enduring capabilities as to honor the bassist. John Foster's barrelhouse piano playing is revelatory, especially the ways he conjoins with Joe Chambers' drums on the faster segments. Bobby Jones confirms his rightful place in the band with a second tenor solo that takes nothing away from Ammons but anchors Mingus' music in the present.

Honey Gordon then joins the band for "Eclipse." Her delivery of the older song is appropriately haunting, but rather overwrought and tonally challenged. It is redeemed by Sy Johnson's extremely interesting updated arrangement, although it leaves no room for soloists other than Gordon.

"Us Is Two" had apparently never been played before this concert. Unfortunately, it becomes the first casualty of the evening; "our first train wreck," as Sy Johnson states in the liner notes. The tune is an upbeat, bouncy thing in the Ellington mode, with lots of Mulligan's bari sax in the ensemble passages. Bobby Jones' magnificent tenor solo is the first break. Then Ammons heads off on a fine tenor solo but gets lost partway through, which throws off most of the band. McPherson's alto sax improvisation helps to get the tune back on track, and it ends on an uplifting note.

"Taurus in the Arena of Life" is next. The liner notes explain that the original title of the piece was "Number One Grandson," created when Mingus thought he was going to be a grandfather. When that turned out to be a false promise, he changed the title and the direction of the piece. Sy Johnson suggests that Art Tatum and Harry Carney were two of the inspirations for the composition's structure. This live version is almost as interesting as the studio take made for *Let My Children Hear Music*. Eddie Preston's high trumpet work and solo are phenomenal, but Ammons' tenor is definitely out of tune.

Next up is "Mingus Blues," which apparently originated onstage as a spontaneous improvisation by Mingus. Ammons steps up after the first chorus to simmering and wail as only he can do. His interaction with Mingus and Foster sounds as if they had rehearsed the piece a hundred times; this is the mark of professional musicians who know how to listen and respond to one another. Listen especially to the unaccompanied duet section between Mingus and Ammons, a conversation not that far removed from what the leader carried on with Eric Dolphy in "What Love." At the end Cosby calls an intermission.

Mingus composed "Little Royal Suite" for Roy Eldridge, but the aging trumpeter was ill and could not make the concert. This was a hand-delivery from God for young Jon Faddis, who really began his professional career on this night at the age of eighteen. His technique is already close to flawless; he scales the full range of the horn, low growls to high screeches, as easily as brushing his teeth. The performance is not all it could have been, however. In an uncomfortable reflection of the Town Hall disaster, Sy Johnson was still working on this arrangement when rehearsals had already begun. Despite some very interesting French horn passages, the ensemble is a mite unsteady but the performance is redeemed by Faddis' pyrotechnics. Ironically, the young trumpeter's style owes more to Dizzy Gillespie than to Diz' predecessor and the tune's dedicatee, "Little Jazz" Eldridge. All that aside, on this evening a star was born who nearly overshadowed the honoree. A string of solos follows Faddis' lead: Ammons (three times in all), Konitz, Mulligan, and McPherson. The trumpeter naturally has the final say, and he takes the band through the roof on his last wild cadenza.

The second CD of the set begins with Cosby introducing "Strollin'" and bringing Honey Gordon back out. Somehow she manages to suck all the life out of one of Mingus' most infectious melodies. The tempo is slightly too slow, her intonation is questionable again, and she is poorly miked. (True, wanting an out-of-tune singer to be more audible is like the old restaurant joke: "Oh, the food was terrible! And such small portions!") The group loses energy after Gordon finishes, and it takes Eddie Bert's marvelous plungered trombone to kick things up again. Another long tally of overlapping soloists ensues: now Hillyer, Ammons, Mulligan, Jones on a sprightly clarinet (dig the way that he picks up on Mulligan's last motif at 5:50), Richie Perri (very good, and mostly unknown aside from this concert), Bert, Konitz, and Howard Johnson on baritone sax.

Cosby next introduces "The I of Hurricane Sue," another title he can't seem to get right. (He jokes that the tune's original title was "Don't Wanna Dance With Your Father Because Your Mother's Too Tall And Your Shoes Are On Wrong.") McPherson begins the tune with a very long, wavering note before settling into the slurred, sinuous melody. Even without the overdubbed winds and whirled sound-tubes of the studio version, this is a chaotic tune thanks to John Foster's free-jazz piano and the spontaneous horn accents behind the lethargic theme. McPherson, Jones, and Foster are the soloists; the pianist is especially inventive and rhythmically entertaining.

Mingus tears through the intro to "E's Flat, Ah's Flat Too," and the dual baritone saxes of Mulligan and Johnson create a gritty, humorous texture. Ammons gets the first solo again. He loses a bit of steam but blows a satisfactory turn. Joe Chambers stomps and pounds hysterically; he is followed by Hillyer, Milt Hinton, Johnson (a burrier tone than Mulligan, who plays alongside him for a bit), Faddis, Lloyd Michaels, Jones, James Moody (a *fabulous* flute improvisation), the incredible Randy Weston on piano, finally Mulligan and Konitz.

Sy Johnson suggests that Dizzy Gillespie's "Ool-Ya-Koo" was pulled out at the spur of the moment as a feature for the composer. Diz didn't even bring his horn to the show, but he engages in some earth-shakingly rapid scatting. Cosby and Mingus join in the fun after a couple of choruses. It is fully improvised until they get around to the bare-bones melody at 2:26, answered by the sax section.

Honey Gordon returns to the stage for "Portrait," initiated by Mingus' solo bass. She sings the melody about an octave higher than Jackie Paris had in the early 1950s, and still has a devil of a time staying in tune. But the ensemble work is beautiful, and Mingus delivers an exceptional solo. Moody's flute and McPherson's alto sax are exultant.

Mingus pulls his bass strings off the side of the fingerboard, making sitar sounds on the introduction of "Don't Be Afraid, The Clown's Afraid Too." The effect is like the human voice; he seriously seems to be articulating words with his hands. It's a shame that this particular track was omitted from the original LP (along with "Taurus," "Strollin'," "The I...," and "Portrait") because it's one of the best-executed performances of the concert. Aside from a little ensemble glitch around 2:54, the band has their act together and all of the solos are uniformly strong. Mingus is in exceptional form. This concert was truly a shining moment in his career and no doubt gave him the strength to carry on.

* * *

Later in 1972, McPherson, Jones, and Eddie Preston left the band. Jones' was the most acrimonious departure, coming amidst a hail of racist epithets and ill feelings. The saxophonist cut a few good albums under his own name, but emphysema forced him into retirement in 1974 and claimed his life in 1980. Preston went on to explore the freer side of jazz with Roland Kirk, Archie Shepp, McCoy Tyner and unrecorded bands of his own. McPherson formed his own band and has continued to gig successfully as a leader ever since. With its foundation cleared, Mingus had to build his house anew.

His next project, *Mingus Moves*, was recorded in October of 1973 at Atlantic's studios in New York City. Here Mingus led a quintet with trumpeter Ronald Hampton, reedman George Adams, pianist Don Pullen, and a prodigal son: Dannie Richmond, who had quit the rock band Mark-Almond and come back into the fold.

The album was a departure for Mingus on several levels. First of all, not one but *four* of the seven compositions on the original LP release were composed by Mingus' associates. His reasons for including his sidemen's tunes on top of his own are not clear, but it was the first time in years that he had devoted more than a token track to anything other than his works or Ellington's. Second, in Adams and Pullen, he had selected two sidemen who strode further into free jazz than anyone previously in his employment. The leader takes the back seat most of the time: no fist-pounding extended solos, not even a meaty bass intro can be found. Mingus had also, for the time being, forsaken his longtime habit of teaching tunes to his musicians by ear instead of writing them out. One wonders if these changes were the result of insecurity in reemerging after a long absence, or the confident fruit of lessons learned during his hiatus. Whatever the case, the Adams/Pullen era of Mingus' career resulted in some essential and completely unique music.

The opening track of the album, Mingus' own "Canon," harkens back to his Third Stream interests while simultaneously looking into the future of jazz. The first sound heard is the naked tenor sax of Adams, playing a slow, pentatonic modal (C dorian, with B and E) theme that is echoed the second time around by Hampton's plaintive trumpet. By stating the notes of the principal triad in the very first measure, its melody is distantly related to "Work Song" from the 1955 date at the Café Bohemia. The piece sheds new light on the meterless call-and-response of the ancient canon form, reveling in the free-time exchanges between the horns. Pullen takes the role of exhorter, nudging each wind player with his stout chords. The canon's pattern is followed for about two-and-a-half minutes, after which Pullen and Richmond set up a firm throb in 3/8 time for Adams to solo over as Hampton continues the original theme. After another minute or so the call-and-response returns and is held until the end, with the players occasionally sailing off on brief tangents before coming home again.

"Opus 4" and "Opus 3" were apparently titled as a result of Mingus' writer's block, as he allegedly couldn't come up with any better names for them. (When it debuted at the Village Vanguard in August 1973, "Opus 4" was actually called "No Name.") At least the final titles complement the classicism of "Canon," although the music certainly doesn't. "Opus 4" starts with an odd, hiccuppy theme in 6/4, switches to a cool 4/4 lope, then flicks back and forth between the two until Pullen's piano solo. It is a difficult piece to navigate, especially since some of the switches only last a bar or two. Pullen's style is complex and magnificent, sounding at times as if the keyboard were a big zipper, flitting between traditional jazz styles and free exploration. Adams is a loose cannon, blowing the kind of hot, heavy rips and flurries associated with saxophonists like John Coltrane and Pharoah Sanders in the mid-1960s. Hampton is the most traditional player, though he meshes exceedingly well with Adams in their many exchanges.

"Opus 3" is a more straightforward bop tune, definitely Mingusian in its tonality, bashing accents, and the freedom given the horns to spread out into new realms. At a couple of points Hampton brings out the wah-wah (Harmon) mute, adding the element of Ellingtonia even as Adams is soaring toward the sky. If this chord progression sounds familiar, it should. In another self-reference, Mingus borrowed the chords of his earlier tune "Pithecanthropus Erectus" and composed this highly effective contrafact.

The tune "Moves" was written by Doug Hammond, who had been the quintet's drummer before Richmond returned. Apparently there were no hard feelings, as Mingus not only agreed to record the tune but let Hammond sing it alongside Honey Gordon. Too bad it's not a more memorable piece; the words fall rather flat and are quickly superseded by Adams' high, fluttering flute. "Wee," a waltz by arranger Sy Johnson, is so similar in spirit to "Moves" that it almost seems to be a continuation of that prior track. Eventually it comes into its own and is revealed as a rather compelling piece, particularly when the bustling 4/4 section arrives. In fact, "Wee" is anything but wee and is probably better suited to a larger ensemble, but Mingus' quintet does it reasonable justice.

Adams' "Flowers For a Lady" is a more sprightly bop tune, with some daunting trills in the horns and excellent cymbal work by Richmond. The drummer was still a consummate listener, shifting on a dime in response to his cohorts, plugging in the ideal nudges and highlights. Pullen's tune, "Newcomer," apparently pays homage to the birth of a child. It roils with restrained anticipation in the beginning, the flute and trumpet rising and falling on Richmond's cymbal waves. The main theme is gentle and lovely, stated in unison by trumpet and tenor sax, and Adams' flute solo contains the essence of energetic beauty. Mingus also takes an attractive solo, still understated compared to his past practices.

The 1993 CD reissue of *Mingus Moves* adds two tracks that were omitted from the original LP for spatial and thematic reasons. "Big Alice" is one of Don Pullen's most enduring compositions, a broken theme bouncing along on an infectious Bo Diddley beat. It was recorded later by Pullen (and, perhaps most memorably, by Howard Johnson's wild tubas-and-rhythm ensemble, Gravity), but this is probably the earliest rendition of this irresistibly catchy tune. All of the players have a great deal of fun with "Big Alice," and Mingus stays firmly in the pocket.

It is not known who composed "The Call," the second unissued tune here. It's lacking in identifiable Mingusisms but it could have been written by either Pullen or Adams, perhaps even someone outside the quintet, although that isn't likely. It begins in suspended time, with long tones from the trumpet and flute accented by finger cymbals. After more than a minute in that vein, then a moderate silence, a quick bop theme pops out with Pullen's piano simmering underneath. "The Call" is perhaps the fieriest tune of the session, with Hampton and Adams in ferocious competition. Around 5:30 the bottom drops out and the band falls back into suspended quietness.

*   *   *

Baritone saxophonist Hamiet Bluiett, later to make a name for himself within the World Saxophone Quartet, served briefly with Mingus from 1972 through 1974. He had already been working with the bassist when *Mingus Moves* was recorded but was not in on the session for some reason. Perhaps the leader had enjoyed what Gerry Mulligan had brought to the band. The only legit document of "Bunny" Bluiett's tenure with the bassist is *Mingus at Carnegie Hall* (Atlantic), recorded at that celebrated venue on January 19, 1974. The album is a mixed blessing, consisting of extended jams on "C Jam Blues" and "Perdido" from the Ellington book. The full first set of this evening's concert—"Peggy's Blue Skylight," "Celia," "Fables of Faubus," Pullen's "Big Alice," played by the quintet of Mingus, Adams, Pullen, Richmond, and Bluiett—was recorded but never released by Atlantic. According to the liner notes, the performances were simply not up to snuff. The second set as represented on this album is excellent, but also atypical of Mingus' usual form because they are guest-heavy jams on compositions other than his own. He always had the deepest appreciation for Ellington's book, to be sure, but there is very little of the Mingus character in these tracks. The leader doesn't even solo on this album. There was apparently a finale recorded after "Perdido" but that, too, has never been issued and may be lost by now.

That said, one couldn't ask for much better alumni/guest artists than trumpeter Jon Faddis and saxophonists Rahsaan Roland Kirk (he had taken on his mysterious additional name by this time), John Handy, and Charles McPherson. Pullen plays the first figure of "C Jam Blues" with one hand, and Mingus soon backs him up with his powerful walking bass style. The full band and guests play the bone-simple melody line, then John Handy takes the first solo on tenor sax. His improvisation runs a full fifteen choruses, with some occasional support riffs from the other players. Handy maintains freshness in his stream of ideas, sometimes playing repetitive variations of motifs in the style of Joe Henderson, other times digging deep into his blues bag or blowing as speedily as Eric Dolphy could. Bluiett, the next soloist, begins with a straight blues/bebop affectation to his playing but soon begins to stray into free-jazz liberty; from about 4:40 on, listen to the way he starts to smear the edges of his notes. It would have been extremely exciting to hear Bluiett's interaction with kindred spirits Pullen and Adams in the smaller group, one can imagine. Even as he moves away from the microphone at 5:55, he continues to blow sandpapery multiphonics (producing more than one note at a time). Next, Adams steps up for his nine hot choruses, going as far out as Bluiett had. From the extremely high, long squealing at 6:55, Adams rockets up to the stratosphere and rarely descends until his final chorus. A very long improvisation by Kirk includes tips of his hat to a number of saxophonists: Adams (9:52), Sonny Rollins (around 10:18), John Coltrane (11:43; dig the quote of "A Love Supreme" at 12:35), Illinois Jacquet (12:45), Dexter Gordon (13:15), and finally Ben Webster. The blind reedman does a brilliant job of imitating the styles and tones of each of these master players. He fades back from the mike on a long scream, then sidles back up to finish his thought before Jon Faddis steps up with his dead-on Dizzy Gillespie impersonation, his muted trumpet buzzing and wheezing in the highest register. Next up is McPherson, whose Parkerian inclinations are a good complement to the faux Dizzyisms of Faddis. His, however, is one of the most introspective, least energetic solos of the night. He finally perks up by about the fourth chorus, becoming the McPherson we once knew. The ensemble returns to the theme after the altoist's solo, and the coda is stretched out to about four minutes in length. Kirk prods on the other players with continual screeches, bass notes, and riffs, Mingus bows whining high-note figures, and a general sense of free mayhem pervades the hall until everyone runs out of steam. Even in the final exhausted minute Mingus, Pullen, and Bluiett won't relent.

"Perdido" is introduced in a jaunty fashion by Pullen, and the rest of the band is eager to go. They botch the first chorus a bit, but Handy and Faddis improvise lines that keep up the spirit. The first solo is Handy's, riding fleet and very high, smearing the top end of his range like sweet butter on a biscuit. Bluiett is curmudgeonly in tone, muscular and aggressive and blowing altissimo honks almost as high as Handy's. He ends his turn with a series of low, off-tempo honks and blats. Kirk's first improvisation is on tenor sax alone, pretty straightforward but soon spreading out into rapid Coltrane-like phrases. He pushes the energy ever upward until he receives a loud ovation. Richmond sounds as if the sticks are about to fly out of his hands as he fights to keep up with Kirk's wild momentum. It should be mentioned that Kirk is a master of circular breathing, the difficult technique of keeping a constant reservoir of air in one's cheeks and mouth, enabling musicians to play for extended periods of time without drawing a hard breath. McPherson, Adams, Faddis, and Pullen follow on their own solo turns, each offering their own special, energized take on the Ellington legacy but reflecting little of Mingus' inspiration. Pullen does the nicest job of bridging the gap between traditional and contemporary jazz forms, weaving Cecil Taylor, Art Tatum, and Ellington into one vivid piano tapestry.

In 1974, Bluiett left the quintet and was replaced by a young white trumpeter named Jack Walrath. Mingus, who hadn't been especially tolerant of white musicians over the years, recognized a huge trove of talent within Walrath and showed him great respect for the remainder of Mingus' life. With the exception of Dannie Richmond, no one enjoyed a longer unbroken tenure with the bassist.

Walrath remembers, "I believe it was in September of 1974 that I moved to New York from California. I was driving across country, and I wanted to play with either Mingus or Joe Henderson. And it just happened that as I was driving to New York, Joe Henderson was flying to Oakland. So that was that, but I always kept Mingus in mind. Later, Paul Jeffrey had a little band and I was playing with him. I got to know Paul very well because he lived close to me in Coney Island. I mentioned to him about Mingus, and he said he was writing some music for him. So one day he said, 'Mingus wants to hear you. Come on down and play with him.' I had just gotten off a Latin gig, and I sat in with him. He liked the fact that I could read his music, because he was writing some fairly hard tunes then. Two or three days later I got the call to go to the Village Vanguard with him. We were there for one or two weeks, I think."

Mingus had the reputation of being harder on white musicians, but Walrath says that wasn't really the case. "I didn't really get any grief from Mingus for being the white guy. In fact, he would defend me. One time he got pissed off because a guy wrote a bad review about me. I used to have a tooth that stuck out and would cut my lip in half, and that whole time I was pretty much in pain. One time it swelled up and I had cold sores and stuff, and I could hardly get a note out. I got a bad review, and Mingus cussed out the reviewer onstage, saying, 'The guy is up here trying to play his heart out.' Then he said, 'Now we're going to play music by five black people!' So I was an honorary black guy for a moment. There was only one time that he came up with some stuff. He had been razzing me for a while, and I finally had to reproach him. We were very clear on the race thing. Sometimes people in the band would act stereotypically, that whole 'Jim Crow' thing about a black man's penis being longer than anyone else's, and he would get onto them. He was a very smart guy. He always wanted to go to Africa but he never did. He had four days off in Rome and a guy told him there was a festival in Nigeria. Mingus was up for it, but then the guy told him he had to leave the white guy at home. Mingus told him off and didn't do the gig. He had a lot of principles. In the early 60s, if a black man stood up for himself in any way, they thought he hated all white people. It used to be considered revolutionary, or at least uppity."

Walrath continues: "I had just come from working with Ray Charles, who frankly was a lot harder to work with than Mingus, so I was ready for just about anything. Right before I left Oakland I saw him on a TV show, and his band was sounding good. It was a sextet or something; it might have been an older tape. I had never seen Mingus live, and one day I sat on the steps of the Village Vanguard. To tell you the truth, it was pretty bad-sounding, no energy. Mingus looked like a zombie because he was taking medication at the time. Dannie Richmond wasn't playing drums with him at that time, either. It must have been almost six months or a year later that I got the call. I always had a kind of concept of changing tempos or doing whatever instead of just having a blowing vehicle, so I seemed to just take to it. Also, I had a better time reading that music because when music is more challenging it's more interesting to me to play or read. Whereas if I was playing in a dance band, if you're sitting there and you play one note on the end of beat three, that makes me uptight more than playing some of his difficult tunes. I was kind of ready for it because I had spent years thinking that way anyway. He did it much better, I thought."

Mingus had abandoned his old principle of teaching his compositions by ear, and had returned to writing out his scores. He was still asking his sidemen to contribute their own tunes to the band's book. Walrath says, "That was supposed to be a concept of the Jazz Workshop anyway. But let's face it, the guy was the leader and he wanted to play his music. He did ask us if we wanted to bring in some tunes, so I brought in three. We recorded one of them, one we played on a gig, and the other one we just rehearsed." The leader remained flexible when it came to the arrangements, Walrath recalls. "Things just happened over the years with certain tunes. He'd usually change things if there was a new guy in the band. Or, one time Dannie Richmond was gone for a couple of weeks and we played without a drummer, and some things came out of that because it was so different. He would hold things back to see where we might go, or something would happen by accident and we might keep it in."

*   *   *

At that time Sue was the publisher of a magazine called *Changes*, and Mingus himself was certainly enduring some changes of his own. Having walked far away from the Ellington model, he was now pulling back toward that ideal while trying to keep a sense of newness in his music. Like Miles Davis, Mingus was faced with the specter of irrelevance in the jazz-hostile 1970s; unlike Miles, he wanted to stay in touch with those elements of jazz' past that had been his continual inspiration. He was fortunate to have, in Adams, Pullen, Walrath, and Richmond, the perfect band to assist him through those difficult changes.

Changes One and *Changes Two* were both recorded for Atlantic a few days after Christmas 1974, and were issued simultaneously on October 1, 1975. The old political spirit was back again, fired by the inmate riots at Attica State Penitentiary in New York. When Governor Rockefeller sent in the National Guard to quell the uprising, it fueled the fury of black Americans who recognized the mistreatment of minority prisoners at Attica as another flare-up in national racial tensions. The opening track of each album was an unsubtle nod at the matter: "Remember Rockefeller at Attica" had previously been titled "Just For Laughs, Saps" (and would be again a couple of years later), while "Free Cell Block F, 'Tis Nazi USA," which was strange enough to seem some sort of anagram, was simply a harsher assertion on Mingus' part. It was also a retitling, previously known as "Jive Five, Floor Four" due to its alternating 5/4 and 4/4 meters. According to Andrew Homzy, Mingus had originally planned to rename "Rockefeller" as "Cell Block F, 'Tis Nazi USA," which makes all the name-switching even *more* confusing.

An upbeat piece, "Remember Rockefeller" reflects little of its title's negative connotation. It does, however, contain a passage that directly acknowledges the "dit-dah, dit-dah" rhythm of "Fables of Faubus," which is a good enough linkage. "Take the 'A' Train" and Mingus' own "Duke Ellington's Sound of Love" (which we will touch upon in just a moment) are also referenced. This is a very engaging performance, particularly thanks to Pullen's brilliance as an improviser. Mingus' solo is muscular with a tambura-like vibrancy to it, though not quite as animated as before his hiatus.

Ronald Hampton had been a commendable improviser, but Walrath's playing couples immediacy with a bright, exceptionally clear tone that smoothly complements Adams' tenor sound. When muted, as on certain sections of "Sue's Changes," Walrath's trumpet can be as gentle as velvet. Mingus maintained that "Sue's Changes" was about the woman's mood swings, as opposed to her publication, and this composition cycles through a staggering number of phases: gentle, jaunty, abrasively free. In the liner notes for *Changes One*, Nat Hentoff suggests that "Sue's Changes" was a real cornerstone of Mingus' body of work because of its virtuosic scope. That might be the case, although in live performance it tended to run on well beyond the patience limits of many listeners. The studio version here, however, is a true masterwork realized by one of the bassist's finest ensembles. The tonal mutations of Adams and Walrath really sell the piece, morphing almost seamlessly from custard to sandpaper to vinegar and back again. Pullen exhibits the same kind of flexibility in his solo, an almost schizophrenic cluster of moods and forms welded together succinctly.

Changes One switches tracks immediately from "Sue's Changes" into "Devil Blues," a hard blues song by Clarence "Gatemouth" Brown for which Adams wrote a new melody. After a strident bass solo from the leader, Adams howls out the lyrics about the devil as a drifter on a black stallion. It's both shocking and hilarious, completely out of character when compared to the previous two tracks. Adams is every inch the wild-eyed blues shouter, punctuating his words with tribal screams and ululations that conjure images of warpaint in the studio. Mingus claimed that this song came about when the quintet was slated to perform at Max's Kansas City in New York, a rock nightclub that would later become (in)famous as one of the birthplaces of punk. With so many singing groups on the club's roster, Mingus thought it would be good if Adams had a song to sing, and this was the end result. It feels good to have a solid Mingus blues again, and this is one of the best.

The final track of *Changes One* is "Duke Ellington's Sound of Love," which Mingus had composed shortly after Ellington's death in 1974. Specifically, this one is the instrumental version, as a separate vocal take with Jackie Paris appears on *Changes Two*. "Sound of Love" is exactly the kind of homage one would expect from a composer who had been inspired by Ellington since childhood. It bears several hints at, or outright quotes from, the Ellington songbook, most clearly the ascending snippet of "Lush Life" that ends the thematic statement. As Hentoff observes in the liner notes, Adams seems fully conscious of tenorman Ben Webster's legacy in the Ellington orchestra, and he pulls off a simply magnificent solo turn that says everything that needed to be said.

As mentioned several times throughout this volume, Mingus' love of vocal music was compromised by his difficulty in writing singable lyrics to match his compositions. The vocal rendition of "Duke Ellington's Sound of Love" on *Changes Two* is yet another affirmation of that difficult balance. Jackie Paris' delivery is tender, smooth, and warm, even as he has to fight his way through clunky, purple lyrics such as, "I was young and carefree, not a song had found my soul," and "Sad clown with his circus closed down, lost on my merry-go-round." Even in an autobiographical piece like this, Mingus had a hard time articulating what was in his heart and head. Nevertheless, these shortcomings are easily outdone by the exceptional melody, a stellar performance by the band, and the mere aura of the great Jackie Paris.

The rest of *Changes Two* is on equal par with the first volume. "Free Cell Block F" has a killer theme with wonderful tumbling triplets in 5/4 time, passages in bossa-nova rhythm, clashing tonalities and Mingus' signature off-beat accents. Few bands could pull off such a complicated work without a drummer as sensitive and flexible as Richmond, who is yet a background presence on the track.

Jack Walrath's composition here, "Black Bats and Poles," was originally entitled "Rats and Moles." As he explained the title, "I had just moved from California, and the idea was like city rats and country moles. But Mingus had to change the title. I've noticed that any big-time bandleaders that I've played with, they always want to get their two cents in. He thought 'Black Bats and Poles' was dirtier, so there it was." The declamatory sound and high range of the theme convey a sense of urgency, and Walrath's solo is a highlight of his career. It is an amazing piece of work that sounds like nothing else in Mingus' catalog.

Sy Johnson's composition "For Harry Carney" is dedicated to the veteran baritone saxophonist, who contributed one of the most recognizable sounds in Duke Ellington's orchestra. If Adams had a bari sax handy on this session, or if Hamiet Bluiett had tackled the piece during his short stint with Mingus, it might have had a more profound impact. But the trumpet-and-tenor version here is rich and poignant, testimony enough to the baritonist's influence upon Mingus and the history of jazz. It projects a Middle Eastern air, like Ellington's timeless "Caravan" and "Isfahan."

The real centerpiece of *Changes Two*, "Orange Was the Color of Her Dress, Then Silk Blue" is addressed with a slower, more deliberate precision than it was in the 1960s, though the mid-theme tempo shifts and "American in Paris" piano bustle are kept intact. Mingus and his men had worked through this tune so many times that they effortlessly nailed it down in one take, resulting in perhaps the definitive rendition. The firm self-confidence of everyone, even newcomer Walrath, is palpable from the first long, relaxed tones through energetic free passages and rock-crushing improvisations. The exchanges of riffs between Adams and Walrath, about six minutes long, boost Pullen to a new creative height. It's hard to imagine that this amazing track was done in a single take.

To realize just how far this tune had evolved over more than a decade, listen to any of the versions from the 1964 tour, then spin this one for comparison. Missing is the funky piano intro that Jaki Byard had announced so well. Gone, too, is the repetitive horn riff that used to burst out during the double-time passage and continue until the signature quarter-note triplet. Few jazz compositions have ever benefitted from this level of complete metamorphosis. In the 1970s and 1980s, bandleader and arranger Gil Evans consistently included "Orange Was the Color" in his own repertoire. Each time he, too, did something significantly different with it, sometimes even beginning the piece in the middle. Despite Hentoff's stumping for "Sue's Changes," and the favoring of "Better Get Hit In Your Soul" by others, I believe that this one might be the single most essential composition to pour forth from the mind of Mingus.

*   *   *

The quintet performed at the Montreux International Jazz Festival on July 20, 1975, closing out the festival with some impressive moments. The set is documented, warts and all, on the DVD *Charles Mingus: Live in Montreux 1975* (Eagle Eye Media/ Montreux Sounds). The first image we behold is an overweight and tired-looking Mingus playing a deep, strong bass solo that leads into "Devil Blues." Adams sings with a real Chicago zest, a gravelly near-scream that he punctuates with primal ululations. The song sets the lingering feeling that Adams is the true star here, regularly stealing the spotlight with fiery tenor solos that shred the air around him. Walrath seems time-bound, looking like Gabe Kaplan in a denim suit; his solos are well-sculpted, upbeat, and unpredictable. Pullen delves into the encyclopedic well of jazz knowledge that made him such an asset, reaching back to James P. Johnson and upward to Cecil Taylor in the course of the same improvisation. The ascotted Dannie Richmond looks a little stoned at all times, his arms nearly as thin as the drumsticks he expertly wields.

From a purely creative standpoint, "Free Cell Block F" is probably the highlight of this set. All of the solos and illuminations are outstanding. "Sue's Changes," on the other hand, is dragged on almost interminably and would have been more successful at half its length. At heart it's one of Mingus' most interestingly constructed later works, alternating between sort of a "Lush Life" feeling and various other tempos and moods. Walrath's trumpet intro is simply gorgeous, and the band members handle all the shifts and turns as if they'd played the piece a thousand times before. Mingus often delivers a basic, light bass pulse that evolves into brisk walking. The tune gradually becomes more atonal along a descending chord pattern as the tension builds; Pullen and Adams handle these subtleties especially well. As Walrath does the slow burn through his solo, Mingus lights up a cigar and relaxes for a bit. Pullen and Adams make good contributions, too, but it's just the mind-numbing length of the piece that causes us to fidget in our seats as the band works back through the themes once or twice too often.

Baritone saxophonist Gerry Mulligan and trumpeter Benny Bailey join the quintet for a wrenching "Goodbye Porkpie Hat" that Mulligan makes his own. As I mentioned earlier, there is a little section of this work that seems to be of indefinite tonality. Once again, the harmony about halfway through the theme is handled a bit differently than on prior versions. Mulligan and Bailey remain on hand for the closing number, "Take the 'A' Train," as Adams and Walrath step back and give full spotlight to the guests. At one point Mingus begins trading fours with Mulligan, getting into good humor, but Bailey intrudes upon their fun by going into a solo just as the bari sax and bass are getting worked up. It's all taken out by the inimitable Richmond, whapping and flailing as effortlessly as ever.

*   *   *

Around this time Mingus received some devastating news from his physician. He had been feeling weak and lacking energy for a while, to the point that his bass playing was being adversely affected. The diagnosis was sobering: amyotrophic lateral sclerosis (ALS), also known as Lou Gehrig's disease. The incurable, largely untreatable illness involves the progressive wasting away of the muscles and nerves. It had killed the baseball star who gave the disease its popular name, and there was little doubt that sooner or later it would claim Mingus' life as well. Charles was informed that he would slowly lose his ability to play bass, to walk, and eventually to move at all. Sue was supportive, and together they began seeking homeopathic medicine and other forms of treatment to prolong his life and capabilities.

Mingus' next project brought him back to the world of film soundtracking. The two main tracks on *Cumbia and Jazz Fusion* (Atlantic), recorded in the spring of 1976 and 1977, could not be further apart in their character. Jack Walrath remains dissatisfied with the way the title section was recorded by Atlantic: "The part that was recorded in Italy, the 'Todo Modo' material, is just so gorgeous. Then when we went into the studio for Atlantic, things were poorly recorded and hacked up. There's one ugly edit from a different track where the tempo changes, and it's not smooth at all. I wish it had been done better." This is one of the most unusual items in Mingus' discography, but the edits here are not as glaring as some committed in the past by Teo Macero.

The title track, recorded in 1977, may have led a number of Mingus fans to scratch their heads and wonder just what kind of record had ended up in their cardboard sleeve. It is, as the title indicates, a fusion of jazz and the *cumbia*, a rhythm indigenous to Colombia but now popular throughout Latin America. The basic *chick-chicka, chick-chicka* pulse underscores this extremely exotic tune, which is unlike anything ever crafted by Mingus before or after.

The first sounds heard are tropical birds, and the rhythm creeps in subtly from the jungle. At 0:40 the basic thematic riff is stated by the oboe (Paul Jeffrey) and soprano sax (Mauricio Smith) while a bevy of percussion is beaten, shaken, and flogged by Candido Camero, Alfredo Ramirez, Daniel Gonzalez, Ray Mantilla, Bradley Cunningham (the owner of Bradley's club in New York City), Ricky Ford, Jack Walrath, and Mingus himself. The remainder of the ensemble includes Jimmy Knepper on tenor and bass trombones, Gary Anderson on bass and contrabass clarinets, Gene Scholtes on bassoon, Bob Neloms on piano, and Dannie Richmond on drums. Jeffrey and Ford also play tenor saxes; Mauricio Smith is on flute, piccolo, and alto sax besides the soprano.

This rainforest pulse drives on for a couple of minutes, with Mingus chanting about the *cumbia* now and then and the birds chirping all about. The pulse shifts at 2:35, and at 2:53 Mingus and the contrabass clarinet begin to play a bass ostinato. The soprano sax, oboe, and bassoon trade off different phrases of the composition, then the same is done by Walrath, Knepper, and the tenor saxes. The band cycles through these permutations for a long period. Then suddenly, at 5:14, everyone makes a seamless transition to a hot bebop rhythm. Now we're in more familiar Mingusian territory, with a rich, multilayered stream of modern jazz pouring out. After a chorus or so, the Latin percussionists are integrated with the jazz wave, and Walrath takes a lung-busting trumpet solo with plenty of Latin inflection. He trades off with Ford for some time, then lets the tenorman have the floor. The musicians on this session clearly know how to listen to one another, given the flow of energy and the responses they make to each other's creative impulses. At 9:02 a new ensemble section is heard, a more positive, major-key head with complex jazz rhythms. This leads up to a new tenor solo by Paul Jeffrey, who sticks closer to the bop continuum than the more free-minded Ford had. Another ensemble passage pops out at 10:43; this sounds like a bad edit, just appearing out of nowhere. The pace slows to a ballad feeling; all semblance of Latin influence drains out and we're left amidst one of Mingus' languid reveries. Bob Neloms takes an opulent piano solo, bubbling and cascading like a brook. He gradually introduces Latin-isms back into his playing, ending with a loud flourish of keys. At 13:00 an almost goofy rhythmic motif is taken up, Mingus playing a hokey slap bass pulse while Knepper, Walrath, and the others spout disconnected old-jazz clichés. The backing horns begin to blow low, long notes to underscore the random improvisers at 14:15, very slowly building to a riff-tide. The soprano sax and oboe return at 15:37 for a simple passage that is joined by Walrath; this is followed by a quick bass riff from the leader, then an unexpected martial rhythm from Richmond that is accentuated by Latin percussion. The drummer spreads out into a solo, trading off with the conga players in a brilliant culture-clash exchange. The ensemble comes back in at 18:52 with another series of riffs and melodic ideas. But at 19:20 Mingus gets back to the hokum bass riff, singing "Who said Mama's little baby likes shortenin' bread? Who said Mama's little baby likes shortenin', shortenin' bread? That's some lie some white man made up and said..." He goes on to inform us that Mama's little baby much prefers truffles, African gold mines, integrated schools (a nod to "Fables of Faubus"), freedom, and all the finer things in life. Richmond and some of the other band members join in the dialogue, which finally attempts to tie in this unusual composition with the rest of Mingus' *oeuvre*. After the twenty-one-minute mark the ensemble returns, and Mingus takes a vibrant bass solo with some Latin overtones. The next ensemble passage has more lush, jazzy orchestration, followed by Knepper's bright trombone improvisation and a fine offering by pianist Neloms. Mingus' next solo turn is embedded within the ensemble passages, and we can sense the impending return to the *cumbia*. It comes after twenty-seven minutes, the *chick-chicka* gliding in during a series of climbing horn riffs, but then drops back in favor of more jazz harmonies. This little tease leaves us hanging; the full Latin feeling never does return, only a great bebop fadeout.

The other principal tune, "Music For 'Todo Modo'," was composed for an Italian film soundtrack and recorded in Rome on March 31, 1976 and April 1, 1976. The core band of Mingus, Richmond, Walrath, Adams, and Danny Mixon (subbing for the unavailable Pullen) is augmented by altoist Quarto Maltoni, Anastasio Del Bono on oboe and English horn, bass clarinetist Roberto Laneri, bassoonist Pasquale Sabatelli, and Dino Piana on trombone.

This, too, is significantly different from Mingus' usual fare, starting off with Walrath's lone, plaintive trumpet. Rattlesnake noises resound behind the modal-sounding theme. After the initial chorus the other horns enter with dissonant harmonies, adding to the extreme tension. George Adams' tenor sax solo is a rush of frantic air-bursts and tremulous moans. At 2:56 we hear a horn drone and Mixon's ominous, funeral-parlor organ before the slow ensemble passage returns. A minor ballad theme is played by the alto sax and trombone at 4:08; the trombone plays a solo cadenza, then the slow horn line once more. At 4:58, with a quick flash of the drums, a medium-tempo swing passage is fired up, supporting a charming alto sax solo by Maltoni. As he had with "Cumbia," the composer/bassist took a while to get around to revealing the Mingus we all know, but this is an engaging creation nonetheless. Adams' tenor sax solo is infectious, with low vibrations and tumbling higher figures. Trumpeter Walrath skitters joyfully about like a hyperactive child, obviously having a ball with this section of the piece, and Mixon on piano rollicks with equal abandon. At precisely 9:00 the swing feel disappears as quickly as it came and is replaced by the solemn dirge. Maltoni and Walrath carry out their benediction with all seriousness, then at 10:29 the band switches to an Ellingtonian slow swing motif with the alto sax still in front. That, too, eventually fades back into the two-horn dirge, only to be annihilated yet again by a new, up-tempo swing section at 12:37. This portion of the tune nods to some prior Mingus pieces; Walrath, Mixon, and Adams again turn in bright, witty solos. Mingus' improvisation at 16:58, backed by light piano and drums, is high-spirited and marvelously executed. It is impossible to tell that his illness had begun to affect his playing ability. The bass solo is followed by the return of the swing theme, then another slow passage leading to a beautiful reverie between Mingus' bowed bass and Adams' alto flute. After a fashion Mingus begins a quiet Latin pulse on his bass, then puts down the bow and accompanies Adams with gorgeous pizzicato until the end.

The 1994 Rhino/Atlantic CD reissue adds on two unusual tracks: a pair of short solo piano performances of the traditional Wedding March, performed by Mingus in his usual shape-shifting style. The first one begins with appropriate bombast and flair, before he spreads out into a slow, slightly jazz-inflected waltz. An Art Tatum-like jazz section gets a progressively heavier dose of bebop flavoring. The second take is very similar, but Mingus' jazz explorations are more extensively developed. The reason behind Mingus' documenting of these miniatures is unclear. They don't add a whole lot to his discography but are interesting reminders of his piano skill and the influence of Art Tatum on his musical conception. One fragment, however, does turn up in the next odd installment of Mingus' late period.

Denouement

Mingus' music and career continued to take some strange turns even as his illness progressed. Atlantic Records began making more decisions about the recording process that did not always sit well with the leader nor his sidemen, but at this point Charles didn't have a great deal of leverage. He knew that things were going downhill, and he just wanted to be able to make as much music as possible in his remaining days.

*   *   *

Charles' next album for Atlantic was *Three or Four Shades of Blues*, recorded on March 9, 1977. The first track, "Better Get Hit In Your Soul," begins with the fine bass introduction, as usual. But the very next thing we hear comes as a shock to the system: the strident, metallic sound of Larry Coryell's electric guitar blasting through the theme. Mingus had moved into the electric-jazz era, pioneered by Miles Davis and Gary Burton in the late 1960s, and at first his fans didn't know what to think. Mingus had not recorded with a guitarist since *The Black Saint and the Sinner Lady*, fourteen years past, and Jay Berliner's jazz and Spanish chops back then had been an entirely different animal than Coryell's amplified crash. Some suspected that Atlantic Records had forced the guitarist upon Mingus, but Jack Walrath remembers that "Mingus liked Larry and really wanted to hire him for the band."

The core quintet at this time was Mingus, Walrath, Dannie Richmond, Ricky Ford on tenor sax, and pianist Bob Neloms. The special guests on the record include Coryell, Philip Catherine, and John Scofield on guitars; altoist Sonny Fortune; George Coleman on alto and tenor saxes; pianist

Jimmy Rowles; and bassists Ron Carter and George Mraz. It is debatable whether Mingus really needed the extra bass support due to his condition, or whether they were invited to join for other reasons. Whatever the case, over time *Three or Four Shades of Blues* became the biggest-selling album of the bassist's career. The pat record production techniques of the 1970s are audible, giving an undefinable sheen to the drums and guitars.

Besides Coryell's lead line, "Better Get Hit" boasts a new vocal chorus sung by Mingus and his bandmates. Unfortunately the singers are a bit mush-mouthed, but we can gather it's a joyful verse about Jesus walking on water and raising the dead. Coryell takes a guitar solo so acidic and jubilant it just about peels the paint off the walls. Catherine joins in with a second guitar line as Coryell begins to wind down, then it's Ricky Ford's turn to flush out the spirits of gospel, bebop, and beyond. On a purely energetic level, this performance might be the fullest realization of the composition's intended spirit.

George Mraz plays the bowed melody of "Goodbye Porkpie Hat," and is then joined by Coryell and Catherine on dual acoustic guitars. This is a beautifully fragile rendition of Mingus' greatest ballad theme, and Coryell's pyrotechnic technique comes off as more of a flamenco influence than the prior shredding. Catherine draws from the Gypsy-jazz legacy of Django Reinhardt in the next solo, with lots of note bending and flourishes, and the improvisations by Coleman and Mingus (still vibrant) move back toward modernity. The Coryell/Catherine duet epitomizes the sheer virtuosity of the two young musicians.

Things move in a completely different direction on "Noddin' Ya Head Blues," featuring the luxurious piano stylings of Bob Neloms. He is right at home in the midst of Mingus' traditionally swinging composition, tinkling and thundering away rapturously on the solo introduction. He seems to inspire the guitarists to stick to traditional thoughts, which they flawlessly do on the melody as Mingus (or is it Mraz?) and Richmond offer firm support. In a subsequent chorus, and during Coleman's flighty alto sax solo, Coryell plays hot, bent-note asides to further egg the players on. His own solo turn is knee-deep in the blues, a reflection of his status as a pioneer in the 1960s jazz-blues-rock crossover. Ricky Ford, who won't be outdone, contrives his own passionate blues statements, with a seeming nod of approval from Coryell and Catherine. The Belgian guitarist has a more trebly tone than his American partner, but no fewer chops and an equal appreciation for the blues. Both guitarists carry the chorus out together in exultant brotherhood. Mingus' solo at 7:59 is humorous, starting with human-like grunts and moans in the lowest range and building to lithe, swooping phrases. The band saunters out with the final choruses, led by the elated twin guitars.

The twelve-minute title piece is one of Mingus' multifaceted suites, moving from Ellington to Basie, Bird, and "caucasian folk blues." It begins with an assured walking rhythm under a relatively short melodic statement, followed by Walrath's bright trumpet solo. After Bob Neloms' piano improvisation, we hear one of Mingus' "Wedding March" interpretations, as tacked onto the *Cumbia and Jazz Fusion* CD. Immediately thereafter follows a pristine piano solo by Jimmy Rowles. One of the greatest accompanists in jazz, Rowles had backed singers such as Billie Holiday, Ella Fitzgerald, Carmen McRae, and Peggy Lee after assisting in the development of the West Coast "cool school." Mingus' walking bass kicks back in, then Neloms gets another turn at the piano. At 4:25, an Afro-Cuban rhythmic pastiche, with some Asian elements blended in, becomes the foundation for Walrath's next exploration. He really gets into the feel of this section, screeching and flourishing like a toreador. Prior to Ford's solo the rhythm and supporting horns get even funkier, with Coryell picking out a taut supporting line. After his searing solo comes a stiffly swinging section around which Mingus builds his own stiff improvisation. At this point it becomes more apparent that he has lost some of his facility, even if the lines he plays are toned down to suit the rhythm. George Coleman's tenor sax improv is smooth and professionally crafted, while John Scofield's signature chorus-pedaled guitar is in the more contemporary vein.

The final up-tempo bopper, "Nobody Knows (The Bradley I Know)," is dedicated to Bradley Cunningham, the New York clubowner who played some percussion on *Cumbia* and was one of the bassist's biggest supporters. It's built upon the idea of the old standard "Nobody Knows the Trouble I've Seen," which is hinted at in the basic theme and directly quoted at 0:20 in an altered-harmony approach. Ron Carter's bass has a very strange, tuba-like buzzing quality to it, as if it were recorded through a distorted amplifier. Sonny Fortune sets the house afire with a strong alto sax solo, clearing the way for John Scofield to blaze through with a cleaned-up guitar sound. Walrath's improv is sweet and emotive, perfectly suited to the quick Mingus groove. Philip Catherine's guitar is just a bit distorted, just enough to give his reflexive playing a rough edge as he solos. As the horns swell around him, he finishes up with a high, percussive riff. Ricky Ford is their cleanup man, taking the final solo with a good deal of energy and flow. The horns seem to bobble just a bit during the last choruses, but this is one great way to wind up a disc. One can almost hear Mingus singing along on the band's last run-through. He and Carter close with a neat, free bass duet.

The last session in which Mingus played bass was held at the bequest of Lionel Hampton, Charles' long-ago employer. Hamp had committed to producing a new series of albums for the Who's Who in Jazz label, and Mingus was one of his primary choices. Although weakened severely by ALS, the bassist opted to record for the vibraphonist in November of 1977.

The album was initially released by Who's Who under the title *Lionel Hampton Presents Charles Mingus*. It's mildly ironic because, while the title might have been more appropriate thirty years prior, in 1977 Mingus hardly needed to be "presented" to the jazz public by Hampton or anyone else. Subsequent legal and bootleg pressings have emerged under a number of different titles: *His Final Work*, *Lionel's Sessions* and others. For our consideration, the track order will be based upon Bluenite Records' *Free-Jazz Moods*, the most inappropriately skewed of the reissue titles (there is little, if anything, in a free jazz vein here). Besides that CD being the one the author has on hand at the moment, it will serve to show how screwed up some of Mingus' reissue catalog has been.

The ensemble includes Mingus, Richmond, Hampton, baritone saxophonist Gerry Mulligan, tenormen Ricky Ford and Paul Jeffrey, Jack Walrath on trumpet, and pianist Bob Neloms, as well as French horn player Peter Matt who is uncredited on many issues. The record is heavy on the older material, rearranged for more modern times, with a couple of newer pieces thrown in. "Caroline Keikki (sometimes spelled 'Keki') Mingus" is one of those, a dedication to one of his daughters. It's a pretty melody, with Hampton's vibes acting as the lead voice, and the arrangement is nicely subdued for a late-period Mingus chart. It was actually arranged by Paul Jeffrey, who most often tried to match the typical structure and energy level of Mingus' works. Walrath solos quite nicely on this subdued material, the kind of tune that was relatively scarce in Mingus' contemporary book.

This album has a particular conundrum to it that, for some reason, has never been adequately addressed in writings about Mingus. It should be obvious to the listeners that Rodgers and Hammerstein's "It Might As Well Be Spring" is out of place in this set, not because it's the only non-Mingus composition, but because the instrumentation on this track is completely different from the rest of the album. There is a trombone in the lead of what sounds like (and is) a quintet with electric piano, and there is no trombonist at all on the other Mingus tracks. The answer? This version of "It Might As Well Be Spring" was recorded by Danish-born trombonist Kai Winding for his own installment of the Who's Who *Lionel Hampton Presents* series. Why this ended up amongst the Mingus tracks is a mystery, but it has apparently been left intact on most releases, both official and bootleg, of the Hampton/Mingus material. It's a perfectly enjoyable tune, of course, but one must wonder why its presence here hasn't been questioned more often.

"Peggy's Blue Skylight" is perhaps taken a little faster than usual, and the band doesn't seem to latch onto it as well as prior incarnations had. Hampton's vibes are not as well-matched in this arrangement; his tinkle-tankle, low-vibrato approach doesn't suit the modernistic composition as much as it did "Caroline." Mulligan is silken-smooth, as he was in almost any situation; Walrath bops mightily, and Mingus manages a sturdy bass solo despite his waning technique. In clubs he had already been forced to start playing through an amplifier, and while his creative mind was still as fertile as ever, his fingers and arms were beginning to weaken considerably.

"Duke Ellington's Sound of Love" is another slow, traditionally minded piece that better suits Hampton's old-fashioned style. Peter Matt's French horn is prominent in the group, a nice textural element, and the ensemble passages are just flawless. Mulligan gets another featured spot, showcasing his one-of-a-kind ballad technique that made the large horn seem like a soprano sax. Walrath and Hampton solo in turn, each interpreting this beautiful ballad in their own personal fashion.

The astute listener will notice that "What Is This Thing Called Love" on the *Free-Jazz Moods* CD is related to the version Mingus had recorded on *Jazzical Moods*, back in 1954. The *more* astute listener will recognize that this *is* the 1954 version, not an updated version from 1977 as we might expect. Unlike "It Might As Well Be Spring," this track is not included on most of the Hampton reissues, but it illustrates the level of deception that has gone into repackaging Mingus' material on CD.

A strange alteration has taken place with "Fables of Faubus," specifically a hard rock backbeat played by Richmond (listen at 0:11). It doesn't work too badly, but it is one more unexpected twist in Mingus' later works. Aside from some further dissonance in the horn parts, the arrangement is otherwise close to normal. The solo order is the same as always: Mulligan retains his usual hip style; Walrath blurts and blasts while he dodges tempo and rhythm change-ups; and Hampton hammers out speedy vibraphone lines as if he were still a kid in Benny Goodman's band.

"Slop" begins with a hard, old-fashioned horn riff that drops an octave, rockets up again, and repeats until Neloms begins his barn-burning piano solo. Aside from the 3/4 meter, it's hard to tell at first that this is the same gospel-blues cousin to "Better Get Hit In Your Soul." The melody doesn't arrive until after Hampton's vibes improvisation, and then it all comes clear to us. The bridge harmony is slightly altered at 1:41; perhaps Jack Walrath blew the wrong notes, but it sounds like a simple, effective switch in the chart. Lots of good jazz but few surprises in the solos by Mulligan, Walrath, and Hampton—it would have been nice if the solo order had been tossed around at least a little bit. The vibraphonist's responses to the horn passages are well-crafted. The bridge at 4:25 is again different from the *Mingus Dynasty* version, so we can assume it was a deliberate decision. An interesting take on an older work that Mingus had ignored for some time.

Perhaps the most fascinating arrangement here is "So Long Eric," which becomes a major-key celebration of Dolphy's life instead of the minor-toned mood of the original. Again, one can't even tell it's the same tune until ten seconds into the piece. Walrath's higher trumpet part on the trills also helps alter the flavor. Hampton gets the first solo this time around, followed by Mulligan who seems exceedingly comfortable with the groove. So do the tenor soloist—probably Ricky Ford—and Walrath. The regular melody returns, then at 3:38 we hear the brief second theme which precedes

Hampton's second solo turn. He sets the vibraphone ablaze this time, flailing unaccompanied except for sporadic held chords from the horns.

"Farewell Blues," a.k.a. "Farewell, Farwell," was composed by Mingus in honor of his departed friend, painter Farwell Taylor. It's an appropriately tender ballad, exotic in its harmonies and structure. Hampton plays the forlorn theme on vibes while the horns blow long notes and choppy phrases behind him. The ensemble section about one minute in tips its hat to the tune's predecessor, "Far Wells, Mill Valley," though at a slower pace. Richmond keeps up a quiet but jaunty drum pattern, giving a sense of hope amidst loss. It is mostly a showcase for Hampton's charming vibraphones, but Mulligan takes a warm, thoughtful solo at 3:58.

"Just For Laughs" is broken into two parts, presumably to overlap the two sides of the initial LP release. This is the same tune as "Remember Rockefeller at Attica," which was originally named "Just For Laughs, Saps." It features nods to "Shave and a Haircut" and "Fables of Faubus," not to mention some of the most hellacious triplet sets in the Mingus canon (0:24). Again we hear much of Peter Matt's rich French horn in the ensemble, and again Mulligan takes the first solo. He and Hampton both make references to the theme, and everyone clearly has fun on this recent composition.

The second part of "Just For Laughs" begins with Bob Neloms' piano solo. It is not clear whether this was really intended as part of the first section, or whether it is from a second take. The first part ends on a pretty definitive note, so this one might have been cut separately. Whatever the case, Neloms' solo is followed by Mingus trading off with Dannie Richmond. The bassist definitely seems to be having trouble getting out his ideas. The tune closes with a final statement of the complex, layered theme and a thundering piano flourish.

*　　*　　*

By the end of 1977 Mingus was confined to a wheelchair, barely able to move. Atlantic Records nevertheless pressed on with Charles' final record sessions, on January 18, 19, and 23, 1978. The leader himself wasn't able to play a note. The two resulting albums, *Something Like a Bird* and *Me, Myself an Eye* (the latter named after the eye of God, which Mingus felt was watching him in his final days) seem more like homages to the genius of Mingus than anything that the master would have come up with himself.

Given Mingus' condition, the collaborative process to make the music for these sessions was much different. Jack Walrath recalls: "Ricky Ford and I went up and spent a while at (Mingus') house, and he was coming up with all this stuff. This one drum tune, 'Three Worlds of Drums,' was something that (Rolling Stones drummer) Charlie Watts was supposed to play with us. I came up with the concept for the introduction. Mingus gave me a tape where he was doodling, and it wasn't really a tune. So he said, 'Here, take some of my licks and make a song out of it.' We had a shout chorus where I played the bottom notes on the piano and Mingus improvised a solo which I transcribed. Then I put a bunch of counterpoint on it. I wish that there was a better recording of that, because the Atlantic recording is so bad that you can't hear everything that's going on with it."

Walrath claims that there was some acrimony between arranger Paul Jeffrey and the other parties. "I arranged 'Devil Woman' myself. 'Three Worlds of Drums' was more of a collaboration, but mostly I arranged it. And Ricky Ford arranged 'Farewell Farwell'; that's his introduction in the beginning. But there was such jealousy from people who had been writing the music before, like Paul Jeffrey. He caused a bunch of commotion behind our backs because he'd been doing all the writing before. He ended up getting us fired during all that. I wanted to pay Paul back because he was the one who steered me to the gig. But Mingus didn't really want to work with him anymore, and he had wanted me to conduct it."

The machinations of Atlantic Records to add more musicians onto the ponderous project didn't help matters. "The thing involved so many people," Walrath says. "First it was only supposed to be ten or eleven people, but it got so complex that I didn't want to have to play and conduct at the same time, so I thought it was a good time to get Paul involved again. Then Paul took Ricky's arrangement and managed to get him put off the thing altogether. He was also basically using Ricky's arrangements and mine when he did the Lionel Hampton record. He condensed them down for that. There was some strange stuff going on that to this day I don't think we really had closure on."

The veteran beboppers, studio musicians, and students who were less familiar with Mingus' music had extreme difficulty with the charts. Says Walrath: " 'Something Like a Bird' was so complicated that people were getting up and leaving the session because it was so hard. Paul asked me to write a brass soli for it, so I just made up my own thing, a 32-bar soli with a melody I came up with. Then I got a call from him after that: 'I want you to sign something saying that I composed the brass soli.' I said, 'Screw that. I'm the arranger; that's what I do.' There were other people who had some trouble with Paul, and a lot of friendships were busted because of things I've rarely seen grown men do. It was a very intense record session. During the rehearsals people would walk out saying, 'Man, you can't do this!' Then they would hear the recording and say, 'Oh, yeah, that's how it works!' "

"The older, more established guys were the ones who bitched the most. Paul was teaching at Juilliard, and he had to bring in some of his students to get the parts played. It was interesting to see how people acted, people that you've admired. Sometimes you see how limited they are, and they can be jealous of the younger people who come along. One of the guys said, 'This isn't a chord!' It was an F open 5th, and underneath it was an F# open 5th/9. It was just like a Phrygian (modal scale) thing, but that was in

Mingus' nomenclature. Younger guys like Mike Brecker had no problem at all, but the older guys get more closed. Some of the people my age didn't extend ourselves because, frankly, some of them didn't treat us very well. Even Mingus himself, sometimes he would come in and sound like it was the first time he picked up the bass. Everyone can have a bad night, so you come to find out that these guys are full of shit, too. You don't enjoy their music any less, but they're human now. There was an attitude with the older beboppers against the younger people. 'Oh, you young guys, all you want to do is play all this new music'."

The collective personnel on these sessions was enormous: Ken Hitchcock on alto and soprano saxes; Lee Konitz, Akira Ohmori, and Yoshiaki Malta on alto; Daniel Block, Michael Brecker, Ricky Ford, George Coleman, and John Tank, tenors; Pepper Adams, Ronnie Cuber, and Craig Purpura, baritone saxes; Jack Walrath, Randy Brecker, and Mike Davis, trumpets; Jimmy Knepper, Slide Hampton, and Keith O'Quinn, trombones; Larry Coryell, Jack Wilkins, Ted Dunbar, and Danny Toan, guitars; Bob Neloms, piano; Kenny Werner, electric piano on "Something Like a Bird"; Eddie Gomez and George Mraz on basses; Joe Chambers, Steve Gadd, and Dannie Richmond, drums; and Sammy Figueroa and Ray Mantilla, percussion. Paul Jeffrey conducted all of the performances.

According to one manuscript in the author's collection, "Three Worlds of Drums" was also performed at some point as "Two Worlds of Drums," featuring Richmond and Steve Gadd, a studio drummer who had made some pop hits with artists like Steely Dan and Paul Simon. The rendition on *Me, Myself An Eye* includes veteran bebopper Joe Chambers as a third drummer; Gadd only appears on this track. The volume of sound is tremendous almost from the get-go, beginning with a slow throb in the lower instruments and trills which turn into strident wails in the higher horns. Coryell picks out forceful single-note lines on his guitar as the drums boil and pound beneath him. After a collective free-jazz passage, Joe Chambers' drum solo comes at 1:23. He begins from nearly nothing, a tom pulse rising in volume and power, a snare roll and some hard shots, then down to silence again. At 2:20 the ensemble bursts in again with a frightening fanfare, heralding Dannie Richmond's turn at center stage. His solo is quicker and more unpredictable, skittering all about the kit. The fanfare hits again at 3:30, and it's time for Steve Gadd to lay down his funkier concepts. Gadd is clearly rooted in fusion, pop, and R&B styles, all of which are poured out from his double-bass-pedaled kit. He plays some fast fluttering patterns on the hi-hat, bows out for a moment, then we hear the Latin percussion of Ray Mantilla and Sammy Figueroa (actually bringing us into *four* worlds of drums: Chambers' bebop, the post-bop of Richmond, Gadd's contemporary jazz, and the Latin jazz continuum). The ensemble rides in on a funky electric groove courtesy of the three guitarists, all of whom are playing different riffs and figures. At 6:48 the trombones blurt outward, then the rest of the horns follow in a rich polyrhythmic stew. Walrath's trumpet is the lead instrument on this complex ensemble section. It spreads out a bit into a different series of rhythms, and suddenly Walrath leaps out into his solo at 8:38. His improvisation is loose-limbed, tonally and rhythmically free over the band's ostinato, sometimes leaning toward Latin motifs. Randy Brecker follows seamlessly with his own trumpet solo. Around 11:27 the ever-swelling ensemble riffs build to a climax, quoting one of Mingus' prior works, then it's time for George Mraz' impressive but light-toned bass solo. At about 12:54 he begins to play some sliding double-stops that are unlike Mingus' usual style but still provide a nice homage. Another crushing ensemble riff lands at 13:21 then immediately makes way for George Coleman's Latin-inflected tenor sax solo. Listen to the way that Mraz keeps up the sliding bass figures to complement the saxophonist's rhythms. When Coleman is done we're still only halfway through the marathon half-hour track. Other solos follow by Eddie Gomez, Michael Brecker, Coryell (an absolutely insane, rock-inspired and distorted improvisation, at 18:20), and finally the three drummers, rotating in the same order they initially appeared: Chambers, Richmond, Gadd. This trio of stickmen cycles through ideas for more than five minutes, with the horn bursts eventually pushing their turns closer together. The Latin percussionists join back in at 25:40, and the full band's final push begins about one minute later. Around 28:25 the rhythm matrix begins to melt, and a slower, more somber horn line is carried through to closure. Walrath has likened this last section to "a funeral march, like an omen."

"Devil Woman" begins almost as a continuation of "Three Worlds," with a like sober feeling, but is soon recognizable as a slow blues. Coryell plays accentuating guitar lines against the horn passages, and the melody arrives at 0:46 with the guitarist and the Brecker brothers in front. Coryell's solo from 2:41 is pure, incendiary electric blues, the evolution of Muddy Waters and Eric Clapton into a contemporary jazz mode. He melds back into the ensemble without a hitch. Michael Brecker roars outward at 5:33, his tenor sax creaking at first like a rusty hinge in the wind. He moves on to fast cascades of notes before finding a hard blues groove. Brother Randy takes over on trumpet at 6:24, using a plunger mute to fine effect without getting into the stale novelty-sound bag. The siblings engage in a magnificent trade-off when the band reenters, continuing until the final theme. Coryell once again sprinkles the orchestra with sweet blue fairy dust.

The new version of "Wednesday Night Prayer Meeting" features an introduction of hand-claps and wordless vocals, a great addition that moves it further into church mode. Coryell again leads the horns through the melody, and for once the percussion is too subdued on this tune. Perhaps it's a combination of production values and the sheer mass of other instruments, but the drums just seem a bit too quiet. Eddie Gomez' twangy bass is the ideal fuel, however, meshing with the drummers and nudging soloists such as Walrath, the Breckers, Ricky Ford, and Coryell to work their hardest. The bassist's own solo, as it builds from a brisk walk at 6:43, would do the master proud. Gomez is one of the most phenomenal technicians to come in Mingus' wake, and this solo announced his claim to the jazz bass throne. The ensemble section that precedes the theme's return seems sloppy, even more than when Mingus would dictate arrangements by mouth. The singing and hand-clapping carries us out to the end.

Lee Konitz is the featured performer on the lovely rendition of "Caroline 'Keki' Mingus," which is almost overwhelmed by the number of players in the band. A theme as tender and fragile as this one calls for a lighter hand, and the orchestration really seems to wear it down compared to the Lionel Hampton version. Alto saxophonist Konitz knows his way around a ballad, and so manages to hold everything together splendidly. Michael Brecker's solo is a thing of complete beauty, impeccably suited to the spirit of Mingus' composition. Larry Coryell subdues his passion to turn in his prettiest solo of the whole session, proving that he's infinitely more than a shredder and free jazzer.

*   *   *

As a record album, *Something Like A Bird* was severely unbalanced: a half-hour extended work accompanied by one of only seven minutes' length. It continued the sense of bittersweet homage initiated by *Me, Myself An Eye*, having basically come from the same sessions.

The title track is a contrafact on the standard "Idaho," the same chordal source as "Four Hands" from 1954's *Jazzical Moods*. It's poignant that Mingus' career would end in roughly the same place as his life in New York's jazz scene had begun. There is much of the spirit of Charlie Parker present, as to be expected from the title. According to the liner notes, Mingus originally called this piece "Something From the Past" but Walrath convinced him that Parker's legacy was still alive and well in ensembles like Supersax. It also contains a subtle nod to the late Clifford Brown; the four descending pairs of notes at 0:06 are drawn from the trumpeter's "Joy Spring." The solos are clustered by instruments: the tenors of Michael Brecker, Ricky Ford, and George Coleman, first in consecutive order and then trading off; Walrath and Randy Brecker on trumpets; Ronnie Cuber and Pepper Adams on baritone saxes; and the basses of Eddie Gomez and Mraz. Finally, Part 1 unites the age-old concept of a full-band jam session with a duly modern touch at the end of the solo-stream: Bob Neloms divulging the history of the acoustic piano in jazz, contrasted with young Kenny Werner's bracing electric piano. The two men end up in one accord, dovetailing their ideas before ending in a mutual crash. The ensemble returns at 18:55 to carry out a truly beautiful interpretation of the melody.

Part 2 of "Something Like a Bird," which is left seamless on the CD edition, kicks off with the trombones of Jimmy Knepper and Slide Hampton in the same scenario: solo, solo, duel, and camaraderie. At last we have the alto saxophones of Charles McPherson, Lee Konitz, George Coleman, and Akira Ohmori, respectively representing the influences of Bird, cool jazz, hard bop, and the contemporary scene. It perfectly summarizes the alto sax continuum in jazz history, even if it bears little flavor of Mingus.

"Farewell Farwell," led by the guitars and Knepper, carries a completely different air than the Hampton version had. Bits and pieces are reminiscent of past works such as "The Shoes of the Fisherman's Wife." The orchestra resists any semblance of swing until 1:53, when Ricky Ford's tenor sax solo arrives. It is ideally smooth, softly eloquent, and a bit nostalgic, like the composition itself. Coryell, on the other hand, prefers an overdriven sound that doesn't suit the mood as well. The guitar solo is simply too pyrotechnic for a ballad of this sort, even during a more up-tempo section. Lee Konitz brings things back down to earth, and Eddie Gomez turns in the final solo of Mingus' last hurrah with a wonderfully melodic improvisation. Similar to the bandleader, Gomez' bass playing had the qualities of a human voice, and Mingus no doubt saw reflections of himself in the younger man's talents. In his final days, his instrumental legacy seemed secure.

Coda

Prior to his death, Mingus began a most unexpected collaboration. He had taken an interest in the music of folk-rocker Joni Mitchell and eventually contacted her about doing some work together. By that time Mingus was a shell of his former self, but he still had many compositional ideas in his head. He submitted several tunes to Mitchell and asked her to have some arrangements worked out.

Mitchell took to the project excitedly and assembled a rehearsal band to develop some of the tunes. Among the musicians she initially hired were Dannie Richmond, alto saxophonist Phil Woods, baritone saxophonist Gerry Mulligan, bassists Eddie Gomez and Stanley Clarke, and two members of the fusion group Mahavishnu Orchestra: guitarist John McLaughlin and keyboardist Jan Hammer. Elektra Records did not initially like the direction the project was taking, although they apparently approved of the fusion angle. Over time the label talked Mitchell into going with a contemporary ensemble featuring several members of the red-hot fusion band Weather Report: soprano saxophonist Wayne Shorter, electric bassist Jaco Pastorius, and drummer Peter Erskine. Also on hand were electric pianist Herbie Hancock and percussionists Don Alias and Emil Richards.

*   *   *

Charles Mingus died on January 5, 1979, in Cuernavaca, Mexico, where he and Sue had gone to consult a traditional healer. At his bequest, Sue and her son Roberto then traveled to India, where they scattered Charles' ashes in the Ganges River. One of jazz' greatest bassists, composers and personalities had passed away, but his legacy would live on until the present day.

Joni Mitchell's *Mingus* (1979, Elektra) was released a few weeks after Charles' death. It bore little resemblance to the original vision of the recording, and Mitchell has subsequently credited this album with the downturn in her career. Despite all of the bad vibes surrounding *Mingus*, it is actually a fine album and a most impressive tribute to its namesake.

Scattered throughout the album are audio clips from the last months of Mingus' life: sounds of a birthday party, and quotes by the man himself about his life experiences. Four of the six tracks were composed by Mingus, with words added by Mitchell. "Chair in the Sky" is perhaps the most enduring of the originals, having been picked up later by some of the Mingus "ghost band" repertory groups. It's perhaps the most Mingusian of the tunes. "Sweet Sucker Dance" is rather confusingly structured; it might have worked better in the bassist's own hands, but here it comes off as a bit of a muddle. "Dry Cleaner from Des Moines" is a fun tune about a guy who has endless luck at the casino, and Jaco Pastorius' brilliant electric bass playing really sells the tune. However, there is very little to identify it as a Mingus composition. Mitchell's lyrics to "Goodbye Porkpie Hat" tell of Mingus' love for Lester Young, and it ends up as a warm, wonderful homage to both of the passed-on jazzmen. Of the two Mitchell originals, "God Must Be a Boogie Man" is a different kind of homage, inspired by *Beneath the Underdog* and the songstress' own conversations with Mingus. The other original, "The Wolf That Lives in Lindsey," has no apparent association with the bassist. Although it is a very good tune, then, it seems very out of place in this context.

*   *   *

Later in 1979, Sue Mingus, Jimmy Knepper, and George Adams organized a group of Mingus alumni and friends which was, in a nod to his 1959 Columbia record, dubbed Mingus Dynasty. A dynasty it was, indeed: among its rotating members were alumni such as Clifford Jordan, Sir Roland Hanna, Jaki Byard, Dannie Richmond, John Handy, Jon Faddis, Richard Williams, Don Pullen, Randy Brecker, and Ricky Ford. A number of jazz stars and upcoming players occupied the bass chair over the years, including Reggie Workman, Mike Richmond, Charlie Haden, Richard Davis, and Spaniard Aladar Pége.

At the Bottom Line, issued in 1995 by WestWind, was recorded in December 1979, when the band was still trying to solidify its conception. The ensemble includes Knepper, Adams, Ted Curson (barely audible much of the time), John Handy, Charlie Haden, Dannie Richmond, and pianist Hugh Lawson. There are only four tracks, ranging from ten to thirteen minutes: the mistitled "Boogie Stop," "Chair in the Sky," "Mr. Jelly Roll," and "Sue's Changes." The hack-and-slash editing and lousy sound quality keep this from being more than a historical document, but it has moments of reasonable interest.

In May 1980 the Mingus Dynasty recorded their studio debut, *Chair in the Sky* (Elektra). The record included all-instrumental arrangements of four selections from Joni Mitchell's album: "Chair in the Sky," "Sweet Sucker Dance," "Dry Cleaner from Des Moines," and "Goodbye Porkpie Hat," along with "Shuffle Bass Boogie" and "My Jelly Roll Soul." It's possible, but not entirely clear, that these charts may have originated in the rehearsals that Mitchell originally held before settling on the Weather Report offshoot band. Charlie Haden played bass on the debut album but was not available on July 18, 1980, when *Live in Montreux* (Atlantic) was recorded. That live session features Mike Richmond and Aladar Pége in good combination, most effectively on the tremendous "Ysabel's Table Dance." "Sketch Two" is an interesting rarity, composed during Mingus' final days and never recorded in his lifetime.

Knepper quit the Dynasty around 1990, and the leadership was taken over by Jack Walrath. Other dynasty albums of interest include *Live at the Village Vanguard* (1984, Storyville), *Mingus' Sounds of Love* (1988, Soul Note), *The Next Generation Performs New Charles Mingus Compositions* (1991, Columbia), and *Reincarnation* (1997, Soul Note). In 1988 the band was briefly augmented to become Big Band Charlie Mingus. That ensemble recorded a pair of sessions for Soul Note, but the results pale in comparison to the real deal or even the smaller "ghost band."

*   *   *

Researcher Andrew Homzy, who had collaborated with Mingus on *More Than A Fake Book*, unearthed a treasure trove of manuscripts and notes as he helped organize the bassist's archives in 1985. As he sorted and analyzed reams of paper, Homzy discovered eighteen scores with measures that were consecutively numbered, suggesting that they were intended to be some sort of large-scale suite. Mingus had inscribed the title *Epitaph* on these manuscripts. He had once mentioned that he had created a suite to be used "for my tombstone," and apparently this was it.

Epitaph was an expansive compendium of his life's labors, drawn largely from material intended for the disastrous 1962 Town Hall concert. The tunes range from early pieces such as "Chill of Death" to "Pithecanthropus Erectus" (providing the main theme of *Epitaph*), "Better Get It In Your Soul," "Peggy's Blue Skylight," and a number of rarely- or never-before-heard compositions. On the scores, Mingus had gone so far as to specify some of the musicians he wanted to perform this suite someday: Buddy Collette, Charles McPherson, Jimmy Knepper, Eric Dolphy, Willie Dennis, Britt Woodman, Clark Terry, trombonist Jimmy Cleveland, Lonnie Hillyer, Ernie Royal, Dannie Richmond, guitarist Jim Hall, and a number of others. He planned on two bass players, himself and the great Milt Hinton, belying the notion that *Epitaph* was intended for posterity. In total, the ensemble would number thirty players.

The manuscripts presented a daunting prospect for Homzy. They were smudged, illegible, incomplete, and sometimes inaccurately notated. The archivist contacted Third Stream pioneer and old Mingus associate Gunther Schuller to request his assistance in preparing *Epitaph* for performance. About four years later, with production support by Sue Mingus, the full score was performed in concert, recorded, and issued by Columbia Records as the two-disc *Epitaph* set (1989).

Mingus would have been pleased that several of the musicians he had originally specified for the project were actually able to participate in this realization: trombonists Eddie Bert, Paul Faulise, and Britt Woodman; tubaist Don Butterfield; altoist Jerome Richardson (whom Mingus had intended to play baritone sax alongside Pepper Adams); and trumpeter Snooky Young. Besides those players, the 1989 *Epitaph* orchestra included Urbie Green, Sam Burtis, and David Taylor on trombones; Bobby Watson and John Handy on alto saxophones; George Adams on tenor sax; Phil Bodner on tenor sax and oboe; Roger Rosenberg and Gary Smulyan on baritone saxes; Michael Rabinowitz on bassoon; Dale Kleps on contrabass clarinet; Randy Brecker, Lew Soloff, Jack Walrath, Wynton Marsalis, and Joe Wilder on trumpets; Sir Roland Hanna and John Hicks on piano; Reggie Johnson and Ed Schuller on basses; Victor Lewis on drums; Karl Berger on vibes; John Abercrombie on guitar; and Daniel Druckman on percussion. A colossal group for a colossal undertaking.

The liner notes by Schuller, who conducted the concert performance, and Homzy give marvelous details about the resuscitation of *Epitaph*. I will not repeat much of them here for the sake of redundancy and space; instead, I encourage readers to peruse the liner notes for themselves as they play these unique discs.

As mentioned earlier, the "Main Score" of *Epitaph* is built upon the foundation of "Pithecanthropus Erectus." Expanded for more than two dozen musicians, the impact of this titanic structure is nearly overwhelming and sets an impressive pace for the rest of the suite. Beautiful additions, evoking Ellington crossing the open prairie to reach 52nd Street, significantly change the character of the piece. "Percussion Discussion," originally a Mingus/Max Roach duo at Café Bohemia in 1955, was rearranged into a dark, ominous work for four brass, three saxophones, and rhythm section. Part 2 of "Main Score," with an impressive oboe solo by Phil Bodner, leads into "Started Melody," which is a lush set of variations on one of Mingus' favorite standards, Vernon Duke's "I Can't Get Started." After a stiff, formal intro featuring the trumpet section, Bobby Watson emerges to play the familiar theme along with the brass.

A half-minute of collective improvisation precedes the melody of "Better Get It In Your Soul," which sounds just a bit staid in the hands of such a large ensemble. As the nine-minute track progresses, however, the orchestra settles into a more appropriately "churchy" groove. The haunting, previously unperformed "The Soul" is built upon the changes to "Body and Soul," another acknowledgment of the jazz-standard annals. Next is "Moods in Mambo," a piece very unlike Mingus' other works, even *Tijuana Moods*, although it still bears some of his signature marks. "Self Portrait/ Chill of Death" is most unusual in that, as Schuller's notes indicate, every musician in the ensemble contributes some sort of improvised material before the 11½-minute track is done. The narration of "Chill" was not used, mostly because Schuller felt that having anyone but Mingus do it would reduce the impact. "O.P.," Mingus' engagingly upbeat tribute to bop bassist Oscar Pettiford, is missing the stop-time section performed at Birdland in 1962 but is marvelous and much too short. Roland Hanna's piano interlude ushers the orchestra into "Please Don't Come Back From the Moon," another Town Hall remnant. Hanna, George Adams, and Randy Brecker are featured most effectively as soloists in this bustling section.

"Monk, Bunk and Vice Versa," which starts the second disc of *Epitaph*, was also performed at Birdland in 1962. It is subtitled "Osmotin'," Mingus' pun on his osmosis-like fusion of Thelonious Monk and early jazz pioneer Bunk Johnson. The theme manages to fuse, among other things, elements of Monk's "Straight, No Chaser" and the old standard "Tea For Two." A wonderfully swinging dissonant take on "Peggy's Blue Skylight" is peppered with some additional elements not heard in Mingus' earlier versions.

Mingus paid tribute to Jelly Roll Morton in the mid-1960s with "My Jelly Roll Soul" but had rarely performed or recorded any of Morton's compositions. It came as a surprise, then, to find an orchestration of "Wolverine Blues" in the *Epitaph* scores. The sensibilities of early jazz, right down to Morton's "Spanish tinge," are kept largely intact although there is a clear aura of "Chazz" jazz in the harmonies. Solos by Randy Brecker and bassoon virtuoso Michael Rabinowitz send this track tootin' through the roof; one of the many highlights of *Epitaph*. In a completely different vein is the Third Stream heavy "The Children's Hour of Dream," which avoids improvisation and swing altogether. As Schuller notes, this was charted not by Mingus but by an ex-Stan Kenton arranger, Gene Roland. It certainly bears elements of Kenton's ponderous classical-jazz examinations. It may have been intended for Town Hall but was not performed, another casualty of all the bad planning. The composition is minor-key and discomforting, more like Mingus' weird nightmares than some fairy-tale dreamscape.

"Ballad (In Other Words, I Am Three)" was given that name by Schuller as it was untitled in manuscript form. The subtitle is taken from the first words of Mingus' book *Beneath the Underdog*, a conversation with his psychiatrist. The "ballad" theme doesn't occur until after a flaming blues solo by Randy Brecker. When it does arrive, it is given a soulful, lamenting treatment by the amazing Bobby Watson. The concert shifts gears with "Freedom," sort of the bastard child of *Epitaph*. This was inserted at

Andrew Homzy's suggestion because a large section of the score was missing and could not be accounted for. Like much of the rest of *Epitaph*, it had also been performed at Town Hall (entitled "Clark in the Dark" on the original LP release of that concert). Unfortunately, the liner notes do not tell who recited the poem at the 1989 concert, but Mingus' biographer Brian Priestley informs this writer that Jerome Richardson was given the honor. The blues solos by pianist John Hicks and baritone saxophonist Roger Rosenberg are stupendous.

"Interlude (The Underdog Rising)" was perhaps Schuller's greatest triumph in this project. Mingus' score for this particular section was in tatters, with overlays taped on in complete disregard of logic and tonal quality. Schuller literally ended up cutting up and pasting the entire score of "Interlude" into something that was reasonably functional as a performance piece. This was plastic surgery of cosmic proportions, *Frankenstein* in reverse, and Britt Woodman's brilliance on plunger-muted trombone holds everything together nicely. "Noon Night," unrelated to "Tonight at Noon," is rather a reinvention of the gorgeous "Nouroog" theme with George Adams in complete control. Finally, we are back to the up-tempo section of the "Main Score," where Schuller thought Mingus would most likely have wanted to return to bring the suite full-circle. Joe Wilder and Woodman carry on in their most unabashed fashion, reassuring us musically that Chazz would have approved.

*   *   *

With the gradual dissolution of the Dynasty band, Sue Mingus sought other ways to keep her husband's music alive and in the public ear. She organized the Mingus Big Band, and later the Charles Mingus Orchestra, to formally maintain and develop her late husband's imposing body of work. Among the musicians she has contracted to play in the groups are trumpeters Walrath, Randy Brecker, Lew Soloff, and Ryan Kisor; trombonists Ku-umba Frank Lacy and Art Baron; French hornists Vincent Chancey and Tom Varner; saxophonists Craig Handy, Ronnie Cuber, John Stubblefield, Steve Slagle, Seamus Blake, and James Carter; bassists Boris Kozlov and Mike Formanek; pianists Kenny Drew Jr. and Dave Kikoski; and drummer Marvin "Smitty" Smith, Jeff "Tain" Watts, and Donald Edwards.

The Mingus Big Band held a longtime gig at the Time Spot Café in New York before moving to Iridium. They have made a series of albums for the Dreyfus label: *Nostalgia in Times Square* (1993), *Gunslinging Bird* (1995), *Live in Time* (1996), *Que Viva Mingus!* (1997), *Blues and Politics* (1999), and *Tonight at Noon: Three or Four Shades of Love* (2002). The latter album also features the expanded Mingus Orchestra, which has gigged regularly at Joe's Pub. Many of the arrangements performed by Sue's ensembles are straight from the Mingus book, while others have been contributed by the band members. All of their recordings are well worth hearing, although nothing matches the majesty and scope of Mingus' own albums.

*   *   *

Besides the officially sanctioned activities of Mingus Dynasty and Sue's bands, a number of Mingus tribute albums have made the rounds. One of the most visible and yet unusual is *Weird Nightmare: Meditations on Mingus* (Columbia), producer Hal Willner's 1992 crazy-quilt. Since the late 1970s Willner has built a career on such odd homages, having created off-beat tributes to Italian film composer Nino Rota, Thelonious Monk, Kurt Weill, and Disney film scores. *Weird Nightmare* ups the weirdness ante further by including some of the bizarre musical instruments invented by Californian weirdo Harry Partch in the 1930s and 1940s. Partch was an ultracreative soul who came up with his own forty-three-note scale, the "monophone fabric," and developed new instruments out of big glass bottles, scrap metal, and parts of existing instruments. Willner heard these creations played at a Partch retrospective and, for some reason, thought it appropriate to include them in his tribute to Mingus. That point is arguable, but the exotic sounds don't really detract from these distinctive interpretations of the honoree's music.

The core ensemble on *Weird Nightmare* includes guitarist Bill Frisell, trombonist and tubaist Art Baron, bassist Greg Cohen, and percussionists Don Alias and Michael Blair. The group is augmented by guests on different tracks: guitarists Marc Ribot, Gary Lucas, Vernon Reid, and Robert Quine; flautist Henry Threadgill; clarinetist Don Byron; drummer Bobby Previte; Francis Thumm on the Partch instruments; the Uptown Horns; Keith Richards and Charlie Watts of the Rolling Stones; harmonica player Howard Levy; and various vocal spots by Elvis Costello, Hubert Selby Jr., Public Enemy rapper Chuck D, punk-rocker Henry Rollins, Robbie Robertson, Dr. John, Ray Davies of The Kinks (humming only), Diamanda Galás, and folkie Leonard Cohen! It's a typically bizarre mixture of personalities for a Willner disc. The producer himself contributes percussion, samples, and sound effects to some tunes.

Most of the melodies remain relatively unsullied, although a few are mutated into freakish new creations. The album begins with the sound of Art Baron's didgeridoo as the house band dives into "Canon." Frisell's guitar intertwines with Gary Lucas' electric slide guitar on the dual-leveled theme. Baron's trombone comes in as an overdub while the didgeridoo drone continues, augmented by the haunting Partch instruments. Starting a bass player's tribute album with no bass is the kind of subversion expected from Willner, and one of which the equally rebellious Mingus might have approved. The track moves seamlessly into "Meditations on Integration" as Alias sets up a minimalist waltz rhythm. Baron's tuba joins the support structure while the guitars wail like banshees and Ribot's banjo twangs discordantly. After some strident drum-pounding, the second theme of the piece emerges around 1:52. On the third track, astride the return of "Canon," Robbie Robertson duskily recites an excerpt from *Beneath the Underdog* about Mingus playing chess in Bellevue with Bobby Fischer. The core quintet, plus Lucas, blast through "Jump Monk," given a hot and heavy tribal beat by Alias and Michael Blair. No Partch gadgets here, but Art Baron turns in some simply blazing trombone work. The melody is played eventually, and only then in fragments that kick against the rhythmic matrix.

Several of Partch's instruments give an other-dimensional ambiance to "Weird Nightmare," matching the detached coolness of Costello's singing like a 1950s crooner lost in the Twilight Zone. "Work Song" is even more abstract, with no sense of the theme for more than the first minute. The Partchian dreamscape dominates until 1:14, when the walking bass finally strides out from the fog. Baron's tuba and Don Byron's clarinet ooze out the melody while cartoon sound effects smash and dissolve around them. Byron and Baron also hold the lead on a stunningly beautiful "Self-Portrait in Three Colors."

A surprising inclusion is "Purple Heart" from Mingus' earliest Jazz Workshop, a nice tune that he apparently never played after the mid-1950s. Over Alias' period conga groove and the trombone/clarinet front line, Henry Rollins recites an unpublished section of *Beneath the Underdog*, this time involving the history of the word "groovy." Charlie Watts hammers through "Tonight at Noon" in support of the four-member Uptown Horns, with Greg Cohen offering a nice approximation of Mingus' sliding octave riffs. Chuck D brings us back to the unpublished part of *Underdog*, picking up where Rollins left off. The rapper's unmistakable rhythmic delivery is a perfect complement to the rock-hard drumbeats and Frisell's wailing, metallic guitar on "Gunslinging Bird."

After a cool, quiet "Weird Nightmare" interlude by Frisell on acoustic guitar, the band returns with "Reincarnation of a Lovebird." Alias is over-dubbed on both congas and dumbek, creating an unusual Middle Eastern-tinged pulse that evolves into a different, quirky dance beat. It, too, gives way at 1:48 to Frisell's shredding electric blues. Byron takes up the cause at 2:29, his clarinet bubbling and squeaking with joyous abandon. At 3:20 the spastic beat unexpectedly returns, is soon shattered, but reforms once more. A burst of swooshing organ at 3:55 ushers us into a surreal "Haitian Fight Song Montage," with tolling clock tower and cuckoos, angry crowd noises, and Gary Lucas bashing out the melody on his National steel guitar. His last swoop nods directly to "Open Letter to Duke" as delivered by a jubilant folk band: Howard Levy on harmonica, Tony Trischka on banjo, Bob Stewart on tuba, Barry Mitterhoff on mandolin and guitar, Sue Evans on percussion, Kenny Kosek on violin, and Bobby Previte on kazoo, castanets, and spoons. It sounds more like background music for Disneyland's

Frontiertown than anything from the Mingus pen, and in that it works brilliantly. The interactions are remarkable, and this may be the standout piece on the whole amazing disc.

Byron takes up the bass clarinet for "The Shoes of the Fisherman's Wife," with an understated *Underdog* recitation by Hubert Selby Jr. This grouping is more spare, with Art Baron on the woody great bass recorder, Cohen on bass, and Frisell's mist-shrouded guitar. Charlie Watts joins his Stones bandmate, guitarist Keith Richards, and the Uptown Horns for "Oh Lord, Don't Let Them Drop That Atomic Bomb On Me." Bernard Fowler takes it straight to church with his powerful singing, and Richards backs him humorously. Cohen, pianist Chuck Leavell (who has a grand time here), and tenor saxophonist Bobby Keyes round out the ensemble. The pace is as slow and bluesy as a New Orleans funeral procession. The next track, arranged by Art Baron, layers "Chill of Death" on top of the equally old Mingus ballad "Eclipse." It begins with Diamanda Galás wailing eerily over a warped tropical soundscape. Baron then blows the mournful theme on wood flute, and at 2:50 Leonard Cohen chants "Chill of Death" with a zombie-like lack of passion. Tension builds as the electric guitar melody and didgeridoo slowly crescendo, and Galás' groans float outward once more.

A sample from a vintage radio production and Frisell's jangling guitar introduce "Pithecanthropus Erectus," which is saddled with an eccentric martial pace. The pained, jagged guitar of Robert Quine hacks through the trombone's melody as Alias and Blair whack on a chair and assorted metal objects. Having white New Orleans pianist/vocalist Dr. John deliver the chant on "Freedom" is a wacky move, even for this project, and it doesn't exactly work despite the interesting instrumental arrangement. The album wraps up with a short, fading reprise of the otherworldly "Weird Nightmare," leaving us in a mood of suspended animation so typical of Willner's sonic adventures.

In a wholly different vein, equally true to Mingus' creative essence, is guitarist Andy Summers' *Peggy's Blue Skylight* (BMG/RCA Victor, 2000). Summers is one of the greatest guitar players of modern rock, having transcended the huge popularity of his 1970s/80s band, The Police, and moved into many new directions. He has long worn his love of jazz on his sleeve; 1997's *The Last Dance of Mr. X* (RCA) included covers of Mingus' "Goodbye Porkpie Hat," Thelonious Monk's "We See," and other jazz tunes, and in 1999 he recorded a full-on Monk tribute, *Green Chimneys* (RCA).

On *Peggy's*, Summers uses guest artists in a similar manner to Willner, but for the most part the results are more creative and entertaining. With Randy Brecker in tow, the guitarist turns "Boogie Stop Shuffle" into a slow back-alley skulk. His "Tonight at Noon" is a fuzz-laden blast worthy of Hendrix, but with accordion and cello stirred into the mix, while "Reincarnation of a Lovebird" becomes a beautiful electric guitar ballad with John Novello's

B-3 organ and some Indian percussion for color. Novello also cooks on "Opus 3." The short poke at "Cumbia and Jazz Fusion" barely transcends cheese, but the hot Latin take on "Remember Rockefeller at Attica," boosted by Alison Wedding's wordless vocals and a larger ensemble, is a highlight. Summers' tremoloed guitar shimmers in bliss on "Peggy's Blue Skylight" before Blondie frontwoman Deborah Harry's haunting interpretation of "Weird Nightmare," possibly the best on record. The low point comes with a version of "Goodbye Porkpie Hat" that is encumbered by "Where Can a Man Find Peace?" as delivered by rapper Q-Tip from A Tribe Called Quest. The feral collective improvisation by the Jazz Passengers makes a fine fade-in for "Free Cell Block F," but it is a little rigid by Mingus standards once the theme gets going. More effective is the duo of guitar and, surprisingly, electric sitar on "Self-Portrait in Three Colors." The tribute is wrapped up by Sy Johnson's angular, imaginative rearrangement of "Myself, When I Am Real," which teams Summers' echoing acoustic guitar with the Kronos String Quartet. Once the unusual character of this session is assimilated, it's easy to appreciate Summers' unique assay of these formidable works. It's as much a tribute to Mingus' creative spirit as to his compositional legacy.

Not every Mingus tribute has been worth its salt. In October 2005 the Lincoln Center Jazz Orchestra (LCJO), under the direction of trumpeter Wynton Marsalis, issued the tepid *Don't Be Afraid...The Music of Charles Mingus* (Palmetto). LCJO shill Stanley Crouch's liner notes tout the album as "one of the finest gatherings of music by Charles Mingus...truly powerful performances," which is hyperbolous nonsense. Despite being a good talent pool of individual players, all of whom shine as soloists, the LCJO injects almost no Mingusian spirit into this recording. Trombonist Ron Westray's arrangements are acceptably constructed, but the musicians seem intimidated by the material and back off from playing with any real fire or passion. They finally cut to the chase on the closing title track, far too late to be effective. This album is a depressing, unworthy excuse for a tribute.

In 2005 Sue Mingus founded another new label, ostensibly replacing the slow-to-blossom Revenge imprint. Sue Mingus Music debuted in June 2005 with *I Am Three*, an album of new arrangements featuring the three major Mingus repertories: the Mingus Big Band, Mingus Orchestra, and the return of the seven-piece Mingus Dynasty. The dynasty's lineup presently includes bassist Boris Kozlov, saxophonist Craig Handy, trumpeter Alex Sipiagin, pianist Kenny Drew Jr. and trombonist Ku-umba Frank Lacy. *I Am Three* features arrangements by members from each ensemble: "Song With Orange," "Orange Was the Color...," Kozlov's astonishing chart for "Tensions," "Paris in Blue," "MDM," "Free Cell Block F," "Wednesday Night Prayer Meeting," "Chill of Death," "Todo Modo," and "Pedal Point Blues." Three arrangements were written by saxophonist John Stubblefield, who was very ill at the time and could only conduct the ensemble from his wheelchair (he died on July 4, 2005, a few weeks after the album's release). Mrs. Mingus' vision for her label includes not only new recordings by the "ghost bands," but new issues and reissues of archival materials. The most celebrated upcoming release is the 1965 *Music Written for Monterey, Not Played . . . UCLA*, which has never been issued on CD before. She has also uncovered tapes from a concert at Cornell University, featuring Eric Dolphy. And, of course, the Mingus "ghost bands" will continue for as long as time, money, and circumstances allow.

*   *   *

The reinvention of Mingus Music continues in the hands of high-profile fans like Elvis Costello, who recently penned lyrics to the daunting "Hora Decubitus." The track kicks off Costello's 2006 album, *My Flame Burns Blue* (Deutsche Grammophon), recorded live with the Metropole Orkest at the 2004 North Sea Jazz Festival. (The title track is a recasting of "Blood Count" by Billy Strayhorn, a further branch of the Mingusian bloodline.)

Back in Watts, the predominantly black Los Angeles neighborhood where Mingus was raised, his bequest is now coming full circle. In June 2005, the L.A. Cultural Affairs Department began construction on the Charles Mingus Youth Arts Center, adjacent to the Watts Towers that were so significant in his own young life. His expansive vision seems destined to pass on to future generations through projects like the Youth Arts Center, and his widow's unflagging determination to maintain his legacy.

Bibliography

Béthune, Christian. *Charles Mingus*. Montpellier, France: Editions du Limon, 1988. In French.

Bryant, Clora, with Buddy Collette, William Green, Steven Isoardi, Jack Kelson, Horace Tapscott, Gerald Wilson and Marl Young. (eds.) *Central Avenue Sounds: Jazz in Los Angeles*. Berkeley, CA: University of California Press, 1998.

Coleman, Janet and Al Young. *Mingus/Mingus: Two Views*. Berkeley, CA: Creative Arts Book Company, 1989.

Franco, Maurizio. (ed.) *Musica Oggi*, Vol.22. Milano, Italy, 2000. In Italian and English.

Levallet, Didier and Denis-Constant Martin. *L'Amerique de Mingus (Mingus' America)*. Paris: P.O.L. (Collection Birdland), 1991. In French.

Lindenmaier, H. Lukas and Horst J. Salewski. *The Man Who Never Sleeps: The Charles Mingus Discography 1945–1978*. Freiburg, Germany: Jazzrealities, 1983.

Mingus, Charles. *Beneath The Underdog*. Nel King (ed.) New York: Alfred A. Knopf, 1971; Vintage Books/Random House, 1991.

——. *More Than A Fake Book: The Music Of Charles Mingus*; Sue Mingus (ed.), with Andrew Homzy and Don Sickler. New York: Jazz Workshop; distributed by Hal Leonard Publishing Corporation, Milwaukee, Wisconsin, 1991.

Mingus, Sue Graham. *Tonight At Noon: A Love Story*. New York: Pantheon, 2002.

Olivier, Stéphane. *Charles Mingus*. Paris: Musipages, 2000. In French.

Priestley, Brian. *Mingus: A Critical Biography*. London: Quartet Books, 1982.

Santoro, Gene. *Myself When I Am Real*. London: Oxford University Press, 2000.

Uekusa, Jin'ichi. *Boku tachi niwa Mingus ga hitsuyo nanda (We need Mingus)*. Collected essays, 1959–1970. Japan: Shobunsha, 1976. In Japanese.

Venn, Michael. "Charles Mingus: A Bibliography." in Dr. Charles T. Brown (ed.)
    Jazz Research Papers 1989, pp. 265–300. Manhattan, Kansas: National
    Association of Jazz Educators, 1989.
Weiler, Uwe. *The Debut Label—A Discography*. Norderstedt, Germany, limited
    edition, 1994. In German.
Zenni, Stefano. *Charles Mingus: Polifonie dell'universo musical afroamericano*.
    Viterbo, Italy: Nuovi Equilibri, 2002. In Italian.

Index

Abercrombie, John, 168
"Adagio Ma Non Troppo" (a.k.a. "Myself, When I Am Real"), 104, 134
Adams, George, 140–43, 145–49, 151–52, 166, 168–70
Adams, Pepper, 59–60, 91–92, 95, 160, 162, 168
Adderley, Julian "Cannonball," 34, 36
Adderley, Nat, 113
Ah Um. See Mingus Ah Um
"Ain't Jivin' Blues," 11
"Ain't Nobody's Bizness If I Do" (Grainger/Robbins), 82
Akiyoshi, Toshiko, 90, 92–94
Ali, Rashied, 131
Alias, Don, 165, 171–73
"Alice's Wonderland" (a.k.a. "Diane"), 58, 67
"All About Rosie" (Russell), 46
"All Set" (Babbitt), 46
"All the Things You Are" (Kern/Hammerstein), 22, 32, 37, 77, 129
"All the Things You C#," 37
"All the Things You Could Be By Now if Sigmund Freud's Wife Was Your Mother," 77, 84
"All Too Soon" (Ellington), 124

Allen, Henry "Red," 56
Alternate Takes (Mingus Dynasty), 69–70
Amazing Bud Powell: Jazz at Massey Hall, Vol. 2, The (Powell), 22–23
America Records, 125
"American in Paris, An" (Gershwin), 37, 148
Ammons, Gene, 136–39
Anderson, Cat, 93
Anderson, Edmund, 49
Anderson, Gary, 150
Anderson, John, 12
"Anthropology" (Parker), 9, 33, 78, 109
Antibes Jazz Festival, 73–76
Apollo Theater, 20
"April in Paris" (Basie), 29
Arkestra, 129
Armour, Eddie, 91–92
Armstrong, Louis, 9, 87
"Arts of Tatum and Freddie Webster, The," 126, 128
Astral Weeks (bootleg), 114
At the Bottom Line (Mingus Dynasty), 166
"AT-FW-YOU-USA" (a.k.a. "AT-FW-YOU") (Byard), 110, 120

Atlantic Records, 3, 31–32, 38, 41, 43, 45, 59, 63, 73, 77, 84, 87, 118, 140, 142, 145, 150, 152–53, 158–59, 167
Attica State Penitentiary, 145–46

Babbitt, Milton, 46
"Baby, Take a Chance With Me," 10–11. See also "Honey, Take a Chance On Me"
"Back Home Blues," 47
Bailey, Benny, 82, 149
"Ballad (In Other Words, I Am Three)," 169
Bank, Danny, 26, 92
Barab, Seymour, 67
Baron, Art, 170–73
Barrow, George, 30–31, 34–39
Basie, Count, 8–9, 29, 154
"Bass-ically Speaking" (Mingus), 23
Bates, N.R. "Nat," 10
"Batman" theme (Hefti), 81
"Bebopper" (Feather/Gordon), 21
"Bedspread" (Collette), 12
Bellevue Mental Hospital, 22, 45, 80–81, 172
"Bemoanable Lady," 73
Beneath the Underdog (Mingus autobiography), 2, 73, 133, 166, 169, 172–73
Benson, George, 29
Benton, Bob, 19
Benton, Walter, 81
Berg, Dick, 136
Berg, George, 92
Berger, Karl, 168
Berigan, Bunny, 57–58
Berliner, Jay, 98–100, 153
Bert, Eddie, 34–39, 92, 136, 138, 168
Best, Denzil, 16, 22
Bethlehem Records, 14, 49, 53
"Better Get Hit In Your Soul" (a.k.a. "Better Git It . . . ," "Better Git Hit . . . ," "Better Get Hit In Yo' Soul"), 2–3, 59, 63–64, 66–67, 69, 75–76, 78, 86, 102–3, 131, 148, 153–54, 157, 167–69
"Big Alice" (Pullen), 141–42

Big Band Charlie Mingus (ghost band), 167
Bigard, Barney, 8–9
"Billie's Bounce" (Parker), 55–56 (mistitled "Bounce"), 109, 132
Bird (Eastwood film), 78
"Bird Calls," 3, 63–65, 69
Birdland (club), 17, 90–91, 169
Birth of the Cool, The (Davis), 16, 24, 30
Birth of the Third Stream, The (various artists), 46
Bishop, Walter, Jr., 29, 129
"Bitty Ditty" (Jones), 29
"Black Bats and Poles" (a.k.a. "Rats and Moles") (Walrath), 147
Black Saint and the Sinner Lady, The, 97–102, 104, 153
Blackburn, Lou, 123–24
Blair, Michael, 171–73
Blake, Seamus, 170
Blakey, Art, 27–28, 34, 41, 131
Blanton, Jimmy, 7, 28
Bley, Paul, 18, 27–28, 43, 81
Block, Daniel, 160
Blondie (rock band), 174
"Blue Bird" (Parker), 133
"Blue Cee," 44, 56, 90
"Blue Monk" (Monk), 60
"Blue Moon" (Rodgers/Hart), 19
Blue Note Records, 42, 47, 91, 118, 122
"Blue Tide" (Givens), 19, 26
Bluebird Records, 47
Blues and Politics (Mingus Big Band), 170
Blues and Roots, 3, 58–61, 63, 66, 84, 97
Bluiett, Hamiet, 142–44, 148
Bodner, Phil, 168
"Body and Soul" (Heyman/Sour/Eyton/Green), 19, 31–32, 82–84, 104, 169
Bohemia. See Café Bohemia
"Boogie Stop Shuffle," 3, 64–65, 116, 166, 173; mistitled "Boogie Stop," 166
"Boppin' in Boston," 14
"Bounce" (Parker), 55–56. See also "Billie's Bounce"

Bradley's (club), 150
Bradshaw, Tiny, 41
Brandeis University, 45–46
Brecker, Michael, 160–62
Brecker, Randy, 160–62, 166,
    168–70, 173
Brice, Percy, 29
Brook, Paige, 20
Brown, Clarence "Gatemouth," 146
Brown, Clifford, 162
Brown, Maurice, 67
Brown, Oscar, Jr., 36
Brown, Ray, 131
Bryant, Bobby, 123
Buffington, Jim, 46
"Bugs," 83–84
Bunink, (Floris) Nico, 67–69, 80
Burtis, Sam, 168
Burton, Gary, 153
Butterfield, Don, 72, 91, 98,
    100–1, 168
Byard, Jaki, 44, 91–92, 94–95, 98, 101,
    104, 107–21, 123–26, 132, 134,
    148, 166
Byron, Don, 171–73

"C Jam Blues" (Ellington), 142
Cadena, Ozzie, 30
Café Bohemia (club), 34–39, 41–42, 44,
    56, 140, 168
Café Wha? (club), 78
Caine, Eddie, 26
"Call, The" (composer unknown), 142
Callender, Red, 6–7, 14, 123
Camero, Candido, 150
Candid Records, 65, 73, 76–79,
    81–84, 133
"Canon," 3, 36, 140, 171–72
"Caravan" (Ellington/Tizol/Mills), 148
"Carnegie Blues" (Ellington), 93
Carney, Harry, 137, 147–48
Caro, Herb, 14–15
"Caroline 'Keikki' Mingus" (a.k.a.
    "Caroline 'Keki' Mingus"), 156, 162
Carr, Helen, 14
Carr, Lady Will, 12, 14
Carter, James, 170
Carter, Ron, 154–55

Cassavetes, John, 57–58, 65, 67
Catherine, Philip, 153–55
"Celia," 50, 101–2, 142
Central Avenue (Los Angeles), 8, 16
"Chair in the Sky" (Mingus/Mitchell),
    166–67
Chair in the Sky (Mingus Dynasty), 167
Chambers, Joe, 136–37, 139, 160–61
Chancey, Vincent, 170
Changes magazine, 145
Changes One, 145–47
Changes Two, 145, 147–48
Charles, Ray, 144
Charles, Teddy, 46, 67–68
Charles "Baron" Mingus: West Coast,
    1945–49 (compilation), 10
Charles Mingus (Tempo di Jazz)
    (bootleg), 90
Charles Mingus and Cecil Taylor
    (bootleg), 91
Charles Mingus and Friends in Concert,
    136–39
Charles Mingus at Birdland: The
    Complete Sessions (compilation),
    90–91
Charles Mingus' Finest Hour
    (compilation), 13, 23
Charles Mingus in Paris (bootleg), 132
Charles Mingus: Live in Montreux,
    1975 (video), 148–49
Charles Mingus: Live in Norway, 1964
    (video), 111
Charles Mingus Octet, 26
Charles Mingus Orchestra (ghost band),
    170, 174
Charles Mingus Presents Charles
    Mingus, 76–78, 84
Charles Mingus Quintet + Max Roach,
    37–39
Charles Mingus Records, 123, 125
Charles Mingus: The Complete Debut
    Recordings (compilation), 18–29
Charles Mingus Youth Arts Center, 175
Charlie Mingus Sextet Live (bootleg),
    132–33
Charlie Parker with Strings (Parker), 78
Chazz. See Charles Mingus
    Quintet + Max Roach

"Chazzanova," 25, 29
"Chelsea Bridge" (Strayhorn), 12
"Cherokee" (Noble), 22
Childers, Buddy, 14–15
"Children's Hour of Dream, The," 169
"Chill of Death, The," 7, 53, 135, 167,
    169, 173–74
Cirillo, Wally, 27, 30, 32
"Clair de Lune" (Debussy), 37
Clapton, Eric, 161
"Clark in the Dark," 93, 170.
    See also "Freedom"
Clarke, Kenny, 26, 29, 32
Clarke, Stanley, 165
Cleveland, Jimmy, 92, 167
"Cliff Walk" (Little), 81
Clown, The, 38, 43–45, 49, 87, 113
"Clown, The," 45, 127
Club Alabam (club), 9, 11
"Cocktails for Two" (Johnston/
    Coslow), 125
Cohen, Greg, 171–73
Cohen, Leonard, 171, 173
Cohn, Al, 28
Coker, Henry, 11
Cole, Nat "King," 21
Coleman, George, 153–55, 160–63
Coleman, Ornette, 27, 43, 48, 65, 118
Coles, Johnny, 107–21
Collette, Buddy, 6–7, 9–10, 12–13, 29,
    92, 94, 123–25, 167
"Colloquial Dream, A," 53. See also
    "Scenes in the City"
Coltrane, John, 89, 98, 141, 143
Columbia Records, 9, 31, 45–46, 63,
    65–67, 70, 76, 91, 104, 133, 136,
    166, 168, 171
Complete, 1945–1949 West Coast
    Recordings (compilation), 15
Complete Candid Recordings of Charles
    Mingus, The (compilation), 84
Complete Town Hall Concert, The,
    92–96
"Compositional Theme Story: Medleys,
    Anthems and Folklore," 105
Concertgebouw (Dutch venue), 109
Concertgebouw Amsterdam, Volumes 1
    and 2 (bootleg), 109

"Consider Me" (Hughes/Mingus), 56
Contemporary Records, 43
"Conversation," 49–50
Cornell University, 175
Coryell, Larry, 153–55, 160–63
Cosby, Bill, 136–39
Coss, Bill, 29
Costello, Elvis, 171–72, 175
"Cotton Tail" (Ellington), 33
Crouch, Stanley, 174
"Cryin' Blues," 59–60
Cuber, Ronnie, 160, 162, 170
"Cumbia and Jazz Fusion,"
    150–52, 174
Cumbia and Jazz Fusion, 150–52, 155
Cunningham, Bradley, 150, 155
Curson, Ted, 71, 73–78, 80–83, 166
Cusson, Lorraine, 72

D, Chuck, 171–72
Dameron, Tadd, 22, 33, 38, 127
"Darn That Dream" (Delange/Van
    Heusen), 19
Davies, Ray, 171
Davis, Maxwell, 10
Davis, Mike, 160
Davis, Miles, 16–18, 23–24, 29–30, 34,
    41, 73, 79, 109–10, 145, 153
Davis, Richard, 166
"Day Dream" (Strayhorn), 21
Debussy, Claude, 109
Debut Records, 9, 15, 18, 20, 22–29,
    34–35, 37, 39, 121, 126
"Deep in the Heart of Texas" (Hershey/
    Swander), 116
Del Bono, Anastasio, 151
Dennis, John, 18
Dennis, Kenny, 56
Dennis, Willie, 24–26, 59, 64, 92, 167
DeRosa, Clem, 33
"Devil Blues" (Brown/Adams), 146–49
"Devil Woman," 85, 90, 159, 161
"Diane" (a.k.a. "Alice's Wonderland"),
    58, 67, 69
Dickenson, Vic, 56
Diddley, Bo, 141
DiDomenica, Robert, 46
"Dixie" (traditional), 57

"Dizzy Atmosphere" (Gillespie), 131
Dizzy Atmosphere: Live at Historic Slug's, Vol. 1, 131
"Dizzy Moods," 2, 47–48, 55, 66
"Do Nothing Till You Hear From Me" (Ellington/Russell), 72–73
Dolphins of Hollywood Records, 13–14
Dolphy, Eric, 6, 14, 31, 42, 58, 73–78, 80–83, 92–93, 95–96, 101, 103, 107–24, 138, 142, 157, 167, 175; death, 122–23
"Donna Lee" (Parker), 9, 78
"Don't Be Afraid, The Clown's Afraid Too," 45, 126–27, 134, 139
Don't Be Afraid . . . The Music of Charles Mingus (Lincoln Center Jazz Orchestra), 174
"Don't Come Back," 94. *See also* "Duke's Choice"
"Don't Let It Happen Here," 126–27
Dorham, Kenny, 82
Dorr-Dorynek, Diane, 58, 67
Dorsey, George, 136
Dorsey, Tommy, 28, 88
Dotson, Hobart, 14, 126–28
"Double G Train," 56, 66. *See also* "GG Train"
"Down by the Riverside" (traditional), 86
"Dream Montage" (Hughes/Mingus), 56
Drew, Kenny, Jr., 170, 174
Dreyfus Records, 170
Druckman, Daniel, 168
"Drum Conversation" (Roach), 22
"Drums" (Mingus/Roach), 38–39
"Dry Cleaner from Des Moines" (Mingus/Mitchell), 166–67
Duke, Vernon, 57, 168
"Duke Ellington's Sound of Love," 3, 45, 146–47, 157
"Duke's Choice" (a.k.a. "Don't Come Back"), 3, 54–55, 65, 94
Dunbar, Ted, 160
Dunlop, Frankie, 47

"E's Flat, Ah's Flat Too" (a.k.a. "Hora Decubitus"), 44, 56, 59–61, 88, 101, 139

Earland, Charles, 131
East Coasting, 49–50, 79
"East Coasting," 49
East Coasting Records, 126
"East St. Louis Toodle-Oo" (Ellington), 6, 11
Eastwood, Clint, 78
"Eat That Chicken," 78, 86–87, 90–91
"Ecclusiastics," 86, 90, 137
"Eclipse," 15, 26–27, 53, 72, 78, 137, 173
Eddie Condon's (club), 34
Edwards, Donald, 170
Edwards, Teddy, 10
Elders, Lonnie, III, 53
Eldridge, Roy, 81–84, 138
Elektra Records, 165–67
Ellington, Edward Kennedy "Duke," 2–4, 6–9, 11–12, 20, 22, 25–26, 31, 33–34, 36, 43–44, 49–50, 54–55, 58, 65–69, 71–73, 79–80, 91, 93, 95, 98–99, 102, 104, 112–13, 116, 119–20, 123–24, 128, 132, 135, 137, 140–43, 145, 147–48, 152, 154, 168
Ellington, Mercer, 68
Ellis, Don, 67, 69
"Elusive" (Jones), 29
"Embraceable You" (Gershwin), 22, 44, 125
Ennis, Skinnay, 14
Epitaph, 91, 167–69
"Epitaph" (suite), 91, 93–95, 167–68
Ericson, Rolf, 92, 98, 100, 102
Erskine, Peter, 165
Ertegun, Nesuhi, 59, 87
Ervin, Booker, 57–60, 63–65, 67–69, 71–76, 80–86, 88–90, 101–3, 132, 135–36
"E.S.P.," 137. *See also* "Extra-Sensory Perception"
"Eulogy for Rudy Williams," 31, 94
Evans, Bill, 46, 49–50, 109
Evans, Gil, 23, 30, 39, 73, 100, 148
Evans, Sue, 172
"Everything But You" (Ellington), 12
"Everything Happens to Me" (Dennis/ Adair), 116
"Exactly Like You" (Fields/McHugh), 71

Excelsior Records, 10
"Extra-Sensory Perception" (a.k.a.
  "E.S.P."), 19, 137

"Fables of Faubus" (a.k.a. "Original
  Faubus Fables," "New Fables"), 47,
  64–66, 76, 78, 90, 107, 113–16, 119,
  121, 131–32, 137, 142, 146, 151,
  157–58
*Fables of Faubus: Live at Historic Slug's,
  Vol. 2*, 131
Faddis, Jon, 136, 138–39, 142–43, 166
Fantasy Records, 18, 21, 23–24
"Far Wells, Mill Valley," 7, 68, 158
"Farewell Blues" (a.k.a. "Farewell,
  Farwell"), 158
"Farewell, Farwell" (a.k.a. "Farewell
  Blues"), 7, 158–59, 163
Farlow, Tal, 16–17
Farmer, Art, 46
Farrell, Joe, 71
Faubus, Orval, 65
Faulise, Paul, 92, 168
Feather, Leonard, 56
Fentone Records, 13–14
"Fifty-First Street Blues," 50, 79. *See
  also* "MDM"
"52nd Street Theme" (Monk), 23, 95
Figueroa, Sammy, 160
Fischer, Bobby, 172
Fitzgerald, Ella, 155
Five Spot (club), 56
"Flamingo" (Anderson/Grouya), 49
Flanagan, Tommy, 81–84
"Flowers for a Lady" (Adams), 141
"Foggy Day, A" (Gershwin), 37, 39,
  42–43, 54
"Folk Forms No., 1," 75–76, 84, 97
Fontana Records, 122
"For Harry Carney" (Johnson), 147–48
Ford, Ricky, 150–51, 153–60,
  162–63, 166
Formanek, Mike, 170
Fortune, Sonny, 153, 155
Foster, John, 136–39
"Four Hands" (Mingus/LaPorta), 32,
  34, 162

4 Star Records, 12
4 Trombones (Johnson/Winding/Green/
  Dennis), 24
Fowler, Bernard, 173
"Frankie and Johnny" (TV ballet),
  67, 69
"Free Cell Block F, 'Tis Nazi USA"
  (a.k.a. "Jive Five, Floor Four"), 3,
  146–47, 149, 174
*Free Jazz: A Collective Improvisation by
  the Ornette Coleman Double Quartet*
  (Coleman), 77, 118
Free-Jazz Moods (bootleg), 156–58.
  See also *Lionel Hampton Presents
  Charles Mingus*
"Freedom," 92–93, 103, 169–70, 173
Freeman, Russ, 14
Frisell, Bill, 171–73

Gadd, Steve, 160–61
Galás, Diamanda, 171, 173
Galbraith, Barry, 46
Garofalo, James, 34
Gayle, Herb, 14
George, Karl, 12
Gershwin, George, 21, 33, 37, 42,
  117, 121
Gershwin, Ira, 57
"Getting Together," 31
Getz, Jane, 121–22
Getz, Stan, 8, 28
"GG Train" (a.k.a. "Double G Train"),
  64, 66
"Ghost of a Chance" (Young), 125
Gillespie, Dizzy, 9, 13, 17–18, 21–25,
  33, 47, 55, 81, 83, 109–10, 127–28,
  136, 138–39, 143
Gilmore, John, 129
"Girl of My Dreams" (Clapp/Mingus),
  63–64, 66
Gitler, Ira, 25
Giuffre, Jimmy, 45–46
Givens, Spaulding, 9–10, 18–20, 24–26
"God Must Be a Boogie Man"
  (Mitchell), 166
"God's Portrait," 14. *See also* "Portrait"
"Godchild" (Wallington), 16

"Golden Sword, The" (Wilson), 13
Golson, Benny, 67
Gomez, Eddie, 160–63, 165
Gonzalez, Daniel, 150
"Goodbye Porkpie Hat" (a.k.a. "Theme for Lester Young"), 63–65, 101, 149, 154, 166–67, 173–74; lyrics added by Joni Mitchell, 166; mistitling of "So Long Eric," 116
Goodman, Benny, 13, 157
Gordon, Dexter, 6, 143
Gordon, Honey, 21, 67, 69, 136–39, 141
Gordon, Nat, 69
Gordons, The, 21
Granz, Norman, 19
Gravity (band), 141
Great Concert of Charles Mingus, The, 120
Green, Bennie, 24
Green, Urbie, 168
Green Chimneys (Summers), 173
"Greensleeves" (traditional), 132
Greer, Sonny, 43
"Gregarian Chant," 31
Grimes, Henry, 90
Grouya, Ted, 49
Guaraldi, Vince, 86, 89
"Gunslinging Bird" (a.k.a. "If Charlie Parker Were a Gunslinger, There'd Be a Whole Lot of Dead Copycats"), 67–68, 172
Gunslinging Bird (Mingus Big Band), 170

Haden, Charlie, 166–67
Hadi, Shafi (Curtis Porter), 43–44, 47–50, 54–57, 63, 65, 87–89
Hafer, Dick, 98–102
Haig, The (club), 16
"Haitian Fight Song" (a.k.a. "II B.S."), 2, 38, 43–44, 59–60, 85, 101
"Haitian Fight Song Montage," 172
"Half-Mast Inhibition," 7, 73
Hall, Jim, 167
"Hallelujah" (a.k.a. "Jubilee") (Youmans), 22
Hamilton, Chico, 6–7

Hammer, Bob, 54–55, 92, 94, 101
Hammer, Jan, 165
Hammond, Doug, 141
"Hamp's New Blues" (Hawes), 47
Hampton, Lionel, 2, 12–13, 15, 26, 72, 87, 135, 155–59, 162–63
Hampton, Ronald, 140–42, 146
Hampton, Slide, 160, 162
Hancock, Herbie, 165
Handy, Craig, 170, 174
Handy, John, 56–60, 63–66, 68–69, 87, 121, 123–24, 126, 142–43, 166, 168
Hanna, (Sir) Roland, 67–69, 71–72, 134, 166, 168–69
Hardman, Bill, 54, 131–32
Harry, Deborah, 174
Hawes, Hampton, 47
Hawkins, Coleman, 19, 32, 83, 104
"He's Gone," 14–15
Hefti, Neal, 81
Henderson, Fletcher, 81
Henderson, Joe, 109, 142, 144
Hendrix, Jimi, 173
Hentoff, Nat, 54, 102, 146–48
Herman, Woody, 8, 16, 26, 132
Hicks, John, 168, 170
Hill, Teddy, 81
Hillyer, Lonnie, 78, 80, 82–84, 92, 123–27, 129, 134, 136–39, 167
Hines, Earl "Fatha," 15
Hinton, Milt, 56, 92, 136, 139, 167
His Final Work (bootleg), 156. See also *Lionel Hampton Presents Charles Mingus*
Hitchcock, Ken, 160
Hite, Les, 9
"Hobo Ho," 135
Hodges, Johnny, 9, 12, 69, 73, 98
"Hog Callin' Blues," 85, 90
Holiday, Billie, 8, 15, 26, 30, 72, 155
Holiday, Shirley, 15
Homzy, Andrew, 3, 12, 146, 167–69
"Honey, Take a Chance On Me," 12. See also "Baby, Take a Chance With Me"
Hooray for Charles Mingus (bootleg), 90–91

"Hora Decubitus" (a.k.a. "E's Flat, Ah's Flat Too"), 44, 56, 61, 101, 103, 175
Horowitz, Vladimir, 104
"Hot House" (Dameron), 22, 33
"How High the Moon" (Hamilton/ Lewis), 9
"Hucklebuck, The" (Alfred/Gibson), 24
Hughes, Langston, 53, 56, 66

I Am Three (Mingus Dynasty/Mingus Big Band/Charles Mingus Orchestra), 174–75
"I Can't Get Started" (Duke/Gershwin), 28, 47, 57–58, 94, 104, 125, 131, 168
"I Get A Kick Out of You" (Porter), 16
"I Got Rhythm" (Gershwin), 33
"I Left My Heart in San Francisco" (Cory/Cross), 133
"I of Hurricane Sue, The," 135–36, 138–39
"I X Love," 101–2. See also "Nouroog"
"Idaho" (Stone), 34, 162
"If I Love Again" (Murray/Oakland), 23
"If I Should Lose You" (Robin/ Rainger), 131
"II B.S.," 101. See also "Haitian Fight Song"
"I'll Remember April" (DePaul/ Johnston/Raye), 24–25, 29, 38–39, 75
"I'm An Old Cowhand" (Mercer), 38
"I'm Beginning to See the Light" (Gershwin), 117
"I'm Getting Sentimental Over You" (Bassman/Washington), 104
Impulse Records, 97, 101, 104
"In a Mellotone" (Ellington), 95
"In a Sentimental Mood" (Ellington), 124, 131–32
In Concert (bootleg), 90
"Indiana" (Hanley/McDonald), 9
Ink Spots, The, 21
"Inspiration," 14, 19, 25. See also "Portrait"
"Interlude (The Underdog Rising)," 170
Introducing Paul Bley (Bley), 27
Intrusions. See Jazzical Moods
"Invisible Lady," 87–88
Iridium (club), 170

"Isfahan" (Ellington/Strayhorn), 148
"It Ain't Necessarily So" (Gershwin), 119, 121
"It Might As Well Be Spring" (Rodgers/ Hammerstein), 156–57
"I've Got It Bad (And That Ain't Good)" (Ellington), 123
"I've Lost My Love," 19

"Jack the Bear" (Ellington), 7
"Jack the Fieldstalker" (Pettiford), 28
Jackson, Quentin "Butter," 44, 92, 98–100
Jacquet, Illlinois, 135, 143
Jarrett, Keith, 28
Jazz Artists Guild, 81
Jazz Composers Workshop, 3, 27, 29
Jazz Composers Workshop, 30–33
Jazz Crusaders, 85
Jazz Experiments of Charles Mingus, The. See Jazzical Moods
Jazz Messengers (band), 27, 34, 41, 131
Jazz Passengers (band), 174
Jazz Portraits (a.k.a. Wonderland, Mingus in Wonderland), 57, 60, 67, 69
Jazz Workshop (label), 125–26
Jazz Workshop (organization), 3, 12, 30, 34, 80, 94, 145, 172
Jazz Workshop (venue), 121–22
Jazzical Moods, Volumes 1 and 2 (a.k.a. Intrusions, The Jazz Experiments of Charles Mingus), 32–33, 157, 162
"Jeepers Creepers" (Mercer/Warren), 19
Jeffrey, Paul, 144, 150–51, 156, 159–60
"Jelly Roll" (a.k.a. "My Jelly Roll Soul," "Jelly Roll Jellies," "Mr. Jelly Roll"), 3, 60, 63–64, 66, 69
"Jet" (Benjamin/Revel/Weiss), 21
Joe's Pub (club), 170
John, Dr., 171, 173
Johnson, Bunk, 93, 169
Johnson, Howard, 126–27, 136, 138–39, 141
Johnson, J.J., 18, 24–25, 45, 83
Johnson, James P., 149
Johnson, Osie, 56
Johnson, Reggie, 168

Johnson, Sy, 134, 137–39, 141, 147, 174
Jones, Bobby, 132, 134, 136–39
Jones, Elvin, 21
Jones, Hank, 21, 29
Jones, Jo, 81–82
Jones, Quincy, 29
Jones, Thad, 18, 21, 29, 33, 94
Jones, Willie, 34–37, 41
Jordan, Clifford, 107–22, 166
Josie Records, 47
"Joy Spring" (Brown), 162
"Jubilee" (a.k.a. "Hallelujah")
   (Youmans), 22
"Jump Monk," 3, 34–35, 39, 42, 56,
   136–37, 172
"Jumpin' Punkins" (Ellington), 7
"Just For Laughs" (a.k.a. "Just For
   Laughs, Saps," "Remember
   Rockefeller at Attica"), 146, 158
"Just Squeeze Me" (Ellington), 93

"Kai's Day" (Winding), 25
Kenton, Stan, 8, 16, 169
Keppard, Freddie, 9
Keyes, Bobby, 173
Kikoski, Dave, 170
"King Fish," 91. See also "Monk, Bunk
   and Vice Versa"
King Records, 125
Kinks, The (rock band), 171
Kirk (Rahsaan) Roland, 84–90, 104,
   137, 139, 142–43
Kisor, Ryan, 170
Kleps, Dale, 168
Knepper, Jimmy, 14, 18, 43–44, 46–50,
   54–56, 59, 64, 66, 68–69, 72, 80–90,
   101–2, 150–51, 160, 162–63, 166–67
"Ko-Ko" (Parker), 132
Konitz, Lee, 18–19, 136–39, 160,
   162–63
Kosek, Kenny, 172
Koutzen, George, 19
Kozlov, Boris, 170, 174
Kronos String Quartet, 174
Krupa, Gene, 81

Lacy, Ku-umba Frank, 170, 174
Lacy, Steve, 30

"Lady Bird" (Dameron), 38
Lambert, Dave, Singers, 23
Laneri, Roberto, 151
LaPorta, John, 27, 30–34, 46
Last Dance of Mr. X, The
   (Summers), 173
Last Date (Dolphy), 122
Lateef, Yusef, 71–72, 78, 90
"Laura" (Mercer/Raksin), 47
Lawson, Hugh, 166
Leavell, Chuck, 173
Lee, Peggy, 155
Legge, Wade, 43–45, 87–89
Lennie's-on-the-Turnpike (club), 129
Let My Children Hear Music, 104,
   133–36
"Level Seven" (Cirillo), 32
Levitt, Al, 19
Levy, Howard, 171–72
Lewis, John, 24–26, 30, 45
Lewis, Victor, 168
Lighthouse, The (club), 16
"Like Someone in Love" (Burke/Van
   Heusen), 28
Lincoln, Abbey, 82
Lincoln Center (venue), 136
Lincoln Center Jazz Orchestra
   (band), 174
Lionel Hampton Presents Charles
   Mingus, 155–58
Lionel's Sessions (bootleg), 156. See also
   Lionel Hampton Presents Charles
   Mingus
Liston, Melba, 92–93
Little, Booker, 81
Little Richard, 11
"Little Royal Suite," 138
Live at Birdland, 1962 (bootleg), 90–91
Live at the Village Vanguard (Mingus
   Dynasty), 167
Live in Copenhagen: The Complete
   Concert (bootleg), 114
Live in Montreux (Mingus
   Dynasty), 167
Live in Time (Mingus Big Band), 170
"Lock 'Em Up (Hellview of Bellevue),"
   80, 84
"London Bridge" (traditional), 115

"Lonesome Woman Blues" (Griffin), 10
Los Angeles Junior Philharmonic, 5
"Los Mariachis," 48
"Love Chant," 39, 42
"Love is a Dangerous Necessity," 133
"Love Supreme, A" (Coltrane), 143
"Low and Behold" (Pettiford), 29
Lucas, Gary, 171–72
"Lullaby of Birdland" (Shearing), 22
Lunceford, Jimmie, 11
"Lush Life" (Ellington/Strayhorn),
    147, 149
"Lyon's Roar," 14
Lyons, Jimmy, 123

Macero, Teo, 26–28, 30–34, 46,
    133–34, 136, 150
Machito, 47
Mahavishnu Orchestra (band), 165
"Main Score" (*Epitaph*), 168, 170
"Main Stem" (Ellington), 50, 79–80. *See
    also* "MDM"
"Make Believe," 3, 12, 20
Malta, Yoshiaki, 160
Maltoni, Quarto, 151–52
"Man Who Never Sleeps, The," 132
Mangione, Chuck, 27
Mantilla, Ray, 150, 160
Mariano, Charlie, 92, 95–96,
    98–100, 102
Mark-Almond, 140
Marsalis, Wynton, 27, 168, 174
Massey Hall, 21–23, 35, 75
Matt, Peter, 156–58
Max's Kansas City (club), 146–47
McCracken, Charles, 134
McCusick, Hal, 46
McLaughlin, John, 165
McLean, Jackie, 41–44, 59–60
McLean, John, 41
McPherson, Charles, 78–84, 90–94,
    123–29, 131–32, 134–40, 142–43,
    163, 167
McRae, Carmen, 155
"MDM (Monk, Duke and Me)," 3, 50,
    79, 84, 174. *See also* "Fifty-First
    Street Blues," "Main Stem,"
    "Straight, No Chaser"

"Me and You," 82, 84
Me, Myself an Eye, 158, 160–62
"Meditation on Inner Peace," 126
"Meditations" (a.k.a. "Meditations on
    Integration," "Meditation (on a Pair
    of Wire Cutters)," "Praying with
    Eric"), 105, 107–8, 113–15, 118–19,
    121–24, 171–72
"Meditations for Moses," 105
Meditations on Integration
    (bootleg), 113
Mehegan, John, 20
"Melody from the Drums," 78, 84
*Memoirs of a Half-Schitt-Colored
    Nigger*, 5. See also *Beneath the
    Underdog*
"Memories of You" (Blake/Razaf),
    49, 104
Metronome magazine, 29
Michaels, Lloyd, 136, 139
Mingus (Candid album), 79–80
Mingus (film), 128–29
Mingus (Mitchell), 166
Mingus, Celia Gemanis (wife), 15,
    17–18, 47
Mingus, Charles, Jr.: blues influences, 2,
    34, 53, 58–59, 75, 84; as
    businessman, 3; classical influences, 6,
    8, 14, 37, 45–47; compositional style,
    3, 10, 25, 31, 58, 68, 73, 78–79, 91,
    102; death, 2, 7, 165–66;
    development as bassist, 6–7, 10–11,
    19, 29, 35–36, 60, 72; Ellington
    influence, 2–3, 65, 71, 73, 98; gospel
    and church influences, 2, 5, 58–59, 64,
    84, 86, 102; in high school, 6–7;
    interest in Hinduism, 7; Latin
    influences, 10, 13, 17, 150; Lou
    Gehrig's disease (ALS), 2, 149, 155,
    158; piano playing, 33–34, 84–85,
    89–90, 104–5, 127, 152
Mingus, Charles, Sr. (father), 5–6
Mingus, Harriet (mother), 5
Mingus, Jeanne Gross (wife), 9
Mingus, Mamie (stepmother), 5
Mingus, Sue Graham Ungaro (wife),
    116, 125–26, 135, 145, 149, 165–66,
    168, 170–71, 174–75

Mingus, Vivian (sister), 5
Mingus, Yanine (daughter), 15
Mingus Ah Um, 54, 56, 60, 63–67,
    69–70, 97
Mingus at Antibes, 73–75
Mingus at Carnegie Hall, 142–43
Mingus at Monterey, 123–26
Mingus at the Bohemia, 34–37
Mingus Big Band (ghost band), 133,
    170–71, 174–75
"Mingus Blues," 138
Mingus Dynasty, 66–70, 80, 157
Mingus Dynasty (ghost band), 69,
    166–67, 170–71, 174–75
"Mingus Fingers," 10, 13, 26, 72
"Mingus Fingus No., 2," 72
Mingus in Amsterdam, 1964
    (bootleg), 109
Mingus in Wonderland. See *Jazz
    Portraits*
*Mingus, Mingus, Mingus, Mingus,
    Mingus*, 101–4, 132
Mingus Moves, 36, 140–42
Mingus Plays Piano, 104–5, 134
Mingus Revisited. See *Pre-Bird*
Mingus x 5. See *Mingus, Mingus,
    Mingus, Mingus, Mingus*
Mingus' Sounds of Love (Mingus
    Dynasty), 167
"Minor Intrusions," 34
"Miss Blues," 26
Mitchell, Joni, 165–66
Mitchell, Oradell, 10
Mitterhoff, Barry, 172
Mixon, Danny, 151–52
"Moanin'," 2–3, 60
Modern Jazz Concert (Schuller et al.), 46
Modern Jazz Quartet, 24, 26
*Modern Jazz Symposium of Music
    and Poetry, A*, 43, 53–55, 65,
    101, 131
Moe, Sharon, 136
Money Jungle (Ellington/Mingus/
    Roach), 91
"Monk, Bunk and Vice Versa" (a.k.a.
    "Monk, Funk and Vice Versa,"
    "King Fish," Osmotin'"), 3,
    90–91, 169

Monk, Thelonious, 3, 19, 23, 34, 49–50,
    60, 79, 86, 93, 104, 124, 169,
    171, 173
"Montage," 20
Monterey Jazz Festival, 123, 126, 134
Monterose, J.R., 41–44
Montreux International Jazz
    Festival, 148
"Mood Indigo" (Bigard/Ellington/
    Mills), 69, 101–2, 124, 132
"Moods in Mambo," 169
Moody, James, 134–36, 139
"Moonboy," 91. *See also* "Please Don't
    Come Back from the Moon"
Moore, Brew, 8
Moore, Melvin, 123
More Than a Fake Book (Mingus/
    Homzy), 4, 167
Morel, Ysabel, 48
Morgan, Lee, 27
Morrison, Peck, 81–82
Morton, Ferdinand "Jelly Roll," 3, 60,
    87, 169
Mosaic Records, 84
Mosley, Robert, 10–11
"Move" (Best), 16, 24
Move! (Norvo), 16
"Moves" (Hammond), 141
"Mr. Jelly Roll," 166. *See also*
    "Jelly Roll"
Mraz, George, 154, 160–62
Mucci, Louis, 46
Mulligan, Gerry, 30, 136–39, 142, 149,
    156–58, 165
Murray, Sunny, 131
Music for Brass (Schuller), 45–46
"Music for 'Todo Modo'," 150–52, 174
*Music Written for Monterey, 1965, Not
    Heard . . . Played in its Entirety at
    UCLA, Volumes 1 and 2*, 125–26,
    134, 175
My Favorite Quintet, 125–26
My Flame Burns Blue (Costello), 175
"My Jelly Roll Soul" (a.k.a. "Jelly
    Roll," "Jelly Roll Jellies," "Mr. Jelly
    Roll"), 59–60, 66, 167, 169
"My Search" (a.k.a. "The Search"),
    91, 94

"Myself, When I Am Real" (a.k.a.
  "Adagio Ma Non Troppo"), 104,
  134, 174
"Mysterious Blues," 81, 84
Mysterious Blues, 83–84

Navarro, Fats, 13, 127
Neloms, Bob, 150–51, 153–58, 160, 162
Nessa, Chuck, 15
"New Fables," 121. *See also* "Fables of
  Faubus"
New Jazz Conceptions (Evans), 49
"New Now Know How," 68–69, 80
New Tijuana Moods, 47. See also
  Tijuana Moods
"New York Sketchbook" (a.k.a.
  "Tourist in Manhattan"), 43, 54
"Newcomer" (Pullen), 141
Newport Jazz Festival, 43, 54, 91
Newport Rebel Festival, 81
Newport Rebels (various artists), 81–83
*Next Generation Performs New Charles
  Mingus Compositions* (Mingus
  Dynasty), 167
Nichols, Rudy, 30–32
Nick's (club), 34
Nielsen, Jon, 15, 17
Night in Birdland, Live Volume, 2, A
  (bootleg), 91
"Night in Tunisia, A" (Gillespie), 22, 110
Nimitz, Jack, 123
"No Private Income Blues," 58
"Nobody Knows (the Bradley I
  Know)," 155
"Nobody Knows the Trouble I've Seen"
  (traditional), 155
"Noddin' Ya Head Blues," 154
Nonagon Art Center, 57–58, 60, 67
"Noon Night," 170
Norvo, Red, 15–18, 24
"Nostalgia in Times Square" (a.k.a.
  "Strollin'"), 57, 69
Nostalgia in Times Square (Mingus Big
  Band), 170
"Nouroog," 54–55, 65, 101–2, 170
Novello, John, 173–74
"Now's the Time" (Parker), 24

"Ode to Bird and Dizzy," 127
"Oh Lord, Don't Let Them Drop That
  Atomic Bomb On Me," 86, 90, 173
"Oh Susanna" (Foster), 119
Oh Yeah, 45, 84–87, 104
Ohmori, Akira, 160, 163
"'Old' Blues for Walt's Torin," 87–89
Old Fellow Palaet's (Danish venue), 114
"Old Gray Mare, The" (traditional),
  116, 119, 121
"Old Portrait," 105, 125. *See also*
  "Portrait"
Oliver, Sy, 28
"On Green Mountain" (Shapero), 46
"Once Upon a Time There Was a
  Holding Corporation Called Old
  America," 127–28, 134. *See also* "The
  Shoes of the Fisherman's Wife Are
  Some Jive-Ass Slippers"
Onttonen, Esa, 90
"Ool-Ya-Koo" (Gillespie), 139
"O.P.," 3, 91, 132, 169
"Open Letter to Duke," 3, 53–54,
  63–65, 172–73
"Opus 1" (Bley), 28
"Opus 3," 140–41, 174
"Opus 4" (a.k.a. "No Name"), 140–41
O'Quinn, Keith, 160
"Orange Was the Color of Her Dress,
  Then Blue Silk" (a.k.a. ". . . Then Silk
  Blue"), 2, 68, 110–12, 114, 118, 120,
  124, 131–32, 148, 174
"Orange Was the Color of Her Dress,
  Then Silk Blues" (mistitling of "Song
  With Orange"), 105
Original Dixieland Jazz Band, 9
"Original Faubus Fables," 76–77, 84.
  See also "Fables of Faubus"
"Ornithology" (Parker), 9
Ory, Edward "Kid," 8
Oscar Pettiford Sextet (Pettiford), 28–29
"Osmotin'," 93, 169. *See also* "Monk,
  Bunk and Vice Versa"
Out to Lunch (Dolphy), 122
"Ow!" (Gillespie/Parker), 25, 109, 120;
  mistitling of "Parkeriana," 110, 112
Owens, Jimmy, 126–28

Paris, Jackie, 18–20, 139, 147

"Paris in Blue," 20, 174

Parker, Charlie ("Bird," "Yardbird"), 3,
    8–9, 15, 21–24, 26, 29, 33–34, 44, 55,
    65, 71, 78–80, 83, 109–10, 120, 124,
    127, 131, 133, 143, 154, 162; billed
    as "Charlie Chan," 22

"Parkeriana" (a.k.a. "Dedication to a
    Genius"), 3, 44, 109–12, 120

"Parker's Mood" (Parker), 44

Parlan, Horace, 33, 54–56, 59–60, 63,
    65–66, 115

Partch, Harry, 171–72

"Passions of a Man," 87, 89

"Passions of a Woman Loved," 45, 87,
    89–90

Pastorius, Jaco, 165–66

Patchen, Kenneth, 79

Paul, Gene, 117

"Pedal Point Blues," 63–64, 66, 174

Pége, Aladar, 166–67

"Peggy's Blue Skylight," 78, 87, 89–90,
    93, 113, 117–18, 129, 131, 133, 142,
    156, 167, 169, 174

Peggy's Blue Skylight (Summers),
    173–74

"Pendulum at Falcon's Lair, The"
    (Pettiford), 28

"Pennies from Heaven" (Burke/
    Johnston), 14

Penque, Romeo, 92, 94

Pepper, Art, 14

"Percussion Discussion" (Mingus/
    Roach), 35–36, 168

"Perdido" (Tizol), 22, 31, 75, 142–43

Period label, 32

Perkins, Walter, 101–2

Perri, Richie, 136, 138

Peterson, Oscar, 27

Pettiford, Oscar, 3, 15, 18, 21, 28–29,
    34, 126–27, 169

Pettis, Everett, 10–11

Philharmonic Hall (venue), 136

Piana, Dino, 151

"Pink Topsy," 26

Pinkerton, Phyllis, 19

"Pipe Dream," 11–12. See also "Weird
    Nightmare"

"Pithecanthropus Erectus," 42, 50, 78,
    93, 132–33, 141, 167–68, 173

Pithecanthropus Erectus, 37, 39, 41–43,
    49, 54

"Please Don't Come Back from the
    Moon" (a.k.a. "Moonboy"), 91,
    94–95, 169

Police, The (rock band), 173

Pollock, Edmund, Dr., 98–99

Polygram Records, 56

Porter, Cole, 33

Porter, Curtis, 43. See also Hadi, Shafi

Porter, Roy, 10

"Portrait" (a.k.a. "God's Portrait,"
    "Inspiration," "Old Portrait"), 2,
    14–15, 19–20, 78, 94, 105, 129, 139

"Portrait of Bud Powell, A"
    (Waldron), 39

"Portrait of Jackie," 43

Powell, Bud, 15, 18–19, 21–23, 75, 83,
    87, 104

Pozo, Chano, 47

"Prayer for Passive Resistance,"
    71–72, 74

"Praying with Eric," 108.
    See also "Meditations"

Pre-Bird (a.k.a. Mingus Revisited), 26,
    61, 71–73, 103

"Prelude in C# Minor"
    (Rachmaninoff), 37

Prestige Records, 25, 82, 120, 125, 133

Preston, Eddie, 101, 132, 136, 138–39

Previte, Bobby, 171–72

Priester, Julian, 81

Priestley, Brian, 2, 93, 129, 170

"Prisoner of Love" (Columbo/Gaskill/
    Robin), 31

Public Enemy (rap group), 171

Pullen, Don, 140–43, 145–46, 148–49,
    151, 166

"Purple Heart," 30, 172

Purpura, Craig, 160

"Pussy Cat Dues," 63–64, 66

"Put Me In That Dungeon," 69

Q-Tip, 174

Que Viva Mingus (Mingus Big
    Band), 170

Quebec, Ike, 30
Quine, Robert, 171, 173
Quintet of the Year: Jazz at Massey Hall
(Mingus/Parker/Gillespie/Powell/
Roach), 22

"R&R," 82–84
Rabinowitz, Michael, 168–69
Ramirez, Alfredo, 150
Raph, Alan, 134
Ray, Floyd, 7
"Ray's Idea" (Brown), 131
Reese, Lloyd, 6, 8
"Reets and I" (Harris), 90
Reichman, Thomas, 128–29
Reid, Vernon, 171
Reincarnation (Mingus Dynasty), 167
"Reincarnation of a Lovebird," 3, 44,
78, 82, 84, 133, 172–74
Reincarnation of a Lovebird
(Candid), 82
Reincarnation of a Lovebird
(Prestige), 133
Reinhardt, Django, 154
"Remember Rockefeller at Attica"
(a.k.a. "Just For Laughs," "Just For
Laughs, Saps"), 146, 158, 174
Rene, Leon and Otis, 10
"Revelations, First Movement," 46–47
Revenge!, 116–17, 120
Revenge Records, 116
Rey, Alvino, 8
"Rhapsody in Blue" (Gershwin), 21
Rheinschagen, Herman, 7
Ribot, Marc, 171
Richards, Emil, 165
Richards, Keith, 171, 173
Richardson, Jerome, 67, 92–93, 95,
98–103, 168, 170
Richmond, Dannie, 28, 43, 47–49,
54–60, 63–66, 68–69, 71–81, 83–84,
86–92, 94, 96, 98–101, 107, 109–21,
123–27, 129, 131–33, 140–45, 147,
149–51, 153–54, 156–58, 160–61,
165–67
Richmond, Mike, 166–67
*Right Now: Live at the Jazz
Workshop*, 121

Riverside Records, 49
Roach, Max, 18, 20–24, 35–39, 81–82,
85, 91, 168
Robertson, Robbie, 171–72
Rockefeller, Nelson, 145
Rodia, Simon, 1
Roland, Gene, 92, 169
"Roland Kirk's Message," 104
Rolling Stones, The (rock band), 158,
171, 173
Rollins, Henry, 171–72
Rollins, Sonny, 41, 65, 113, 143
"Rose Geranium" (Cirillo), 32
Rosenberg, Roger, 168, 170
Ross, Margaret, 46
Rota, Nino, 171
Rowles, Jimmy, 16, 154–55
Royal, Ernie, 26, 92, 94, 167
Royce Hall (venue), 126
Russell, George, 46, 49

"'S Wonderful" (Gershwin), 33
Sabatelli, Pasquale, 151
Salle Wagram (French venue), 116, 120
"Salt Peanuts" (Gillespie), 22, 44
Sanders, Pharoah, 141
"Santa Claus is Coming to Town"
(Coots/Gillespie), 28
Santoro, Gene, 2
Savoy Records, 30–31
"Say It Isn't So" (Berlin), 10, 14
"Scenes in the City" (Mingus/Elders/
Hughes) (a.k.a. "A Colloquial
Dream"), 53–54
Scholtes, Gene, 150
Schuller, Ed, 168
Schuller, Gunther, 45–46, 73, 91,
168–70
Scofield, John, 153, 155
Scott, Hazel, 18
Scott, Tony, 49
"Search, The," 91. *See also* "My
Search"
"Secret Love" (Webster/Fain), 129
Selby, Hubert, Jr., 171, 173
"Self Portrait/Chill of Death," 169
"Self-Portrait in Three Colors," 64–65,
78, 172, 174

"September in the Rain" (Dubin/ Warren), 36

"Septemberly," 36–37

"Serenade in Blue" (Gordon/Warren), 35

Severinsen, Doc, 28

Shadows (Cassavetes film), 57–58, 65, 67, 69

Shapero, Harold, 46

Shaughnessy, Ed, 28

"Shave and a Haircut" (traditional), 158

Shaw, Clarence, 47–50, 54–55

"She's Funny That Way" (Whiting, Moret), 125, 132

"She's Just Miss Popular Hybrid," 104

Shepherd, Jean, 45

Shepp, Archie, 139

"Shoes of the Fisherman's Wife Are Some Jive-Ass Slippers, The" (a.k.a. "Once Upon a Time There Was a Holding Corporation Called Old America"), 78, 127, 132, 134, 163, 173

"Shortenin' Bread" (traditional), 151

Shorter, Wayne, 27, 165

Showplace (club), 73, 78

"Shuffle Bass Boogie," 3, 11, 64, 167

Silver, Horace, 28, 34

Simon, Paul, 160

Sims, Zoot, 8, 28, 92, 95

Sipiagin, Alex, 174

"Sketch Two," 167

Sketches of Spain (Davis/Evans), 73

Slagle, Steve, 170

"Sleepy Lagoon" (Coates/Lawrence), 88

"Slippers," 54–55, 65

"Slop," 2–3, 21, 67, 69, 157

Slug's (club), 131

Smith, Marvin "Smitty," 170

Smith, Mauricio, 150

Smith, Warren, 92, 95

"Smog L.A." (Cirillo), 32

"Smooch," 11. *See also* "Weird Nightmare"

Smulyan, Gary, 168

"So Long Eric," 107–8, 110–12, 120, 125, 131–32, 157–58; mistitled as "Goodbye Porkpie Hat," 116–17

"Solitude" (Ellington), 58, 98

Soloff, Lew, 168, 170

"Sombre Intrusion" (Jones), 29

Something Like a Bird, 158, 162–63

"Something Like a Bird" (a.k.a. "Something From the Past"), 3, 159–60, 162–63

Sommer, Teddy, 46

"Song With Orange," 67–70, 105, 112, 174

"Song With Orange In It, A" (TV show), 67–68

"Sophisticated Lady" (Ellington), 120, 124, 132

"Soul, The," 169

Spann, Les, 92, 94

Speigner, Louis, 12

"Split Kick" (Silver), 28

"Spontaneous Combustion" (Bley/ Mingus/Blakey), 27–28

"Spur of the Moment" (Parlan), 33

"Stardust" (Carmichael), 24

Stars of Swing (group), 10

"Started Melody," 168

Statements (bootleg), 132

Steely Dan, 160

Stewart, Bob, 136, 172

Stewart, Melvin, 53–54

Stewart, Slam, 87

"Stockholm Sweetnin'" (Jones), 29

"Stormy Weather" (Arlen/Koehler), 33, 80, 84

"Story of Love," 13–14, 25, 73

"Straight, No Chaser" (Monk), 50, 79, 169. *See also* "MDM," "Monk, Bunk and Vice Versa"

Strayhorn, Billy, 12, 21, 71, 175

Strings and Keys, 18–19

Strings and Keys (group), 9

"Strollin'" (a.k.a. "Nostalgia in Times Square"), 57, 67, 69, 138–39

Stubblefield, John, 170, 174–75

Sue Mingus Music (label), 125, 174–75

"Sue's Changes," 47, 102, 132, 146, 148–49, 166

"Summertime" (Gershwin), 47

Summers, Andy, 173–74
Sun Ra, 129
Sunenblick, Robert, 15
Supersax (band), 162
"Sure Thing" (Powell), 22
"Suspensions" (Giuffre), 46
"Sweet Georgia Brown" (Bernie/
    Pinkard/Casey), 9
"Sweet Sucker Dance" (Mingus/
    Mitchell), 166–67
"Swingin' An Echo," 10

Tabackin, Lew, 94
"Take the 'A' Train" (Ellington/
    Strayhorn), 11, 66, 71, 90, 111–12,
    124, 129, 131–32, 146, 149
Tank, John, 160
Tate, Grady, 92
Tatum, Art, 8–9, 89, 104, 110, 115,
    128, 137, 143, 152
"Taurus in the Arena of Life" (a.k.a.
    "Number One Grandson"), 135,
    137–39
Taylor, Art, 23–25
Taylor, Billy, 15, 17, 23
Taylor, Cecil, 43, 143, 149
Taylor, David, 168
Taylor, Farwell, 7, 12, 19, 68, 73, 158
Taylor, Faye, 7
Taylor, Sam "The Man," 56
"Tea For Two" (Youmans), 24, 31, 36,
    47, 93, 169
Teagarden, Jack, 132
"Teapot" (a.k.a. "Walkin'") (Bley), 28
"Tenderly" (Shavers), 36
"Tensions," 59–60, 174
Terry, Clark, 72–73, 92–93, 95, 167
"Testament" (Hughes/Feather), 56
"Texas Hop, The" (Mingus/Griffin), 10
Thad Jones (Jones), 29
Theatre de Champs-Elysées (French
    venue), 120
Theatre National Populaire du Palais de
    Chaillot (French venue), 132
"Theme, The" (composer unknown), 28
"Theme for Lester Young," 101, 103.
    See also "Goodbye Porkpie Hat"

"These Foolish Things"
    (Strachey/Link), 13
"They Trespass the Land of the Sacred
    Sioux," 126, 128
"Things Ain't What They Used To Be"
    (Ellington), 67–68
Third Stream movement, 13, 24, 27, 30,
    33–34, 45–47, 49, 140, 168–69
"This Masquerade" (Benson), 29
"This Subdues My Passion," 12
"This Time the Dream's On Me" (Arlen/
    Mercer), 28
Thompson, Eli "Lucky," 10–11
Thompson, Warren, 14
Threadgill, Henry, 171
"Three or Four Shades of Blues,"
    154–55
Three or Four Shades of Blues,
    153–55
"Three Worlds of Drums" (a.k.a. "Two
    Worlds of Drums"), 158–61
"Thrice Upon a Theme," 33
Thumm, Francis, 171
Thurlow, Janet, 26–27
"Tijuana Gift Shop," 48
Tijuana Moods (a.k.a. New Tijuana
    Moods), 47–49, 55, 66, 169
"Tijuana Table Dance," 90. See also
    "Ysabel's Table Dance"
Time Spot Café (club), 170
Timmons, Bobby, 36
Tiomkin, Dimitri, 8
Tizol, Juan, 20, 22, 31, 75
Toan, Danny, 160
"Todo Modo". See "Music for 'Todo
    Modo'"
Todo Modo (Italian film), 150–51
"Tonight at Noon," 43, 45, 87–88, 170,
    172, 173
Tonight at Noon, 45, 87–90, 93, 113
Tonight at Noon: Three or Four
    Shades of Love (Mingus Big Band),
    133, 170
Tonight Show, The (TV), 28
Tormé, Mel, 20
"Tourist in Manhattan," 43, 54. See
    also "New York Sketchbook"

Town Hall, 90–97, 101, 103, 107–11, 113, 121, 126, 138, 167, 169–70
Town Hall Concert (Jazz Workshop), 108–9, 125
Town Hall Concert (United Artists), 92. See also *Complete Town Hall Concert, The*
"Transeason" (Cirillo), 32
Transition Records, 43
Trenier, Claude, 11–12
Trenner, Donn, 14
Tribe Called Quest, A (rap group), 174
Triglia, Bill, 47–49
Trio: Mingus Three (Mingus/Hawes/Richmond), 47
Trischka, Tony, 172
Tristano, Lennie, 17–20, 23, 30, 33, 137
"Trombosphere" (Givens), 24
"Turkey in the Straw" (traditional), 116, 118
Twilight Zone, The (TV), 27
"Two Worlds of Drums," 160. See also "Three Worlds of Drums"
Tyner, McCoy, 139
Tyrone Guthrie Theater (venue), 125

Ungaro, Roberto, 165
United Artists Records, 57, 91
University Aula (Norwegian venue), 110
"Untitled Blues," 23
Uptown Horns, 171–73
Urso, Phil, 28–29
"Us Is Two," 137

Van Gelder, Rudy, 30
Varner, Tom, 170
Vass, Jimmy, 131–32
"Vassarlean," 11, 83–84. See also "Weird Nightmare"
Vaughan, Sarah, 21
Verve Records, 56, 120
Village Gate (club), 126
Village Vanguard (club), 34, 98, 140, 144–45
Vital Savage Horizons (bootleg), 90

Waldron, Mal, 30–31, 34–39, 41–44, 59–60, 115
Waller, Fats, 86, 110, 115, 124
Wallington, George, 16, 34, 41
Walrath, Jack, 4, 144–53, 155–62, 167–68, 170
Waters, Muddy, 161
Watkins, Doug, 84–86, 88–90
Watkins, Julius, 28–29, 126–28, 134
Watson, Bobby, 168–69
Watts, Charlie, 158, 171–73
Watts, Jeff "Tain," 170
Watts Towers, 1, 175
"We See" (Monk), 173
Weary Blues (Hughes), 56, 66
Weather Report (band), 165, 167
Webster, Ben, 113, 143, 147
Webster, Freddie, 128
Wedding, Alison, 174
"Wedding March" (traditional), 152, 155
"Wednesday Night Prayer Meeting," 2–3, 59, 64, 67, 74, 78, 108, 161–62, 174
"Wee" (a.k.a. "Allen's Alley") (Best), 22
"Wee" (Johnson), 141
"Wee Dot (Blues for Some Bones)" (Johnson), 24
Weill, Kurt, 171
Wein, George, 91
Weinstock, Bob, 25
"Weird Nightmare" (a.k.a. "Pipe Dream," "Smooch," "Vassarlean"), 2, 11–12, 53, 72, 83, 172–74
Weird Nightmare: Meditations on Mingus (various artists), 171–73
"Well, You Needn't" (Monk), 93
Werner, Kenny, 160, 162
Wess, Frank, 29
"West Coast Ghost," 49–50
Weston, Randy, 136, 139
Westray, Ron, 174
"Wham Bam Thank You Ma'am," 85–86
"What Is This Thing Called Love" (Porter), 18, 33, 74, 157
"What Love," 74–75, 77, 84, 93, 138

Wheeler, Buzz, 14
"When Johnny Comes Marching
   Home" (traditional), 119
"When the Saints Go Marching In"
   (traditional), 126
"Where Flamingos Fly" (Brooks/Thea/
   Courlander), 73
White, Dupree, Mrs., 108
Who's Who in Jazz Records, 155
Wilder, Joe, 134, 168, 170
Wiley, Jackson, 20, 26–27, 33–34
Wilkins, Jack, 160
Williams, Al, 56
Williams, Fess, 13, 94
Williams, Richard, 67–68, 90, 92,
   94–95, 98, 100–103, 166
Williams, Rudy, 13, 31, 94
Willner, Hal, 171–73
Wilson, Gerald, 13
Winding, Kai, 18, 24, 156
"Wolf That Lives in Lindsey, The"
   (Mitchell), 166
"Wolverine Blues" (Morton), 169
Wonderland. See Jazz Portraits
Woodman, Britt, 6, 10, 12, 14, 80,
   92–93, 95–96, 101–2, 167–68, 170
Woodman, William, Jr. ("Brother"),
   10, 12
Woodman, William, Sr., 6
Woods, Phil, 165
"Woody 'N You" (Gillespie), 33,
   47, 55
"Work Song," 36, 71, 140, 172
"Work Song" (Adderley), 113

Workman, Reggie, 166
World Saxophone Quartet, 142
"Wouldn't You" (Gillespie), 55. See also
   "Woody 'N You"
"Wrap Your Troubles in Dreams"
   (Barris/Koehler/Moll), 81–82, 84
Wright, Herman, 90
Wyands, Richard, 15, 57–58

"Yankee Doodle" (traditional),
   114–15, 119
"Yesterdays" (Kern/Harbach), 19,
   25, 47
"You And Me" (Feather/Gordon), 21
"You Don't Know What Love Is"
   (DePaul/Raye), 29
"You Go To My Head" (Coots/
   Gillespie), 21
Young, Lee, 8–9, 12
Young, Lester ("Prez"), 8–9, 14, 28, 31,
   64–65, 95, 103, 166
Young, Snooky, 92, 134, 168
Young Rebel, The (compilation), 15
"Ysabel's Table Dance" (a.k.a. "Tijuana
   Table Dance"), 48, 116, 120–21,
   135, 167

Zegler, Manuel, 46
Zenni, Stefano, 2
Zimmerman, Fred, 46
"Zing! Went the Strings of My Heart"
   (Hanley), 16
"Zoo-Baba-Da-Oo-Ee," 13
"Zootcase" (Cohn), 28

About the Author

TODD S. JENKINS is the author of *Free Jazz and Free Improvisation: An Encyclopedia* (2004, Greenwood Press), and a contributor to *Down Beat, All About Jazz, Signal to Noise* and *Route 66 Magazine*. He is also a director of the American Jazz Symposium, a non-profit arts organization.

pull
9/25   DATE